Lecture Notes in Computer Science 14765

Founding Editors

Gerhard Goos
Juris Hartmanis

The series Lecture Notes in Computer Science (LNCS), including its subseries Lecture Notes in Artificial Intelligence (LNAI) and Lecture Notes in Bioinformatics (LNBI), has established itself as a medium for the publication of new developments in computer science and information technology research, teaching, and education.

LNCS enjoys close cooperation with the computer science R & D community, the series counts many renowned academics among its volume editors and paper authors, and collaborates with prestigious societies. Its mission is to serve this international community by providing an invaluable service, mainly focused on the publication of conference and workshop proceedings and postproceedings. LNCS commenced publication in 1973.

Daniel Dietsch · Andrey Rybalchenko ·
Martin Schäf · Thomas Wies

Editors

On the Pursuit of Insight and Elegance

Essays Dedicated to Andreas Podelski on the
Occasion of His 65th Birthday

 Springer

Editors
Daniel Dietsch
University of Freiburg
Freiburg, Germany

Andrey Rybalchenko
Microsoft Research
Cambridge, UK

Martin Schäf
Amazon
New York, NY, USA

Thomas Wies
New York University
New York, NY, USA

ISSN 0302-9743   ISSN 1611-3349 (electronic)
Lecture Notes in Computer Science
ISBN 978-3-032-13710-4   ISBN 978-3-032-13711-1 (eBook)
https://doi.org/10.1007/978-3-032-13711-1

This Springer imprint is published by the registered company Springer Nature Switzerland AG
The registered company address is: Gewerbestrasse 11, 6330 Cham, Switzerland

If disposing of this product, please recycle the paper.

Preface

Andreas Podelski is one of the leading researchers in formal verification and software engineering. He embarked on his academic journey working on automata and formal languages, culminating in a Ph.D. from the University of Paris 7 in 1992, under the guidance of Maurice Nivat. His doctoral thesis on Tree Automata laid the foundation for his subsequent explorations and innovations in the field. From 1992 to 1994, he expanded his research horizon at DEC PRL (Digital Paris Research Laboratory) as part of the LIFE project, delving deeper into the intricacies of automata theory with Hassan Aït-Kaci.

In the mid-90s Andreas was a Research Group Leader in the Programming Logics Group led by Harald Ganzinger at the Max Planck Institute for Computer Science. During this time, he pioneered several groundbreaking studies, including his work on the analysis of logic programs and constraint solving in 1997. His paper, "Set-Based Analysis of Logic Programs and Reactive Logic Programs," marked the beginning of a prolific period of research that would redefine the boundaries of software model checking.

The turn of the millennium was a particularly fertile period for Andreas. Together with Thomas Ball and Sriram K. Rajamani, he worked on two seminal papers that provided the theoretical underpinning of the software model checker SLAM, which became part of Microsoft's Windows Device Driver Development Kit. SLAM was one of the first automatic software verification tools to have a large-scale impact in industrial use. Bill Gates said at the time about the broader impact of the SLAM project:

Things like even software verification, this has been the Holy Grail of computer science for many decades but now in some very key areas, for example, driver verification. We are building tools that can do an actual proof about the software and how it works in order to guarantee the reliability.

The highly cited TACAS 2001 paper "Boolean and Cartesian Abstraction for Model Checking C Programs" retrospectively placed the SLAM analysis algorithm in terms of the framework of abstract interpretation. The paper derived the algorithm by successive abstraction of a program's semantics, thereby providing a deeper understanding of its trade-off between precision and scalability. The subsequent TACAS 2002 paper "Relative Completeness of Abstraction Refinement for Software Model Checking" further provided new insights on the theoretical completeness guarantees of software model checking algorithms based on abstraction refinement, which remains one of the predominant algorithmic techniques used in software model checkers up to this day.

Around the same time, Andreas embarked on his long-term research project of tackling a quintessential problem of computer science: the Halting Problem. Andreas' work on termination analysis began in the early 2000s. Together with Andrey Rybalchenko, he published two highly influential works on termination analysis in 2004: their LICS paper on "Transition Invariants" and their follow-up VMCAI paper on "A Complete Method for the Synthesis of Linear Ranking Functions". These papers introduced an automated termination proof method based on a novel reduction of liveness to safety verification. Rather than following the classical approach of reducing termination to the problem of finding a single global well-founded ranking function that decreases with each program step, the paper instead proposed to approximate the transitive closure of a program's transition relation with a finite union of relations, each of which can be proved well-founded in isolation. The soundness of this proof method relies on an intriguing application of Ramsey's Theorem. Its compositional nature turned out to be the key ingredient that sparked the work on an entirely new generation of automated termination provers. In particular, it laid the foundation for their subsequent work on the Terminator tool with Byron Cook.

The Terminator tool was a game changer for the analysis of liveness properties as it was the first automated tool to prove termination of real-world systems software. This achievement established a new standard for liveness analysis of software and paved the way for further research in the area. Andreas' work on termination analysis has had a lasting impact on the field. In honor of these achievements, Andreas and Andrey received the LICS Test-of-Time Award in 2024.

In 2006, Andreas joined the University of Freiburg as Professor and head of the Chair of Software Engineering, which he built into a thriving and highly impactful research group. The group's reputation for excellence stems directly from Andreas' core philosophy. Throughout his career, he has demonstrated a remarkable ability to identify and tackle the most challenging problems in software verification, often pushing the boundaries of what is thought to be possible. For example, his work on automata-based software model checking with Matthias Heizmann and Jochen Hoenicke, as described in his 2009 SAS paper "Refinement of Trace Abstraction", has led to the development of highly effective verification tools. This includes the tools in the Ultimate tool family, which have won numerous awards in the software verification competition, SV-COMP. Ultimate has become a benchmark for software model checking, demonstrating the power of automata-based techniques in practice. Ultimate tools went on to win SV-COMP five times, along with 68 medals across various categories, a testament to the world-leading work done in Andreas' research group.

These projects cover only a fraction of Andreas' scholarly accomplishments. In recent years alone, his work has touched on topics as diverse as shape analysis, verification of concurrent and distributed systems, and requirements engineering.

Andreas' scholarly pursuits have been complemented by his commitment to mentoring the next generation of computer scientists. His guidance has shaped the careers of numerous students and postdoctoral researchers, many of whom have themselves made significant contributions to the field.

One of Andreas' most admirable qualities as a mentor is his tireless dedication to distilling an idea to its very essence. This pursuit of clarity is central to his method, consistently challenging his collaborators and students to reach the highest level of academic rigor. Each iteration of review and discussion brings greater focus, often leading to a problem being recognized as fundamentally simple, signaling a major breakthrough. The ultimate reward is the beautifully crisp insight that emerges, bringing a knowing smile to his face. For all of us, this rigorous process instilled his high academic standards, which made the eventual successes deeply rewarding.

Andreas also consistently applied a creative approach to foster his group's well-being. He ensured our physical health by holding seminars in remote huts of the Black Forest that could only be reached on foot, or by carefully planning a group meeting in a location amenable to windsurfing. And he cared for our emotional health by bringing his dog as a mascot to every meeting, seminar, and lecture, and at times, even sending the dog home with his Ph.D. students. (We fondly remember the "office-chair dog sled races" through the university corridors and Andreas' stoic ability to deflect any complaints from the university administration.)

Beyond the confines of academia, Andreas' work has had a profound impact on industry through collaborations with companies such as Bosch, Daimler, and Microsoft. These partnerships have not only translated his research into practical applications, but have also provided real-world challenges that fuel further academic inquiry.

Over a career spanning more than 30 years, Andreas' research has been recognized by numerous honors and awards. But his true legacy lies in the conceptual breakthroughs, analysis tools, and the many researchers he has inspired in the quest to ensure software reliability and security through mathematical reasoning and verification. This Festschrift celebrates Andreas' trailblazing academic career and research contributions. It brings together his collaborators, students, and friends to honor his profound impact on formal methods.

We hope that this volume will inspire present and future researchers to build upon Andreas' pioneering foundations to ensure a future of robust and trustworthy software systems.

October 22, 2025

Daniel Dietsch
Andrey Rybalchenko
Martin Schäf
Thomas Wies

Contents

A Methodology for Modular Termination Verification

K. Rustan M. Leino[(✉)]

Amazon Web Services, Seattle, WA, USA
leino@amazon.com

Abstract. This paper describes a specification methodology for the sound modular verification of termination for programs with dynamically bound methods. The basic idea is to group methods into partially ordered clusters and to give precise termination specifications within each cluster. The paper proposes a general methodology where the grouping is specified manually, and a specialized methodology where the grouping is computed modularly from the call graph and some additional specifications.

1 Introduction

An important part of formally verifying programs correct is to prove that they terminate. In a modular setting, such verification is done module by module, proving for each module that it satisfies its specifications, under the assumption that imported modules satisfy theirs. Modularity is necessary for the verification to scale.

The contribution of this paper is to give a clear account of how to write *specifications* that allow modular formal verification to prove termination. I present a general methodology for understanding the issues at hand, as well as a specialized methodology that can be used with low specification overhead in an automatic program verifier. The overarching approach is to syntactically (that is, without theorem proving) determine clusters of mutually recursive methods and then to semantically (that is, using theorem proving) prove termination of the calls within each cluster.

There are two possible, orthogonal causes for non-termination in a program: infinite loops and infinite recursion. The termination specification for one loop is independent of the termination specifications of other loops. Consequently, how one such loop specification is written does not restrict the possible ways of writing specifications for other loops. In contrast, the termination specification for one method has an effect on the termination specifications of the method's callers and callees. At minimum, this requires some organizing principles—a *methodology*—when applied to a large program. This is especially dicey when the program may contain dynamically bound calls, because then it is not obvious which methods may be mutually recursive. In this paper, I address issues of writing termination specifications to prevent infinite recursion.

I consider a setting where a program is broken into modules. The modules declare dependencies among themselves by acyclic *import* declarations. Borrowing nomenclature from object-oriented programming, I'll refer to the code routines in each module

© The Author(s), under exclusive license to Springer Nature Switzerland AG 2026
D. Dietsch et al. (Eds.): Podelski Festschrift, LNCS 14765, pp. 1–22, 2026.
https://doi.org/10.1007/978-3-032-13711-1_1

as *methods*. In the first several sections of this paper, I'll look at termination and specifications more generally, without concern for modules. In other words, those sections are presented as if the entire program were written in one module. Then, starting in Sect. 6, I'll transition into how to write specifications in the presence of modules and information hiding.

I assume the termination checking is part of a deductive verifier that is capable of formally verifying assertions in programs. These assertions may come from programmer-supplied **assert** statements, but more generally come from proof obligations stipulated by the programming-language definition (like index bounds checks for arrays), proof obligations that arise from programmer-supplied specifications (like method preconditions), and proof obligations that enforce a programming discipline (like a methodology for ensuring termination). There are plenty of deductive verifiers of this kind—Why3 [5], SPARK [2], VeriFast [8], Viper [11], and Dafny [9, 10], to mention but a few.

Andreas Podelski has a long history of advancing the understanding of and state of the art in programming languages, specifications, and program analysis, including important results in the area of program termination. It is therefore an honor for me to contribute this article to the Festschrift volume that celebrates the scientific achievements of Andreas Podelski.

2 Fundamentals of Termination

2.1 Well-Founded Orders

The fundamental idea behind termination proofs, introduced in a seminal paper by Floyd [6], comes down to mapping moments of a program execution to values of a *well-founded order*. A well-founded order $\succ$ is an irreflexive partial order that has no infinite descending chains; that is, there is no infinite sequence of values $a_0, a_1, a_2, \ldots$ such that

$$a_0 \succ a_1 \succ a_2 \succ \cdots$$

To prove the absence of infinite recursion, the moments of interest are method call boundaries. If successive moments that extend the call stack are mapped to decreasing values of the well-founded order, then the program is sure to terminate. In other words, such a construction ensures that no execution has an infinite call stack.

(For loop termination, the moments of interest are the program states at the top of each iteration of the same loop activation. But I will continue to ignore the orthogonal concern of specifying and verifying the termination of loops.)

To apply Floyd's fundamental idea, we include in the specification of each method an expression that is evaluated on entry to the method. I'll refer to this expression as a *(termination) metric*. To prove termination, a deductive verifier then generates, for each call, a proof obligation that the value of the callee's metric is smaller than the value of the caller's metric.

Proposition 0.
Let $(\mathcal{A}, \succ_{\mathcal{A}})$ and $(\mathcal{B}, \succ_{\mathcal{B}})$ be well-founded orders where the domains $\mathcal{A}$ and $\mathcal{B}$ are disjoint. Define $\succ$ on $\mathcal{A} \cup \mathcal{B}$ by

$$x \succ y \quad \equiv \quad x \succ_{\mathcal{A}} y \ \lor \ x \succ_{\mathcal{B}} y$$

Then, $(\mathcal{A} \cup \mathcal{B}, \succ)$ is also a well-founded order. This also holds for infinitary unions.

Proposition 1.
Let $(\mathcal{A}, \succ)$ be a well-founded order and let $\top$ denote an element not in $\mathcal{A}$. Define $\mathcal{A}_\top$ to be $\mathcal{A}$ extended with the element $\top$, and define an order $\succ_\top$ on $\mathcal{A}_\top$ by

$$x \succ_\top y \quad \equiv \quad (x = \top \ \land \ y \neq \top) \ \lor \ x \succ y$$

Then, $(\mathcal{A}_\top, \succ_\top)$ is also a well-founded order.

Proposition 2.
Suppose $(\mathcal{A}, \geq)$ is a partial order and $\mathcal{A}$ is a finite set. Let $\succ$ be the irreflexive counterpart of $\geq$. Then $(\mathcal{A}, \succ)$ is well-founded.

2.2   Programs

I consider programs of the following form, where I'm only expanding those grammar productions that are relevant at this time.

```
Program ::= Declaration*
Declaration ::= Type | Method | ...
Method ::= method Id "(" Param*' ")" ":" Type Specification* Body
Param ::= Id ":" Type
Specification ::= Precondition | TerminationMetric | ...
Precondition ::= requires Expr
TerminationMetric ::= decreases Expr ...
Body ::= "{" BodyFragment* "}"
BodyFragment ::= MethodCall | ...
MethodCall ::= Id "(" Expr*' ")"
```

I will omit the method return type if it is not relevant in examples.

2.3   Generating Verification Conditions

For illustration, let's define $\succ$ as the following well-founded order on any integers x and y:

$$x \succ y \quad \equiv \quad x \geq 0 \ \land \ x > y$$

When x is non-negative, $\succ$ is like arithmetic greater-than, and $\succ$ does not determine a relationship when x is negative. Consider the following method (where I'm only showing the control flow and recursive calls):

```
method M(x: int)
  decreases x
```

```
{
  if x ≤ 0
    ...
  else if x is even
    ...
    ⓪  M(x / 2)
    ...
  else
    ...
    ①  M(x - 5)
    ...
}
```

The method is specified with the termination metric x, as shown by the **decreases** clause. Each call in the method body gives rise to a termination proof obligation. The simplest way to prescribe these proof obligations is to instrument the program with assertions placed just before each call. With reference to the markers in the example program, these are

$$
\begin{array}{ll}
⓪ & x \succ x/2 \\
① & x \succ x - 5
\end{array}
$$

Applying standard weakest preconditions [4], these assertions give the logical verification conditions

$$
\begin{array}{lll}
⓪ & \neg(x \leq 0) \wedge x \text{ is even} & \implies \quad x \succ x/2 \\
① & \neg(x \leq 0) \wedge \neg(x \text{ is even}) & \implies \quad x \succ x - 5
\end{array}
$$

Note that the left-hand side of each $\succ$ is the metric of the caller, as evaluated on entry to the caller. The right-hand side of each $\succ$ is the metric of the callee, instantiated with the actual parameters of the call and evaluated at the time of the call.

As any modern verifier can ascertain, these are valid formulas. By simply supplying this termination metric (that is, **decreases** x) for the method, we thus prove that the program terminates.

From here on, I will take it for granted that each termination proof obligation is generated in the context of the respective call. Therefore, I will mostly just talk about calls from one method to another, leaving implicit the control-flow guards and program changes that occur during the execution of a method body.

2.4 Summary of Well-Founded Termination

I've described the general structure of termination proofs: proving that the metrics decrease with each call, or more precisely, that every new activation record placed on the call stack has a metric that is smaller than the previous. The comparisons (in the previous sentence, "smaller") are always done with respect to some well-founded order that is fixed for the entire program. Since a well-founded order has no infinite descending chains, the proof obligations associated with each call imply the termination of the program.

I'm following the approach of uniformly checking termination with *every* call. This makes it simple to prescribe which two metrics should be compared in the well-founded order. An alternative, which Podelski and his colleagues have made good use of, is to consider paths of calls that lead back to the same method [3].

3   Dynamically Bound Methods

Dynamically bound methods are found in object-oriented languages, where a popular name for them is *virtual methods*. In such languages, a class can declare a method that its subclasses can replace. When the method is invoked on an object, the call at run time is redirected to the method implementation that is given for the allocated type of that object.

The details of which method implementation is selected for the redirection is not relevant to this paper. So, I'll abstract over that selection mechanism and simply view virtual methods as having a *set* of implementations. I'll say *virtual method* to refer to the declaration of a dynamically bound method and speak of each of its implementations as an *override*.

I'll write methods as follows:

```
method StaticallyBound(...) ... { ... }
virtual method DynamicallyBound(...) ...
method DynamicallyBound' overrides DynamicallyBound(...) ... { ... }
```

Giving a new name for each override is convenient for this paper, because it will let me refer to each declaration uniquely by the name it introduces. By convention, I will use a name like M' as the name for an override of a virtual method M. I'll say just "method" to refer to either of these or to a statically bound method.

The redirection performed by a virtual method is akin to a call. That is, it is as if the virtual method had a body that selects one of the overrides and then makes a call to that override. To prove termination, we have to account for this call as well. We could demand that each override have a metric that is smaller than that of the virtual method. However, it is convenient to think of a virtual method and all its overrides as using the same metric. That is what I will do. Formally, one can justify this "stuttering" in various ways; for example, by a lexicographically ordered pair where the second component counts down with every redirection. But the stuttering is also easy to justify by noting that a redirection always immediately follows a call, so the number of stuttering calls is no more than the number of decreasing calls.

4   Adding Structure to the Well-Founded Order

In theory, what I've described is all there is to proving termination of a program with dynamically bound methods. In practice, however, it is useful to impose some structure on the well-founded order. We want the specifications to be easy to use and to be abstract enough to support information hiding and program evolution.

4.1 Lexicographic Tuples

An indispensable tool in writing termination specifications is the lexicographically ordered tuple, or *lexicographic tuple* for short. Such a tuple is ordered component by component, with the left-most component being most significant. For example, given three domains $\mathcal{A}$, $\mathcal{B}$, and $\mathcal{C}$, each with its own ordering $\succ_{\mathcal{A}}$, $\succ_{\mathcal{B}}$, and $\succ_{\mathcal{C}}$, respectively, the lexicographic order $\succ$ on $\mathcal{A} \times \mathcal{B} \times \mathcal{C}$ tuples is defined as

$$
\begin{aligned}
\lfloor a_0, b_0, c_0 \rceil \succ \lfloor a_1, b_1, c_1 \rceil \quad &\equiv \\
(a_0 \succ_{\mathcal{A}} a_1) \; &\vee \\
(a_0 = a_1 \;\wedge\; b_0 \succ_{\mathcal{B}} b_1) \; &\vee \\
(a_0 = a_1 \;\wedge\; b_0 = b_1 \;\wedge\; c_0 \succ_{\mathcal{C}} c_1)&
\end{aligned}
$$

I've used $\lfloor \ldots \rceil$ brackets to enclose the list of components of each lexicographic tuple.

> **Proposition 3.**
>
> If the orders for all components of the tuple are well-founded, then so is the lexicographic order of such tuples.

4.2 A Specific Order

I will now be more specific about the well-founded order to be used. The domain of this order will be tuples whose type is

$$
\mathcal{S} \times \underbrace{\mathcal{U}_\top \times \mathcal{U}_\top \times \cdots \times \mathcal{U}_\top}_{k}
$$

for some fixed k. The domain $\mathcal{S}$ denotes a set of *strata*, which, starting in the next section, will be the main subject of the rest of the paper. The domain $\mathcal{U}$ is the union of all types in the program. For example, $\mathcal{U}$ will contain boolean values, integer values, algebraic-datatype values, pointer values, etc. As we saw in Sect. 2.1 (Proposition 1), the subscript $\top$ says that $\mathcal{U}$ is extended with a unique top element, $\top$. By defining a well-founded order on each type of the program, we obtain, by Propositions 0 and 1, a well-founded order on $\mathcal{U}_\top$.

Obtaining $\mathcal{U}$ by defining a fixed well-founded order on each type in the programming language has three advantages. It is a simple way to allow all program values to be part of termination metrics. The ordering is consistent for all programs written in the language. And (unlike the situation in many verification systems based on type theory), it saves users from having to define their own orders and proving them to be well-founded, which is a complicated matter best reserved for experts. The approach to using a single, fixed, language-defined order has shown to be effective in Dafny [9].

4.3 Example

To illustrate the use of lexicographic tuples, here are two methods for computing the sum of the triangle numbers of the elements of a sequence. The triangle number of n is the sum of the first n natural numbers (or is 0 if n is negative). I'm writing $|\mathsf{s}|$ to denote the length of a sequence s. I haven't yet talked about strata, so this example arbitrarily uses the value Yellow for the first component of the termination metric.

```
method SumOfTriangles(s: seq<int>, i: int): int
  requires 0 ≤ i ≤ |s|
  decreases Yellow, |s| - i, ⊤
{
  if i = |s|
    return 0
  else
    return Triangle(s, i, 0)
}
method Triangle(s: seq<int>, i: int, j: int): int
  requires 0 ≤ i < |s|
  decreases Yellow, |s| - i, s[i] - j
{
  if j < s[i]
    return j + Triangle(s, i, j + 1)
  else
    return SumOfTriangles(s, i + 1)
}
```

The termination proof of this program goes as follows: The call from SumOfTriangles to Triangle decreases the third component of the lexicographic tuple, since ⊤ is above every integer. By passing in a larger value for j (bounded by s[i]), the recursive call of Triangle decreases the third component of the lexicographic tuple. Finally, by passing in a larger value for i (bounded by |s|), the call from Triangle to SumOfTriangles decreases the second component of the lexicographic tuple.

4.4   Fixed Tuple Length

When I introduced the ordering in Section 4.2, I said it is to have k components of type $\mathcal{U}_\top$. How is this k determined and how can one make sure that all termination metrics of the program use the same tuple length? For example, suppose the two methods of the SumOfTriangles example are used in a larger program that uses a larger tuple length. Then, is it necessary to change these termination specifications to make their tuples longer?

To address this concern, we'll employ a simple syntactic rewriting: Each programmer-supplied **decreases** clause is implicitly right-padded with ⊤ elements to reach the desired tuple length. For a given program, the number k is picked to be the maximum length of any given **decreases** clause. (Since a program is finite, this will pick k to be finite.) Since all tuples will be extended by just ⊤ elements, it is never necessary to know the exact value of k—to compare two **decreases** clauses, pad them with enough ⊤ elements to make the clauses the same length, and then perform the lexicographic comparison.

With this syntactic rewriting in place, we can simplify the SumOfTriangles example above by removing the explicit mention of $\top$. This turns out to be a natural thing to do for common programming styles.

Remark: The Dafny language uses the top-element padding just described. In an early version of Dafny, the padding had instead used "bottom" elements. However, a lively discussion I had with Andreas Podelski about these matters came to the conclusion that top-padding corresponds to more common programming patterns. As a result of that discussion, Dafny was changed to use top-padding. Thanks, Andreas!

5   Strata

Many methods in a program are not recursive at all. To a programmer, it may be "obvious" that such methods terminate. It would be nice if we could achieve the same simplicity in the corresponding formal justification. Even when methods are recursive, most pairs of methods in a program are not mutually recursive. For two methods that are not mutually recursive, it would be nice to specify the termination of one independently of the termination specification of the other. This is where we'll get help from the strata S that I mentioned in Section 4.2. In a nutshell, the idea is to write termination specifications that place methods into layers, or *strata*.[1]

5.1   Grouping Methods by Stratum

Consider the following example, which for each number x of an algebraic list computes the factorial of Twice(x). Values of the algebraic (inductive) datatype are ordered by structural inclusion, which is well-founded.

```
datatype List<X> = Nil | Cons(X, List<X>)
method Compute(xs: List<int>): int
  decreases Pink, xs
{
  match xs
  case Nil ⇒ return 0
  case Cons(x, tail) ⇒ return Factorial(Twice(x)) + Compute(tail)
}
method Twice(x: int): int
  decreases Pastel
{ return 2 * x }
method Factorial(x: int): int
  decreases Peach, x
{
  if x ≤ 0
    return 1
  else
```

---

[1] *stra·tum*, pl. *strata*. a) A layer of rock in the ground. b) A group of methods that is partially ordered with respect to other groups of methods.

```
    return x * Factorial(x - 1)
}
```

The termination specifications in this program use three strata, which I called `Pink`, `Pastel`, and `Peach`. If these strata are ordered so that `Pink` is larger than `Pastel` and `Peach`, then we can prove that the program terminates. Notice that, other than the respective stratum components, each method just mentions what is necessary to prove that its own recursion terminates. (It is instructive—perhaps even startling—to try to write integer-valued termination metrics—that is, not using strata or lexicographic tuples—for these methods.)

The strata let us organize the methods into groups. Within each group, the rest of the lexicographic components are used to prove termination. Between groups, all we need to know is some ordering relation between the strata. In other words, if the stratum components of the caller and callee are different, then the proof obligation for termination can be phrased independently of the subsequent k components of the caller and callee metrics. On the other hand, if the caller's and callee's strata are the same, then proving termination comes down to (semantically) proving that the other k components exhibit a lexicographic decrease.

So, we're going to allow a program to declare strata and to order them. The order must be verified to be a partial order (which, on behalf of Proposition 2, gives us the well-founded order we need).

The first component of each termination metric is a stratum. In my use of them, this stratum will be fixed for each method. Therefore, it will be natural to speak of "the stratum of a method". In this way, each stratum acts as a name for a group of methods.

5.2 Automatic Stratification

In what I've described so far, the $1 + k$ components of each metric are supplied (by the programmer) as part of the program text. I will continue to build on this foundation. However, for just this subsection, let's consider how the stratum component of every metric can be inferred automatically by a whole-program analysis.

Given an entire program (or, stated differently, a one-module program), here is one way we can assign strata systematically. It makes use of the program's *call graph*, so let me first define it.

The vertices of a program's call graph are the program's (statically bound, virtual, and overriding) methods. There is an edge from method A to method B if the body of A contains a call to B. Also, if A can redirect to B, then the call graph has an edge from A to B as well as an edge from B to A; by making this edge bidirectional, the automatic stratifications in this paper will end up assigning the same stratum to a virtual method and its overrides.

The strongly connected components (*SCCs*) of a directed graph form a partial order. More precisely, in the nomenclature of graph theory, the condensation of a graph under its SCC equivalence relation yields a directed acyclic quotient graph. The SCCs of the call graph are in one-to-one correspondence with nests of mutually recursive methods (modulo the fact that overrides are always in the same SCC as their corresponding virtual method).

The systematic stratification follows a condensation of the call graph: Introduce one stratum for each SCC. Then, for every edge from an SCC S to an SCC T, order the stratum of S above the stratum of T; that is, $S \succ T$. Since the SCCs are partially ordered, we obtain a partial order also for the strata.

The resulting stratification has the following property, which is important enough to deserve a name:

> **Sympathetic Stratification.** For any call from a method A to a method B, either $stratum(A) = stratum(B)$ or $stratum(A) \succ stratum(B)$.

If $stratum(A) = stratum(B)$, then a proof of termination needs to consult the remaining lexicographic components of the termination metrics of A and B. If $stratum(A) \succ stratum(B)$, then the proof obligation for termination is satisfied on account of the strata alone.

The beauty of a sympathetic stratification is that those are the only two cases. This means that the calls whose termination a programmer may consider "obvious" do not require any further specification or proof from the programmer. Furthermore, since we can perform this stratification automatically, the stratum component of termination metrics can be tacit in **decreases** clauses. The strata are used to explain the soundness of the methodology for writing termination specifications, but they need never appear in the programming-language syntax.

Two remarks are in order.

First, it is possible to use fewer strata than this stratification gives rise to. For example, the stratification will give 3 strata for the 3 methods of the Compute example in Section 5.1. But since Twice and Factorial never call each other, those two methods could use the same stratum. There is no benefit to using fewer strata, however. In the other direction, it is not possible to use more strata and still verify the program. The reason is that, if an SCC used more than one stratum, then some call within the SCC will fail the termination proof obligation because the strata do not go in the right direction. In other words, if we use more strata, we will not get a sympathetic stratification. In conclusion, this automatic stratification is as good as we can hope for.

Second, a reminder: the stratification I just described assumes it is possible to compute the call graph of the entire program. Alas, in the presence of modules, information hiding, and modular verification, this is not possible. Next, let us return to having explicit strata in the program and dive into the modularity problem. I'll return to the subject of automatic stratification in Section 9.

6   Modularity

Modularity facilitates organization and abstraction. We'd like termination specifications at module interface boundaries to be expressive enough to be useful for the clients ("importers") of the module, and at the same time be abstract enough to give the module implementation some freedom to evolve.

I'll start this section by reviewing the definition of modular verification. Then, I'll go into key aspects of modules.

6.1 Modular Verification

The *modular verification* of a program consists of the separate verification of each module in the program as well as simple *link-time checks* on the composition of modules. The verification of a module is performed using the contents of the module plus the information it obtains from its imported modules. For this modular reasoning to be well-founded (sound), it is important for the import relation to be acyclic.

The link-time checks are performed on the whole program, but are admissible within the definition of modular verification on the grounds that they are simple enough not to require any logical reasoning. For example, if the programming language separates module interfaces from module implementations, then link-time checks will enforce that every module interface has exactly one implementation and that the program's module import relation is acyclic.

6.2 Module Declarations

To be more precise about how program declarations are partitioned into modules, let me update the grammar:

```
Program ::= Module*
Module ::= module Id "{" Declaration* "}"
Declaration ::= Import | Export | Stratum | Type | Method | ...
```

I will detail `Import`, `Export`, and `Stratum` declarations in the next few sections.

6.3 Imports

If a module M wants to mention a name declared in another module L, then M must first *import* L. This is done with an **import** declaration. I'll write $\supset$ to denote the transitive closure of the import relation (e.g., $M \supset L$) and $\supseteq$ to denote the reflexive closure of $\supset$.

The import ordering of modules in a program must be acyclic. That is, $\supseteq$ must be a partial order.

In typical programming languages, if a module M imports a module L that defines a name x, then this name is written as x inside L and as L.x in M. For brevity in this paper, I will omit the qualification "L." and write just x for uses of x everywhere.

6.4 Exports

To support the good software-engineering practice of information hiding, a module is allowed to restrict which of its declarations are visible to importing modules. In some programming languages, this is done by selectively declaring some of the names defined by the module as "public". In this paper, I will refer to this module interface boundary as the module's *export set*.

An export set controls not only which names importers can see, but also what information about those names is provided to importers. Here, three things are of interest to this paper:

First, whenever the name of a method is exported, so is the signature and specification of the method. However, the body of the method is never exported. In other words, the details of a method's implementation remain private to the module. This allows the module to change the implementation over time without concern of breaking importing modules. A consequence of keeping method bodies private to a module is that it is not possible for importers to build a call graph for the whole program.

Second, the export set allows a module to choose which edges of the import relation are public information. A consequence of allowing imports to be private is that it is not possible for any single module to build the import relation for the whole program. Rather, the acyclicity of the import relation can only be enforced at link time.

Third, an export set can include stratum names separately from stratum ordering information. That is, just because a stratum name is exported does not mean that importers will know anything about the ordering of that stratum with respect to other strata. This lets a module decide which stratum ordering edges to make public.

7 Defining Strata

The declaration of a stratum C has the form

stratum C **below** AA **above** ZZ

where AA and ZZ are lists of previously defined strata. The **below** and **above** lists define edges in the ordering of strata. In particular, the declaration says that $A \succ C$ holds for every stratum A in the list AA and that $C \succ Z$ holds for every stratum Z in the list ZZ. I will omit the **below** or **above** keyword if the list that follows is empty.

The *origin* of a stratum is the module that declares the stratum.

The *upward closure* of a stratum C in a module M is the set of strata B such that $B \succ C$ is in the transitive closure of the $\succ$ relation induced by the stratum declarations given in M.

A stratum C in M is said to be *in the top tier of* M if all strata in the upward closure of C in M are declared in M.

7.1 Ensuring a Partial Order on Strata

Strata are supposed to form a partial order. To make sure that the given ordering clauses indeed define a partial order, a module's stratum declarations are checked, one by one in the order given, to satisfy $A \succ Z$ for every A in AA and Z in ZZ. If this condition holds for all such A, Z pairs, then the new stratum is admitted and its ordering information can be used in the checks for the remaining stratum declarations.

To check a condition $A \succ Z$, a module is allowed to use stratum-ordering information in the export sets of its imported modules, as well as the stratum-ordering information induced by the module's previously admitted stratum declarations.

Discharging the $A \succ Z$ proof obligations requires some care. A simple strategy is to introduce the module's strata in a bottom-up fashion. In many cases, this will mean that each stratum declaration will have an empty **below** list, which makes the ordering check trivial. The one case where it is necessary to use a **below** clause is when the desire is to define the stratum to be below a stratum declared in another module. In that case, it may be necessary to know about the other stratum's relative ordering information.

A module uses a declaration

export C $\succ$ D

to give its importers information about the stratum ordering. The condition in this export declaration is checked once all stratum declarations in the module have been admitted.

7.2 Stratum Ordering Induced by Module Ordering

When information is needed about the stratum ordering, the following inference is allowed:

> **Stratum-Module Axiom.** For any module M and strata C and D,
> $C \in TopTier(\text{M}) \land \text{M} \supset origin(\text{D}) \implies \text{C} \succ \text{D}.$

That is, strata in the top tier of M are above strata declared in modules transitively imported by M. In other words, this axiom dictates that strata in the top tier of M implicitly be ordered above strata introduced by "earlier" modules.

The program stratum information available in one module is limited. If that information is enough to prove A $\succ$ Z in one module, then A $\succ$ Z also holds in light of the additional information available elsewhere in the program. In other words, the modular process I described for admitting stratum declarations results in a partial order for all strata in the program.

8 Composition Requirements

When discharging termination proof obligations in a module, a module has available the stratum-ordering information from the module itself and from (the export sets of) its imports. However, in the presence of method overrides, this is not always enough, even in well-structured programs. Let's take a look through an example.

8.1 Motivating Example

Consider the following program:

```
module Client {
  import Util, Math

  method Process' overrides Process(x: int): int
    decreases Umber
  { ... Sqrt(...) ... }
}
module Util {
  export Umber, Process
  stratum Umber
```

```
  virtual method Process(x: int): int
    decreases Umber
}
module Math {
  export Mauve, Sqrt
  stratum Mauve
  method Sqrt(x: int): int
    decreases Mauve
}
```

The `Client` module uses two other modules, one for various utilities and one for math operations. Since `Process'` is an override for the virtual method `Process`, `Process'` has to use the same **decreases** clause as `Process`. The call from `Process'` to `Sqrt` gives rise to the termination proof obligation

```
Umber ≻ Mauve
```

Unfortunately, this condition is not provable in module `Client`. Indeed, it may not be true at all, for example if `Math` privately imports `Util` and privately declares `Mauve` to be above `Umber`. If a programmer believes that `Util` and `Math` are independent libraries that do not call each other or override each other's methods, then the programmer is often right. But, of course, we want to be sure.

Note that, if `Util` and `Math` are indeed independent libraries, then it is not reasonable to expect that `Util` would declare or export the information `Umber` ≻ `Mauve`. So, a practical methodology for modular verification of termination must allow a module like `Client` to proceed in the absence of knowing `Umber` ≻ `Mauve`.

8.2   The Design of Composition Requirements Declarations

As a way out of the quandary above, I propose allowing a module to declare *composition requirements*. Such requirements are assumed when verifying the module. The composition requirements are enforced at link time.

Here is how it works. Module `Client` needs to prove `Umber` ≻ `Mauve`. However, if we allowed a composition requirement to mention these strata directly, then the link-time checks would need complete information about the program's strata. That seems like too much information for a link-time check. Indeed, the complete stratum ordering information is similar in information volume to the whole-program call graph. So, we reject this candidate design.

Instead, composition requirements will be on modules. After all, link-time checks already have to check the acyclicity of the import ordering (which is far more sparse than the stratum ordering or any whole-program call graph). So, we'll allow `Client` to declare

```
requires Util ⊃ Math
```

which says that `Client` can be composed with other modules only if `Util` ⊃ `Math` is possible. More precisely, the role of the composition requirement is to introduce an edge in the module ordering. If the addition of such an edge leads to a cycle, then the link-time checks will fail and the program will be rejected.

For any stratum C mentioned in a module M, we have $M \supseteq origin(C)$. In our example, we thus have Math $\supseteq origin$(Mauve). The call from Process' to Sqrt has the proof obligation

Umber $\succ$ Mauve

This condition follows from the composition requirement Util $\supseteq$ Math and the Stratum-Module Axiom, *provided* Umber is in the top tier of Util.

8.3 Top-Tier Exports

To determine if a stratum is in the top tier of a module requires knowing all the stratum declarations in that module. This information is available only in the module itself, so the only way to communicate this information to importers is by another export declaration. For this purpose, we need a new kind of export,

export TopTier(C)

which can be declared in the module that declares stratum C. Like the other stratum-ordering export declarations, this one is checked after all the module's stratum declarations have been admitted.

8.4 The Final Program

Applying what I've discussed in this section, we can verify the example program from Section 8.1 by declaring

export TopTier(Umber)

in module Util and declaring

requires Util $\supseteq$ Math

in module Client.

9 Automatic Stratification

Now that we have a general methodology for writing and verifying termination specifications using explicitly declared strata, I will define a specialized methodology that does not use any explicit strata. Instead, the idea is to generate stratum declarations automatically from module-local call graphs and to replace strata by method names in export information. The automatic stratification will be sympathetic, so the termination proof obligation for a call will either come down to the non-stratum components of **decreases** clauses or will hold trivially. Since the stratum component of **decreases** clauses will always be handled automatically, programs need only provide the other components.

9.1 Module-Local Call Graphs

Akin to what we considered in Section 5.2, we first build a call graph. The call graphs here will be computed locally to module. A *module-local call graph* for a module contains all whole-program call-graph edges that either start or end in the module (plus any call-graph information gleaned from exports, as I will describe below).

9.2 Generating Strata

The algorithm to assign strata to a module's methods is as follows. Order the SCCs of the module-local call graph topologically from bottom to top. Then, process each SCC S in order:

Case 0
> If S consists only of external vertices (that is, methods declared outside the module), then the methods in S have already been assigned some stratum. Furthermore, S has no outgoing edges into the current module, because the only edges in that direction are bidirectional and S does not contain internal vertices. So, no action is necessary for S.

Case 1
> If S consists only of internal vertices (that is, methods declared inside the module), then introduce a new stratum, say C, and place it above the strata of all of S's outgoing edges. That is, generate the declaration **stratum** C **above** .... Assign the new stratum to all methods in S.

Case 2
> If S consists of both internal and external vertices, then first insist that all external vertices have the same stratum, say C (more about this soon). If it is not possible to determine that these vertices all have the same stratum, then reject the module. Next, assign C to the methods in S. Finally, for every outgoing edge from S, say to an SCC with stratum D, do: If the origin of D is the current module, then augment the declaration of D to add the clause **below** C. If the origin of D is not the current module, then check $C \succ D$; reject the module if this condition cannot be determined.

It is worthwhile to note that the third case applies only if the module contains a method override for a virtual method declared in a different module. Without any such override, all call-graph edges are in the same direction as the module ordering, so no SCC would have both internal and external vertices. So, in the absence of any such inter-module overrides, only the first two cases apply, and they satisfy all ordering relations trivially. (For years, this was the situation in Dafny, because of a restriction on the use of traits [1].)

9.3 Example

To illustrate the algorithm, consider the following example modules (where, for brevity, I'm omitting method parameters):

```
module Car {
  export Operate
```

```
  import Lights, Radio
  method Operate() { ... SenseFog() ... Play() ... }
  method SenseFog() { ... Dim() ... }
  method Play' overrides Play() { ... Mute() ... SelectTrack() ... }
  method SelectTrack() { ... }
}
module Lights {
  export Dim
  method Dim() { ... }
}
module Radio {
  export Play, Mute
  virtual method Play()
  method Mute() { ... }
}
```

The module-local call graph for module Car is

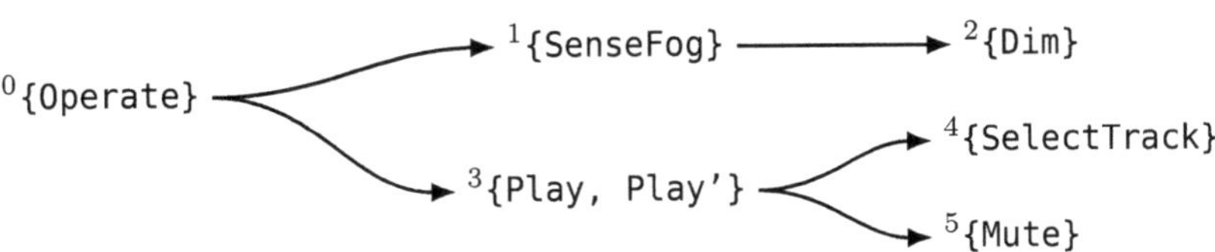

Going bottom-up in this call graph,

- SCC 2 and SCC 5 only have external vertices, so Case 0 applies. I will refer to the strata of those SCCs as E2 and E5, respectively.
- For SCC 1 and SCC 4, Case 1 applies, so we introduce new strata S1 and S4 and declare S1 to be above E2.
- For SCC 3, Case 2 applies, so we assign the stratum of Play, say E3, to Play'. Because of its outgoing edge to SCC 4, we augment the definition of S4 to place it below E3. Because of the outgoing edge to SCC 5, we note that we need to check $E3 \succ E5$.
- Finally, for SCC 0, Case 1 applies, so we introduce stratum S0 and declare it above S1 and E3.

Had the augmentations in the example led to a stratum with other strata both above and below, then we would need to conduct the $A \succ Z$ checks mentioned in Section 7.1 to ensure that the strata form a partial order. Luckily, that works out trivially in this example. For SCC 3, I noted that we need to check $E3 \succ E5$. Unfortunately, there is not enough information to confirm $E3 \succ E5$, so module Car is rejected.

The rejection of module Car is sensible, because nothing rules out the possibility that Mute would call Play, in which case there would be a call cycle among Mute, Play, and Play'.

9.4   Ordering of the Strata of Methods

As the `Car` example reminded us, Case 2 in the algorithm above prescribes some checks on the strata of imported methods. To deal with such checks, it is necessary for modules to share information about the strata of methods. With the explicit strata in Section 7, we had added stratum-ordering exports (Section 7.1). The analogous declaration in the absence of explicit strata is

```
export P > Q
```

where P and Q are methods. This declaration expresses $stratum(\text{P}) \succ stratum(\text{Q})$.

With explicitly named strata, it is immediately clear when two methods have the same stratum. In the absence of explicit strata, such information requires an export that reveals the relationship between such methods. For this reason, we'll allow a declaration

```
export P ~ Q
```

which expresses $stratum(\text{P}) = stratum(\text{Q})$.

As before, these ordering exports need to be checked for each module that declares them. But these two new export declarations play an additional role, which is to *add* edges to the module's call graph. This is necessary if a module wants to force relationships between the strata of its methods, because the module itself may not always contain calls that would add those call-graph edges.

In summary, a module M can use these two kinds of **export** declarations. They affect the construction of M's module-local call graph by adding an edge from P to Q (for **export** P > Q) and adding two edges between P and Q (for **export** P ~ Q). The automatic stratification in M then uses this module-local call graph, as described in the three cases in Section 9.2. As a final step, the information conveyed by the **export** declarations is checked to hold in the module-local call graph.

9.5   Car Example Revisited

To verify module `Car` in Section 9.3, module `Radio` must export more information. In essence, `Radio` must ensure and reveal that `Mute` does not call `Play`. To allow overrides of `Play` to call `Mute`, we add

```
export Play > Mute
```

to module `Radio`. Now, the importing module `Car` has enough information to confirm $\text{E3} \succ \text{E5}$, so that module is now accepted.

As a variation of the example, suppose `Radio` does want to call `Play` from `Mute`. Then, the export declaration above would be rejected, since

$$stratum(\text{Play}) \succ stratum(\text{Mute})$$

would not hold in the call graph for `Radio`. We would then have to remove this export declaration (in which case module `Car`, with its call from `Play'` to `Mute`, would be rejected, as we saw in Section 9.3) or we can instead add

```
export Play ~ Mute
```

With this export declaration, the call graph in Radio places Play and Mute in the same SCC, so these methods need to be given **decreases** clauses to enable the termination proof of the call from Mute to Play. In other words, the termination proof needs to look beyond the stratum component of the termination metric.

Moreover, if Radio exports Play ~ Mute, then the call graph in Car would change to

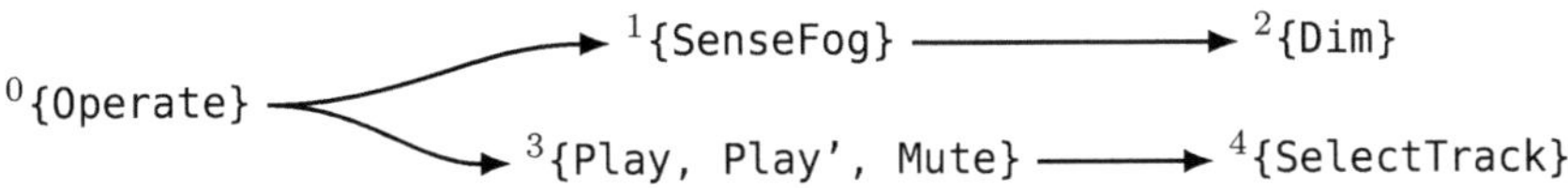

This, in turn, will cause of the automatic stratification to assign to Play' the same stratum as Play and Mute. Therefore, the termination of the call from Play' to Mute will also need to consult the **decreases** clause. In other words, it is now recognized that the call from Play' to Mute is a mutually recursive call.

9.6   Top-Tier Methods

Lastly, the export declaration for top-tier strata from Section 8.3 needs an analogous form for methods. A direct analog would be to support **export** TopTier(stratum(P)) for any method P. However, since most strata *are* top tier, a more frugal alternative is to insist that every exported method *without* a top-tier stratum be exported together with that information. More precisely, if a module M exports a method P that is either statically bound or virtual (that is, not a method override) and the stratum of P is something other than a top-tier stratum of M, then this has to be declared in the export set. This will be declared using

export M > P

And with that, we have a full methodology for writing termination specifications. It uses no explicit strata, and, for accepted modules, the initial stratum component of **decreases** clauses is generated automatically to be a sympathetic stratification.

9.7   Top-Tier Examples

As a final variation of the Car example from Section 9.3, suppose module Car wants to export method SelectTrack. With the frugal approach to top-tier exports, an attempt to declare only **export** SelectTrack would be rejected on the grounds that this method is not top tier. To remedy the situation, module Car also has to declare

export Car > SelectTrack

Under the frugal top-tier approach, exported methods are exported as top tier by default. In light of that default, automatic stratification, and a composition requirement, here are all of the declarations needed to verify the modules from Section 8:

```
module Client {
  import Util, Math
```

```
  requires Util ⊃ Math
  method Process' overrides Process(x: int): int
  { ... Sqrt(...) ... }
}
module Util {
  export Process
  virtual method Process(x: int): int
}
module Math {
  export Sqrt
  method Sqrt(x: int): int { ... }
}
```

For this particular program, no **decreases** clauses are needed at all, and the only declaration we had to add to facilitate termination verification is the composition requirement Util ⊃ Math, which has to be checked at link time.

9.8 On Syntax

The syntax I have used in the section above presents the various ordering specifications separately. In a programming language, it may be more natural to fold that information into existing declarations. For example, composition requirements may be better notated as part of import declarations.

10   Related Work

To my knowledge, the only other work that addresses modular termination specifications of dynamically bound methods is by Jacobs et al. [7]. They use as the well-founded order a lexicographic pair. The first component of that pair is a multiset of method names, where method names have a predetermined order inside modules and method names from different modules are ordered according to the module import ordering. The second component of the pair is an ordinal number, which is typically constructed by mapping lexicographic tuples of numbers into polynomials in the limit ordinal ω. Although this second component is formulated in terms of a single ordinal, it is similar to the ready-to-use k components of $\mathcal{U}_\top$ in this paper. The more interesting difference lies in their first component versus the use of strata in this paper.

Using multisets of method names provides more flexibility than the strata proposed in this paper. For example, it is possible to give Process (Section 9.7) a specification that allows Process' to call Sqrt without needing to know anything about the relative ordering of modules Util and Math. On the other side of the ledger, the flexibility comes at a cost. To make use of the full flexibility requires specifications that relate objects to their "dynamic depth" [7].

As a final point of comparison with the work by Jacobs et al. [7], if there are no inter-module overrides (that is, if overrides are always in the same module as the corresponding virtual method), then one can obtain this paper's general methodology using their methodology by defining a stratum to be a multiset consisting of one method name.

(One also needs to adjust their call rule to refund the permissions required to make a call upon return from the call.) However, because their ordering of method names within and across modules is fixed, there is no analogous way to define a **below** A clause where the origin of stratum A is an imported module.

The specialized methodology in this paper does not use strata explicitly. This means that programs need to use **decreases** clauses only to explain why recursion and mutual recursion terminates. To reduce programmer-supplied information even more, the Dafny program verifier [9] uses a default **decreases** clause for any method that doesn't explicitly declare one. The default uses a lexicographic tuple consisting of the method's parameters, in the order given. In practice, this default turns out to be an effective way to reduce explicit termination specifications.

To go even further in reducing explicit termination specifications, one can employ some kind of termination analysis, like that by Cook, Podelski, and Rybalchenko [3]. Such analyses typically require the entire program, which would not qualify as modular verification. However, even applying such an analysis within a module would help reduce explicit specifications.

11   Conclusions

Termination proofs must show a decrease in some well-founded order. In this paper, I proposed using as the domain of that order a lexicographic tuple, where the first component layers methods into partially ordered strata and the remaining components are ordinary expressions of the language. In a verified program, the strata correspond to disjoint sets of methods, where every recursive or mutually recursive call goes between methods of the same stratum. The task of ensuring termination is divided into the subtask of partitioning methods into strata and the subtask of applying theorem proving to calls within each stratum. Calls between strata are non-recursive, so their termination follows trivially.

In the paper, I presented two methodologies for performing the first of the two subtasks. In the general methodology, strata are explicitly introduced by the programmer. In the specialized methodology, the strata are inferred from modular views of call graphs, some additional ordering specifications, and some restrictions. Both methodologies lend themselves to modular verification.

Acknowledgments. I am grateful to Fabio Madge, Dominic Mulligan, John Tristan, Remy Willems, and Stefan Zetzsche for discussions and feedback that improved this paper.

References

1. Ahmadi, R., Leino, K.R.M., Nummenmaa, J.: Automatic verification of Dafny programs with traits. In: Monahan, R. (ed.) Formal Techniques for Java-like Programs, FTfJP 2015. ACM (2015)
2. Chapman, R., Dross, C., Matthews, S., Moy, Y.: Co-developing programs and their proof of correctness. Commun. ACM **67**(3), 84–94 (2024)

3. Cook, B., Podelski, A., Rybalchenko, A.: Termination proofs for systems code. In: Schwartzbach, M.I., Ball, T. (eds.) Proceedings of the ACM SIGPLAN 2006 Conference on Programming Language Design and Implementation, pp. 415–426. ACM (2006)
4. Dijkstra, E.W.: A Discipline of Programming. Prentice Hall, Englewood Cliffs, NJ (1976)
5. Filliâtre, J.-C., Paskevich, A.: Why3—where programs meet provers. In: Felleisen, M., Gardner, P. (eds.) ESOP 2013. LNCS, vol. 7792, pp. 125–128. Springer, Heidelberg (2013). https://doi.org/10.1007/978-3-642-37036-6_8
6. Floyd, R.W.: Assigning meanings to programs. In: Proceedings Symposium on Applied Mathematics, vol. 19, pp. 19–31 (1967)
7. Jacobs, B., Bosnacki, D., Kuiper, R.: Modular termination verification. In: Boyland, J.T. (ed.) 29th European Conference on Object-Oriented Programming, ECOOP 2015. LIPIcs, vol. 37, pp. 664–688. Schloss Dagstuhl—Leibniz-Zentrum für Informatik (2015)
8. Jacobs, B., Piessens, F.: The VeriFast program verifier. Technical report CW-520, Department of Computer Science, Katholieke Universiteit Leuven, Belgium, August 2008
9. Leino, K.R.M.: Dafny: an automatic program verifier for functional correctness. In: Clarke, E.M., Voronkov, A. (eds.) LPAR 2010. LNCS (LNAI), vol. 6355, pp. 348–370. Springer, Heidelberg (2010). https://doi.org/10.1007/978-3-642-17511-4_20
10. Leino, K.R.M.: Accessible software verification with Dafny. IEEE Softw. **34**(6), 94–97 (2017)
11. Müller, P., Schwerhoff, M., Summers, A.J.: Viper: a verification infrastructure for permission-based reasoning. In: Jobstmann, B., Leino, K.R.M. (eds.) VMCAI 2016. LNCS, vol. 9583, pp. 41–62. Springer, Heidelberg (2016). https://doi.org/10.1007/978-3-662-49122-5_2

Liveness to Safety for Distributed Systems

Lenore D. Zuck[(⊠)]

University of Illinois Chicago, Chicago, USA
zuck@uic.edu

Abstract. The paper studies the problem of reducing liveness properties into safety properties for distributed systems with arbitrary topologies. The reduction is based on using justice (weak fairness) properties in liveness proof rules to define a *planner* – sequences of just states that guarantee liveness, and thus replacing the liveness rule with a monitor for the planner, that guarantees that a liveness goal is reached by the time the planner is satisfied. The method is extended to protocols with probabilistic elements.

The method is applied to three protocols, one that induces a spanning tree on a network, one that chooses a leader in each tree of a forest of trees, and one that identifies a maximal independent set in a network.

Dear Andreas: Over two decades ago we found our mutual interest in liveness, and, with Bernhard, ran a "Beyond Safety" workshop in Schloss Ringer. I just looked at the "Liveness Manifestos" we requested. You wrote "The issue [. . .] becomes obsolete once we have shown that the good methods for checking safety are, in fact, methods for checking liveness (we are working on it)." We still are. My offering to you here is more evidence that you were correct. Thanks for years of friendship, being a great co-organizer, many productive work-related arguments, and some amazing dinners.

1 Introduction

We study the problem of verifying liveness of distributed protocols with arbitrary underlying topologies using the "liveness to safety" method. There, instead of using well founded ranking to establish liveness, one reduces liveness to a safety property, and verifies the resulting safety property. The main advantage of replacing liveness by safety is that there are many methodologies and tools for verification of safety properties of distributed systems, while verification of liveness properties is less studied and is considerably more difficult.

We focus on networks of processes with arbitrary topologies where, unless otherwise specified, nodes (processes) can communicate only with their neighbors. The processes run some protocol, often to create coordination or synchronization. The protocols are associated with both *safety* and *liveness* properties. Mechanized proofs of safety properties of such systems have been studied for decades, while focus on mechanization of verification of liveness properties is rather recent.

Let the underlying network be described by the undirected graph $G = (V, E)$, where each node is associated with a single process. There is a protocol that each node

D. Dietsch et al. (Eds.): Podelski Festschrift, LNCS 14765, pp. 23–39, 2026.
https://doi.org/10.1007/978-3-032-13711-1_2

runs, whose goal is to impose some structure among the nodes. For example, choosing a leader. Each node can only communicate with its neighbors. In particular, nodes have no information about the structure of the underlying graph they are part of, but only about the edges connected to them directly. A property ϕ is valid if for every network configuration G where the nodes execute the protocol, the property ϕ holds in every computation of the system. If ϕ is a safety property (for example, $\Box\, p$ where p is a state property), then it suffices to show that for every reachable state satisfies ϕ. We assume (rather optimistically) that we have the tools to verify safety properties for such distributed systems.

The situation becomes more difficult when we consider liveness property. Take, for example, the common response property ψ that claims that "every p-state is eventually followed by a q-state" (in LTL, ψ is $p \Rightarrow \Diamond\, q$). Unless p implies q, proving ψ requires that computations progress. The progress of computations is described by *fairness* properties. One form of fairness, and the only one we will discuss here, is *justice*. Justice properties are state properties that must hold infinitely many times. For example, the justice property r requires that every computation has infinitely many r-states. Liveness is often verified by a well founded ranking of the reachable states. To verify ψ, one assigns a ranking to each state that appears on a q-less computation from a p-state (known as a *pending* state). Then, one proves that the ranking is non-increasing in transitions among pending states, and that the ranking must eventually decrease, unless a q-state is reached. See [MP91] for examples of such rules.

Often, it is justice properties that enforce the eventual decrease of ranking. In slightly more detail, each pending state s is associated with a set of justice properties it violates. Each transition from s that does not decrease the ranking leads into a state s' that violates the same justice properties s does (and perhaps more), while if transition from s into a state s' that satisfies some of the justice requirements associated with s, then s' ranking is lower than that of s.

The use of justice properties in such rules indicates that, in a sense, the liveness property is "bounded" by the justice properties. That is, since the decrease of the ranking depends on the guaranteed (eventual) occurrences of just-states, the liveness property can be recast as a safety property that embeds the required occurrences of the just-states in it. As we show, in many instances it is possible to identify the sequences of helpful justice requirements from the protocol together with the underlying communication graph.

Consider the following simple example (taken from [FMPZ06]) where the processes all have access to a shared boolean variable t which they can all read and write. This bypasses the discussion of the underlying topology, while emphasizing the liveness-to-fairness method.

Example 1 (A Simple Mutual Exclusion Algorithm).
Program SIMPLE in Fig. 1 is a simple mutual exclusion algorithm that guarantees deadlock-freedom access to critical section for any N processes $[1..N]$.

In this version of the algorithm, location 0 constitutes the non-critical section which a process may non-deterministically exit to the trying section at location 1. Location 1 is the waiting location where a process waits until the token (t) is available and then takes it. Location 2 is the critical section, and location 3 is the exit section where the

$$
\prod_{i=1}^{N} P[i] :: \quad
\begin{array}{l}
\textbf{in} \quad N : \textbf{natural where } N > 1 \\
\textbf{local } \ t \ : \textbf{bool where } t = 1 \\
\left[\begin{array}{l}
\textbf{loop forever do} \\
\quad \left[\begin{array}{l}
0 : \textbf{NonCritical} \\
1 : \textbf{when } t = 1 \textbf{ do } t := 0 \\
2 : \textbf{Critical} \\
3 : t := 1
\end{array}\right]
\end{array}\right]
\end{array}
$$

Fig. 1. Program SIMPLE

process returns the token. As we show, the program guarantees that if some processes are waiting to enter the critical section, eventually some process will succeed.

Let ψ be the liveness property $(\exists i.\pi[i] = 1 \Rrightarrow \Diamond \exists j.\pi[j] = 2)$ where $\pi[i]$ denotes the location of process i (in general, $\phi_1 \Rrightarrow \phi_2$ abbreviates $\Box\,(\phi_1 \to \phi_2)$.) The property ψ describes that if *some* process is waiting to enter the critical section, then *some* process eventually enters the critical section. The justice requirements associated with Program SIMPLE are, for every $i \in [1..N]$, $J_1[i] = (\pi[i] \neq 1 \vee t = 0)$, $J_2[i] = (\pi[i] \neq 2)$, and $J_3[i] = (\pi[i] \neq 3)$, that is, no process can stay forever in location 1 with $t = 1$, and no process can stay forever in locations 2 or 3. Assume that the safety property

$$
\phi : |\{i \in [1..N] : \pi[i] \in \{2,3\}| + t = 1
$$

which implies mutual exclusion (at most one process can be at locations 2 or 3) was established using parameterized safety techniques.

Consider ψ and let *pend* be the set of *pending* states, that is, any state on a $(\forall j.\pi[j] \neq 2)$-path originating in a $(\exists i.\pi[i] = 1)$-state. The usual method to establish ψ identifies a well-founded domain, assigns a ranking from this domain to each *pend*-state, and establishes that every transition from a *pend*-state either leads to the goal state or to *pend*-state whose ranking is monotonically decreasing, and that some transitions are guaranteed to lead to the goal state or to a *pend*-state with a lower ranking. Here, we can use $(\{1,2\}, \leq)$ as the well founded domain, and, rank each *pend*-state s with $\delta(s) = 1 + (\exists i.\pi[i] = 3)$.

If the system is in a *pend*-state with $\delta = 2$, then from the safety property it follows that there is a single process, say j, such that $\pi[j] = 3$. It thus follows that $\neg J_3[j]$ holds. Every non-j transition will keep the system in a *pend*-state with $\delta = 2$ and $\neg J_3[j]$, and a j-transition will lead the system to a $J_3[j]$ state with $\delta = 1$. The justice requirement $J_3[j]$ then guarantees that if $\delta = 2$, eventually $\delta = 1$.

If the system is in a *pend*-state with $\delta = 1$, the safety property guarantees that $t = 1$, and *pend* guarantees that $\exists.i\pi[i] = 1$, that is, the set $\{i : \pi[i] = 1\}$ is not empty, and for every i in the set, $\neg J_1[i]$ holds. Fairness now requires that eventually one of processes in location 1, say j, is scheduled and enters location 2, satisfying the goal as well as $J_1[j]$.

The *liveness to safety* (L2S) method calls for forgoing the ranking. This is accomplished by replacing the liveness property with a safety property, or more appropriately, *bounded liveness* property, that implies the original liveness, and captures some upper bound on when it is obtained. Here, we use a bound that is a sequence of justice requirements, and the bound is the computation that meets the justice requirements in the sequence.

Let $J_1, \ldots, J_k$ be a sequence of justice requirements. From fairness it follows that any prefix of a computation must be followed by some finite suffix with a projection $J_1, \ldots, J_k$ of the just states. If after every *pend*-state such a suffix guarantees the liveness goal, then the liveness is guaranteed. Hence, we replace the liveness property by the safety property "it is never the case that a suffix of *pend* that has a J_1-state, then a J_2-state, $\ldots$, then a J_k-state where the liveness goal is not attained."

We call such a sequence of justice properties a *planner*. For Example 1, the planner may consist of two rounds, each consisting of all the justice properties. If there is a process, say j, in location 3, in the first round, $J_3[k]$-state causes the token to be released and to have no processes in location 3. If there is no process in location 3, a single round will move a process from location 1 into location 2. Each "round" here may consist of many states (and transitions). We, however, require that each round satisfies all the justice requirements, in whichever order. The existence of such rounds, in every computation, is guaranteed by fairness.

The L2S method described here was applied to systems with shared variables, such as the one in Example 1, or where the underlying topologies (G) are a ring, a star, a clique, or other symmetric topologies. When there are no shared variables, communication is often restricted to neighbors, the nodes in the system may not know what is the topology, which itself may change over time, or even the diameter of the network (that can often be used to measure progress.) Proving safety properties for such systems is sometimes non-trivial (see [BPZ06]).

To apply our L2S method we employ a non-interfering monitor that tracks the scheduler and ensures the liveness property is attained before the scheduler exhaustes the planer. We first apply it on two examples. One is the Spanning Tree Algorithm inspired by the Asynchronous Spanning Tree of [Lyn96], that induces a directed spanning tree over an undirected network of process starting with a given root. The liveness property is "every node that is reachable form the root eventually has a parent or is the root." The second example is the Leader Election used in IEEE 1934 interface standard for a serial bus (FireEire). The initial configuration there is a tree or a forest of trees, with devices at the leaves. The goal is for each tree to choose a leader, and the process is somewhat similar to that of Lynch's Spanning Tree algorithm. The liveness property is "eventually there is a leader in every tree in the forest."

The third example is Luby's Maximal Independent Set (MIS) [Lub86] that finds a maximal independent set in the network. Unlike the previous examples, this protocol depends on probabilistic choices which must be incorporated into the L2S strategy. We embed the *probabilistic planner* of [APZ03] into the justice-based planner to derive the liveness property of the MIS protocol. Unlike the justice-based planner, a probabilistic planner dictates an exact sequence (of random draws), and its soundness follows from measure theory arguments. Its liveness property is "eventually each connected node declares it self in, or out, of the MIS."

The safety properties of all three protocols were established in [BPZ06].

To the best of our knowledge, this paper is the first to offer a mechanizable proof methodology to verify liveness of these distributed protocols.0

2   Formal Model and Verifying Invariants

We present our computational model and the L2S with planners method.

2.1   Discrete Systems

As our computational model, we take a *discrete system* $S = \langle Var, \Theta, \rho, \mathcal{J} \rangle$, where

- *Var*—A set of *system variables*. A *state* of S provides a type-consistent interpretation of the variables *Var*. For a state s and a system variable $v \in Var$, we denote by $s[v]$ the value assigned to v by the state s. Let Σ denote the set of all states over *Var*.
- Θ—The *initial condition*: An assertion (state formula) characterizing the initial states.
- $\rho(Var, Var')$—The *transition relation*: An assertion, relating the values *Var* of the variables in state $s \in \Sigma$ to the values V' in an S-successor state $s' \in \Sigma$.
- $\mathcal{J}$—A set of *justice* (*weak fairness*) requirements (assertions). A computation must include infinitely many states satisfying each of the justice requirements.

For an assertion ψ, we say that $s \in \Sigma$ is a ψ-state if $s \models \psi$.

A *computation* of a system S is an infinite sequence of states $\sigma : s_0, s_1, s_2, ...$, satisfying the requirements:

- *Initiality*—s_0 is initial, i.e., $s_0 \models \Theta$.
- *Consecution*—For each $\ell = 0, 1, ...$, the state $s_{\ell+1}$ is an S-successor of s_ℓ. That is, $\langle s_\ell, s_{\ell+1} \rangle \models \rho(Var, Var')$ where, for each $v \in Var$, we interpret v as $s_\ell[v]$ and v' as $s_{\ell+1}[v]$.
- *Justice*—for every $J \in \mathcal{J}$, σ contains infinitely many occurrences of J-states.

We say that the system S satisfied an LTL property ϕ, and denote it by $S \models \phi$, if for every computation σ of S, $\sigma \models \phi$.

Asynchronous Composition.   Given two systems, $S_i : \langle Var_i, \Theta_i, \rho_i, \mathcal{J}_i \rangle$ for $i \in \{1, 2\}$. The *asynchronous parallel composition* of S_1 and S_2, denoted by $S_1 \| S_2$, is the system

$$\langle Var_1 \cup Var_2, \Theta_1 \wedge \Theta_2, \rho_1^{\#} \cup \rho_2^{\#}, \mathcal{J}_1 \cup \mathcal{J}_2 \rangle$$

where for every $i = 1, 2$, $\rho_i^{\#} = \rho^i \wedge pres((Var_1 \cup Var_2) - Var_i)$. For any set of variables U, $pres(U)$ abbreviates $\wedge_{u \in U}(u' = u)$. Thus, in the asynchronous parallel composition of S_1 and S_2, each step is a step of one of the participating systems, leaving the variables of the other, that are not common to the two systems, intact.

Synchronous Composition. Given two systems as above. The *synchronous parallel composition* of S_1 and S_2, denoted by $S_1 \| S_2$, is the system

$$\langle Var_1 \cup Var_2, \Theta_1 \wedge \Theta_2, \bigvee_{\tau_1 \in \rho_1, \tau_2 \in \rho_2} \tau_1 \wedge \tau_2, \mathcal{J}_1 \cup \mathcal{J}_2 \rangle$$

Simple Planners. Let $S = \langle Var, \Theta, \rho, \mathcal{J} \rangle$ be a system, and let $J \in \mathcal{J}$ be a justice assertion. Assume σ_0 is a finite prefix of a computation σ of S, that is, $\sigma_0 \prec \sigma$. Since σ is required to contain infinitely many occurrences of J, there is a finite $\sigma_1 = s_k, \ldots, s_\ell$ such that $(\sigma_0; \sigma_1) \prec \sigma$, s_ℓ is a J-state, all for all i, $k \leq i < \ell$, s_i is not a J-states. We denote $\sigma_0; \sigma_1$ by $\sigma_0 \circ J$.

Let a (simple) *planner* be $pln = J_1, \ldots, J_n$, where for every $1 \leq i \leq n$, $J_i \in \mathcal{J}$. We extend the definition of $\sigma \circ J$ to $\sigma \circ pln$ inductively: for every i, $1 \leq i \leq n$, $\sigma_0 \circ pln$ is $\sigma_0 \circ (J_1, \ldots, J_i) = (\sigma_0 \circ (J_1, \ldots, J_{i-1})) \circ J_i$. The resulting $\sigma_0 \circ pln$ is a finite prefix of σ and contains states satisfying $J_1, \ldots, J_n$, in this order, after the prefix σ_0. We denote the extension of σ_0 to $\sigma_0 \circ pln$ by $(\sigma_0 \circ pln)_{|\sigma_0}$. That is, $\sigma_0 \circ pln = \sigma_0; (\sigma_0 \circ pln)_{|\sigma_0}$.

2.2 Monitoring Liveness with Safety Using Justice Sequences

Let S and pln, be as above. Assume a progress property $\phi \colon q \Rightarrow \Diamond r$. It is often the case that, once a q-state occurs (i.e., once the system is in a pending state), after all justice requirements in pln are met in order (not necessarily consecutively), an r-state is met. We then say that the progress property ϕ is *bounded*, with pln being the bound.

Suppose a planner pln for ϕ and assume that for every prefix σ_0 of a S-computation that ends with a q-state, $(\sigma_0 \circ pln)_{|\sigma_0}$ contains an r-state. It then follows that $S \models \phi$. To check that indeed every q-state, once the planner pln is invoked, reaches an r-state, we construct a *non-interfering monitor* $M_\phi(pln)$ that is synchronously composed with S. The monitor is activated when a computation reaches a q-state, if it is not already active. Once active, the monitor traces the justice properties according to pln, and declares "failure" if pln is exhausted before an r-state is reached. If an r-state is reached, the monitor becomes inactive. The verification of ϕ then reduces to a verification that the monitor never declares failure.

The non-interfering *monitor*, $M_\phi(pln) = \langle Var_M, \Theta_M, \rho_M, \emptyset \rangle$, that is synchronously composed with S, is defined by:

Var_M – consists of Var and two new variables: a boolean $pend$ and a variable cur in the range $[1..|pln|]$. The variable $pend$ is set, if not already set, when the system is in a state that follows a q-state, and is reset when the system reaches an r-state. The variable cur marks which justice states in pln where met in order.

Θ_M – $pend = (q \wedge \neg r) \wedge cur = 1$, i.e., initially the current position in pln points to the first position in pln;

ρ_M – ρ_M consists of two conjuncts, one for each of the variables:
  1. $pend' = \neg r' \wedge (pend \vee q')$. This conjunct states that $pend$ becomes true when it was false and $q \wedge \neg r$ is true, and that $pend$ becomes false when r is realized. In all other cases $pend$ is intact;

$$2.\ cur' = \begin{pmatrix} \textbf{if} & \neg pend \vee \neg pend' & \textbf{then } 1 \\ \textbf{else if } J'_{cur} & & \textbf{then } cur + 1 \\ \textbf{else} & & cur \end{pmatrix}$$

The first part states that a new "tracing" of pln starts from pending states when a r-state was not reached. Note that since $r \rightarrow \neg pend$, cur is set to 1 when an r-state is reached. The second part increments cur with a new $(pend \wedge J_{cur})$-state. The third part leaves cur intact when the new state satisfies $(pend \wedge \neg J_{cur})$.

Note the variables in Var are not modified by $M_\phi(pln)$, justifying our description of $M_\phi(pln)$ as "non interfering."

Thus, as long as S is not in a pending state, $pend$ and cur are 0. Once S is in a pending state, $pend$ is set. From thereon, whenever a J_{cur+1}-state is reached, cur is incremented (as long as it does not exceed $|pln|$). Obviously, if cur ever reaches $|pln|+1$), then the goal r was not reached after pln is exhausted, refuting the assumption that ϕ is a bounded-by-pln progress property. This is captured by following claim:

$$(S \| M_\phi(pln)) \models \square \, (cur \leq |pln|) \quad \Longrightarrow \quad S \models \phi$$

Proof. Assume that $S \not\models \phi$. Thus, there exists an S-computation σ such that $\sigma = \sigma_0 ; \sigma'$, σ_0 ends with a q-state, and σ' is a r-less infinite suffix. Consider the behavior of $S \| M_\phi(pln)$ on $\sigma_0 \circ pln$. Since all $(\sigma_0 \circ pln)_{|\sigma_0}$ are pending and not-satisfying r, it follows that $\sigma \models \Diamond \, (cur > |pln|)$. $\square$

2.3 Generalizing the Planner

So far we assumed that the planner consists of an explicit sequence of justice properties, and that each should be met in a separate state. We first remove the second assumption. If a $pend$ state satisfies several consecutive justice condition, J_{cur}, J_{cur+k}, then cur can be incremented by k in the second part of cur's update. More formally, consider the case that $pend' \wedge J'_{cur}$ in the second part of cur's update. Let $k \leq |pln| - cur$ be the maximum such that $J'_{cur}, \ldots, J'_{cur+k}$. Then cur' can be set to $cur + k$ without impacting the correctness of Lemma 1.

It is often the case that one does not want to restrict to a particular sequence, but rather to a set of sequences that, given a set of justice requirements, allows them all to occur in whichever order. To capture such a planner, we assume an interleaving $\|$ operator to regular languages, such that for every $a, b \in \Sigma$ (where Σ is the alphabet), $a \| b$ is the regular expressions describing the language $\{ab, ba\}$. Similarly, for $a_1, \ldots, a_n \in \Sigma$, $\|_{i=1}^{n} a_i$ is the regular expression describing the language that contains all permutations of $a_1, \ldots, a_n$. Armed with this notation we can include sequences of the form $\|_{J \in \mathcal{J}'} J$, $\mathcal{J}' \subseteq \mathcal{J}$, in a planner, indicating that every $J \in \mathcal{J}'$ should be met (at least once) in the finite suffix. This generalizes the work [FMPZ06] where it is assumed that every process is associated with a single justice property, and the planner is of the from $(\|_{J \in \mathcal{J}} J)^K$ for some $K \geq 1$, that is, the suffix has K rounds where each justice property is met. The monitor for this planner is described there.

For a distributed system with arbitrary topology it is often easier to construct *pln* so that it depends on the topology, or on some state property. For the first case, consider a tree where progress starts at the leaves and propagates upwards (see, e.g., Sect. 3.2). It then makes sense to design a planner consisting of rounds, starting with the leaves and going up until the root. For the second case, consider Example 1. When describing the example, we alluded to the planner $(\|_{J\in\mathcal{J}}J)^2$. There, $\mathcal{J}$ consists of $3N$ properties, say $J_\ell[i]$ for $1 \le i \le N$ and $\ell \in \{1, 2, 3\}$, where $J_\ell[i]$ is the justice property associated with process i while in location ℓ. For example, $J_1[i] = \neg(\pi[i] = 1 \wedge t = 1)$. The reason that two rounds are required was to first clear location 3 (first round) and then move a process from location 1 into location 2 (second round). From the safety property it follows that there is at most one process at location 3. Assume this is the case and let i_0 be the id of this process. Then once a $J_3[i_0]$-state is reached, the first time a $J_1[i]$-state is reached, so is the goal. This calls for the simpler planner $pln : \|_{i\in[1..N]}J_3[i] ; \|_{i\in[1..N]}J_1[i]$ which consists of two parts. The first guarantees that

$$\phi_1 :\ (\exists i.\pi[i] = 1) \Rrightarrow \Diamond\, ((\exists j.\pi[j] = 2) \vee (\exists i.\pi[i] = 1 \wedge \forall j.\pi[j] \neq 3))$$

while the second part guarantees that

$$\phi_2 :\ (\exists i.\pi[i] = 1 \wedge \forall j.\pi[j] \neq 3) \Rrightarrow \Diamond\, (\exists j.\pi[j] = 2)$$

In the general case, a planner may consist of several consecutive parts, some consisting of explicit lists of justice properties, and some using the $\|$ operator, indicating that the justice properties can be attained in whichever order.

We described above a monitor for planners that consist of explicit lists of justice properties. Assume a planner P that is of the new form $\|_{J\in\mathcal{J}'}J$. We abuse notation and let P refer the set of justice requirements in this planner. The non-interfering monitor for $\phi : (q \Rrightarrow \Diamond r)$ using the planner P is $M_\phi(P) = \langle Var_M, \Theta_M, \rho_M, \emptyset \rangle$ is defined by:

Var_M – consists of V and two new variables: a boolean *pend* and a set $Q \subseteq P \cup \{\bot\}$ where $\bot \notin \mathcal{J}$. The variable *pend* is as before. The variable Q saves the P-justice states that were already met.

Θ_M – *pend* $= (q \wedge \neg r) \wedge Q = \emptyset$, i.e., initially no justice property in A is met;

ρ_M – ρ_M consists of two conjuncts, one for each of the variables:

1. *pend* is updated as before;

2. $Q' = \begin{pmatrix} \textbf{if} \qquad \neg pend \vee \neg pend' \qquad\qquad\qquad \textbf{then}\ \emptyset \\ \textbf{else if}\ R = \{J' : J \in P\} \wedge Q \subseteq P\ \textbf{then}\ Q \cup R \\ \qquad\qquad\qquad\qquad\qquad\qquad \textbf{else}\ \{\bot\} \end{pmatrix}$

   This conjunct states that a new "tracing" of P starts from pending states when a r-state was not reached. Once in a *pend*-state with some $J' \subseteq P$ are reached, these J's are added to Q. Once $Q = P$, any step sets Q to $\bot$.

Obviously, if Q ever becomes $\{\bot\}$, then the goal r was not reached after A is exhausted, refuting the assumption that ϕ is a bounded-by-A progress property. This is captured by following claim:

$$S \| M_\phi(P) \models \Box\,(Q \neq \{\bot\}) \quad \Longrightarrow \quad S \models \phi$$

Example 2. Consider the synchronous composition of the program of Example 1 with $M_\phi(P_1)$ where $P_1 = \|_{i \in [1..N]} J_3[i])$. Thus q is $(\exists j.\pi[j] = 2)$ and r is $((\exists j.\pi[j] = 2) \vee (\exists i.\pi[i] = 1 \wedge \forall j.\pi[j] \neq 3)$. Denote by Q_1 the set Q used by this monitor.

We obtained the invariant ψ_1:

$$\forall i \neq j.\ Q_1 \neq \{\bot\}\ \wedge\ (\neg pend \vee t = 1 \vee Q_1 = \emptyset)\ \wedge$$
$$pend \to (t = 0 \wedge (\pi[i] = 3 \to \pi[j] \notin \{2,3\} \wedge Q_1 = P_1 \setminus \{J_3[i]\})$$
$$pend \to (\exists i.\pi[i] = 3 \wedge \exists j.\pi[j] = 1)$$

Together with the safety invariant, ψ_1 is an inductive invariant and implies $\Box\,(Q_1 \neq \{\bot\})$. From Lemma 2 it now follows that $simple \models \phi_1$.

An invariant ψ_2 for the monitor that establishes ϕ_2, using P_2 for the planner for this part and Q_2 for the internal variables of the monitor, is:

$$\forall i \neq j.\ Q_2 \neq \{\bot\}\ \wedge\ (\neg pend \vee t = 1 \vee Q_2 = \emptyset)\ \wedge$$
$$pend \to (t = 1 \wedge (\pi[i] \notin \{2,3\} \wedge P_2 \subseteq P_2) \wedge (\exists j.\pi[j] = 1))$$

Which, again, with the safety invariant implies that $\Box\,(Q_2 \neq \{\bot\})$, and, from Lemma 2, that $simple \models \phi_2$.

We could have taken the complete planner, $P_1; P_2$, to obtain an invariant that is a conjunction of ψ_1 and ψ_2. We separated the steps to emphasize that we can define sub-goals and use each "sub-planner" to accomplish one of them.

The idea of separating the attainment of liveness into subgoals, each accomplishes a step towards the goal, is not novel. For example, the liveness proofs in Unity [CM89] are of that nature. There, a liveness proof is broken up into consecutive "chunks" and justice (in fact, a weaker form of the justice defined here) and helpful transitions ensure that each chunk is satisfied. Our planners generalize this idea to more complex patterns, which help shorten and simplify liveness proofs.

3   Examples of Tree Protocols

A Distributed Spanning Tree protocol assumes a bi-directional connected graph with a designated root, and imposes a spanning tree structure on top of it.

The Leader Election is part of the *root contention* protocol used in the IEEE 1394 (formerly known as FireWire) bus specification. IEEE 1394 specifies a network to which devices can be connected and disconnected dynamically. At each point in time, the network is arranged as a tree, or a forest of trees, where the devices are at the leaf nodes. The root contention sub-protocol is invoked during a connection or disconnection event, at which time the root of the each subtree needs to be determined anew.

3.1   Distributed Spanning Tree

The Distributed Spanning Tree protocol studied here is a variant of the Asynchronous Spanning Tree algorithm of Lynch [Lyn96]. There is a distributed system of processes arranged in a bi-directional connected graph $G = (V, E)$, without self loops, where each node represents a process. A node $v_0 \in V$ is designated as the *root* and initiates the protocol whose goal is to impose a (directed) spanning tree on the graph with v_0 as the root.

For a node $v \in V$, let $neigh(v)$ denote the immediate neighbors of v. For simplicity's sake, we bypass the communication model of I/O automata and assume a $V \times V$ matrix $ping$, where process v can write the vth column and read the vth row. The entries of $ping$ are boolean, all initialized to false but for the $(v_0)^{th}$ column which is initialized to true for every (v, v_0) entry where $v \in neigh(v_0)$.

Each process v, has two variables, $parent(v)$ in $V \cup \{\bot\}$, initialized to $\bot$, and a boolean $done(v)$, initialized to false. The variable $parent(v)$ is undefined until v's parent in the tree is determined, and the variable $done(v)$ is set when node v has communicated with all its neighbors. The protocol is described in Fig. 2. There, $ping$ is initialized to true for the $(v_0)^{th}$ column in all $neigh(v_0)$ entries, indicating that v_0 is requesting all its neighbors to be its children in the spanning tree. Thereafter, a non-v_0 node that is assigned a parent sets its $ping$ column to true for all its non-parent neighbors, as a request to be their parent. Each node v can write read and write $parent[v]$ and $done[v]$. It can also write $ping(v, u)$ and read $ping(u, v)$ for every $u \in neigh(v)$.

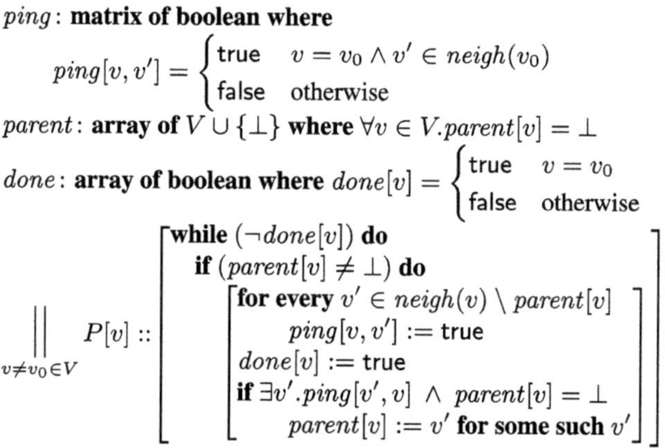

$$ping: \textbf{matrix of boolean where}$$
$$ping[v, v'] = \begin{cases} \text{true} & v = v_0 \land v' \in neigh(v_0) \\ \text{false} & \text{otherwise} \end{cases}$$
$$parent: \textbf{array of } V \cup \{\bot\} \textbf{ where } \forall v \in V.parent[v] = \bot$$
$$done: \textbf{array of boolean where } done[v] = \begin{cases} \text{true} & v = v_0 \\ \text{false} & \text{otherwise} \end{cases}$$

$$\left\|_{v \neq v_0 \in V} P[v] :: \begin{bmatrix} \textbf{while } (\neg done[v]) \textbf{ do} \\ \quad \textbf{if } (parent[v] \neq \bot) \textbf{ do} \\ \quad \quad \begin{bmatrix} \textbf{for every } v' \in neigh(v) \setminus parent[v] \\ \quad ping[v, v'] := \text{true} \end{bmatrix} \\ \quad done[v] := \text{true} \\ \quad \textbf{if } \exists v'.ping[v', v] \land parent[v] = \bot \\ \quad \quad parent[v] := v' \textbf{ for some such } v' \end{bmatrix}$$

Fig. 2. Program SPAN

The progress property of Program SPAN is:

$$\phi: \ \forall v \in V.\Diamond \, (done[v] \ \land \ (v \neq v_0 \to parent[v] \neq \bot))$$

claiming that for every node v, eventually $done[v]$ is set and every $v \neq v_0$ has a parent.

The safety property of Program SPAN is that at any point, the nodes assigned a parent together with v_0 form a spanning tree rooted at v_0. For a set of nodes U, a set of directed edges E', and a node $u_0 \in U$, let $Tree(U, u_0, E')$ denote the predicate that (U, E') is a directed spanning tree, that includes all of U's nodes, whose root is r. (See Sect. 3.3 for a discussion on this predicate.) Then the safety property of Program SPAN is:

$$\square \left(Tree\left(\{v_0\} \cup \{v \in V : parent[v] \neq \bot\}, v_0, \right.\right.$$
$$\left.\left. \{(u, v) : parent[v] \neq \bot \wedge (u = v_0 \vee parent[u] \neq \bot) \wedge parent(v) = u\}\right)\right)$$

That is, that at any point v_0 together with the nodes that are assigned a parent, form a directed spanning tree rooted at v_0 with the parent edges leading from a parent to a child.

Note that proving safety of programs that have such predicates such as $Tree$ has been performed in the past (e.g., [SRW02,BPZ07,BPSZ12,BPZ06]).

For the progress property ϕ, we rely on the safety property and need to establish that eventually every non-v_0 node is assigned a parent. The justice properties of Program SPAN are that every process is scheduled infinitely many times, that is, $\mathcal{J} = \{J_v, v \in V\}$. A possible planner is to schedule nodes in the order of their distance from the v_0. Let $V_0 = \{v_0\}$, and for every $i > 0$, let $V_i = \cup_{u \in V_{i-1}} neigh(u) \setminus \cup_{j < i} V_j$. Then the planner $\|_{v \in V_1} J_v; \|_{v \in V_2} J_v; \dots \|_{v \in V_d} J_v$, where d is the maximum distance between u_0 and any $v \in V$ will guarantee ϕ. If d is not known, then its upper bound, $|V| - 1$ can be used. A less sophisticated planner is the one that, for $|V|$ rounds, schedules all the nodes, that is $(\|_{v \in V} J_v)^{|V|}$.

Let K be the counter for the segment in the planner we use, which may be one of the two described. Assume K is initialized to 0 and is incremented at the end of every segment. Then for both planners we have the invariant:

$$\forall i \leq K, \forall v \in V_i.\ done[v] \wedge (v \neq v_0 \rightarrow parent[v] \neq \bot)$$

3.2   Leader Election

The Leader Election protocol described here is adapted from the protocol used in IEEE 1394 (FireWire). There, the network consists of trees with devices at the leaves. At times, processes (nodes) leave or join the network. When a change happens, a leader needs be elected. The leader election creates a spanning tree in each component it is run, but, unlike the previous case, the creation of the tree is initiated by the leaves (devices) and the root is determined when a tree is created. We do not model the dynamic aspect of the network since it is assumed the network is static for the duration of the protocol. The protocol is to succeed (elect leaders) only in sub-graphs that are themselves trees, otherwise, it makes no guarantees.

The description of the protocol is a simplified version from a similar one in [BPZ06]. One difference is fixing a bug there where the protocol does not start if a leaf node has a leaf sibling. There, only safety was proved, and the bug was not detected. This points to another virtue of proving liveness, namely, that safety proofs, that prove "nothing bad ever happens," may miss that sometimes "nothing ever happens." The other difference is technical. Here we let the *parent* relation to be readable by all, which allows us to describe a node-based protocol, as opposed to edges-based protocol there. The protocol is initiated by the devices, that is, the leaves.

Assume an undirected graph $G = (V, E)$. A subgraph (U, E') for $U \subseteq V$ and $E \subseteq E'$ is a tree if it is connected and $|U| = |E'| - 1$. Leaves are then nodes that have a single neighbor. The goal of the protocol is to elect a leader in each of the trees. We assume that a node, say v, which is not a leader, can become a child of another node, say $u \in neigh(v)$ in one atomic step. We refer to our version of the protocol as *Leader Election*, and present it in Fig. 3. As before, each node v has a variable $parent(v)$ in $V \cup \{\bot\}$ whose role as in the spanning tree protocol, and a boolean variable $leader[v]$, initialized to false, that is set to true once v becomes the leader of the tree is resides in.

$$
\begin{array}{l}
parent: \textbf{array of } V \cup \{\bot\} \textbf{ where } \forall v \in V.parent[v] = \bot \\
leader: \textbf{array of boolean where } \forall v \in V.leader[v] = \textsf{false} \\
\left\|_{v \in V}\ P[v] :: \left[
\begin{array}{l}
\textbf{if } \forall u \in neigh(v).parent[u] = v \\
\quad \textbf{then } leader[v] := \textsf{true} \\
\textbf{if } parent[v] = \bot \wedge |\{u \in neigh(v) : parent[u] = v\}| = |neigh(v)| - 1 \\
\quad \textbf{then } parent[v] := u \textbf{ s.t. } u \in neigh(v) \wedge parent[u] \neq v
\end{array}
\right]
\end{array}
$$

Fig. 3. Program LEADERELECTION

Each node process $P[v]$ performs the following two steps:

1. The first if-statement is executed if all the nodes in $neigh(v)$ have v as their parents. In this case, v becomes the leader by setting $leader$ to true. Note that if v is a singleton, then it becomes a leader;
2. The second if-statement is executed if all of v's neighbor, but for one, have v as their parent. Then v's parent becomes the neighbor of v that doesn't have v as its parent.

The protocol works as follows: Assume the underlying graph is a tree. Initially, all leaf nodes (and no internal node) can execute the second step since they have a single neighbor (that does not have them as a parent). Thereafter, the algorithm "climbs" up the tree, each node executing the second step, until the root, which executes the first step, is reached.

If the original graph consists of a forest of trees, then a leader will be elected in each of the trees. If the original graph has non-tree connected components, then no leader will be elected in these components. The safety property of the protocol therefore states that in each component, there is at most one leader. Formally, this is stated by:

$$\forall u, v \in V : u \neq v \wedge reachable(u, v) \rightarrow \Box \neg(leader[u] \wedge leader[v]) \tag{1}$$

where for every $u, v \in V$, $reachable(u, v)$ holds if there is E-path leading from u to v, i.e., if there are nodes $u = u_1, \ldots, u_k = v \in V$ such that for every $\ell = 1, \ldots, k - 1$, $E(u_\ell, u_{\ell+1})$.

Another invariant of the protocol, is:

$$\forall v \in V.\Box\, (leader[v] \rightarrow parent[v] = \bot)$$

That is, that processes that are leader are not assigned parents.

The progress property of the protocol is that, if G is a forest, then eventually every node will become a leader or be assigned a parent:

$$\forall v \in V. \Diamond \, (leader[v] \vee parent[v] \neq \bot)$$

We described both the spanning tree and the leader election in the same section because they have the same planner, and the resulting invariant is similar. Both also include some reasoning on reachability, which we discuss next.

3.3   On Reachability

For the spanning tree example, we assumed the graph is connected, for if it isn't, then the tree only spans the nodes that are reachable from v_0. In the leader election example, since it explicitly handles forests (that may consist of trees that are not connected), we defined *reachable* and ignored it being a somewhat problematic construct for verification.

The work in [BPZ06] offers a way to bypass the *reachable* predicate. This is accomplished by "coloring" a node, say red, and letting the color propagate to its neighbors, (or alternatively, applying breadth first search from a node) and replacing "reachable" by "eventually red." There is a discussion there on when one should start the coloring. A mechanized proof that eventual coloring of a node is equivalent to it being reachable is still open. The coloring can be replaced by a prophecy that eventually a node is colored red, thus replacing "reachability" with a prophecy variable. That is, a node is reachable iff it is eventually colored red. This in fact replaces the breadth first search inductive definition of reachability by induction over time.

It is sometimes possible to bypass 2nd order predicates when discussing trees. For example, the predicate $Tree(U, u_0, E')$ used in Sect. 3.1 can be described by a procedure that assigns the number 0 to u_0, and for every node whose number is i, assigns $i+1$ to all its neighbors that are not assigned numbers and deletes the corresponding edge. Since this procedure is sequential, its correctness and termination can be established by traditional methods as in [Man03]. If, upon termination, all edges are removed and all nodes are assigned numbers, the graph is a tree. The successful termination of the procedure can replace the $Tree(U, u_0, E')$ predicate. There are other methods to bypass the reachability portion of the $Tree$ predicate.

4   Maximal Independent Set (MIS)

The MIS protocol, due to [Lub86], assumes a bidirectional communication network $G = (V, E)$ where each node represents a process. The goal of the protocol is to define a *maximally independent set* (MIS) among the nodes, that is, a set which is independent (no two adjacent nodes are members of it) and is locally maximal (every node outside the set has a neighbor in the set). The protocol proceeds by letting processes, all of whom are initially undecided, to either enter the set ("win") or give up ("lose"). Processes that are winners or losers halt.

The original protocol is synchronous, consisting of a sequence of rounds, each consisting of three phases. In the first phase, each process draws a number from a fixed range and sends the result to all its neighbors. In the second phase, each process that holds the maximum value among its neighbors joins the set (i.e., wins) and sends a message to that effect to all its neighbors. In the third, each process that receives a message from a neighbor that joins the set declares itself a loser. We present the protocol as asynchronous, however, maintaining the lockstep nature of the phases among the nodes by allowing the phases to be shared among all nodes. To avoid explicit communication, we present the communication, namely, the values drawn and win/lose states, by variables shared among neighbors.

The probability distribution of each draw in the original protocol guarantees fast convergence. Since we are only interested in proving the convergence itself, disregarding how fast it is achieved, we allow the choices to be binary with equal probability, that is, $random(H, L)$ indicates a coin flip, with outcomes H or L, with equal probabilities (1/2).

Each process v has a variable $state[v]$ in $\{playing, lost, won\}$ and a variable $phase[v]$ in $\{0, 1, 2\}$. When $phase[v] = k$, the process is in the $(k + 1)^{st}$ phase of the three mentioned above. The program MIS is represented in Fig. 4. Each process loops as long as $state[v] = playing$. As a first step in the loop body, the process waits until all playing neighbors are in its, or the next, phase.

$$
\begin{array}{l}
state: \textbf{array of } \{playing, won, lost\} \textbf{ where } \forall v.state[v] = playing \\
val: \textbf{array of } \{H, L\} \\
phase: \textbf{array of } \{0, 1, 2\} \textbf{ where } \forall v.phase[v] = 0
\end{array}
$$

$$
\left\|_{v \in V} P[v] :: \left[
\begin{array}{l}
\textbf{while } state[v] = playing \textbf{ do} \\
\quad \left[
\begin{array}{l}
\textbf{await } \forall u \in V(state[u] = playing) \rightarrow \\
\quad phase[u] \in \{phase[v], phase[v]+1 \bmod 3\} \\
\textbf{if } phase[v] = 0 \textbf{ then } val[v] := random(H, L) \\
\textbf{elsif } phase[v] = 1 \wedge val[v] = H \wedge \forall u \in neigh(v).val[u] = L \\
\quad \textbf{then } state[i] := won \\
\textbf{elsif } phase[v] = 2 \wedge \exists u \in neigh(v).state[u] = won \\
\quad \textbf{then } state[v] := lost \\
phase[v] := phase[v]+1 \bmod 3
\end{array}
\right]
\end{array}
\right]
\right.
$$

Fig. 4. Program MIS

The safety properties of MIS are *independence*:

$$
\forall v.\forall u \in neigh(v).\square\,(state[v] = won \rightarrow state[u] \neq won)
$$

and *maximality*:

$$
\forall v.\exists u \in neigh(v).\square\,(state[v] = lost \rightarrow state[u] = won)
$$

The proof of the safety properties (as well as some others) is in [BPZ06].

The liveness property of the protocol is that eventually everybody wins or loses, that is:

$$\phi \colon \forall v \in V. \Diamond \, (state[v] = won \;\lor\; state[v] = lost)$$

This liveness property doesn't always hold, for example, if all nodes keep drawing L, there may will be a winner (or a loser). It is, however, the case that the property holds *with probability 1*, which is all that one can require of liveness in a system that includes probabilistic choices. That is, that the set of computations where the property holds, using a Lebesgue measure on the computations, has measure 1.

The planner we've used so can only refer to justice properties. To handle the probabilities, we use an idea first introduced in [APZ03]. It is based on the observation that in every infinite sequence of random draws (with probabilities bounded from below), every given finite sequence of draws will occur infinitely many times. Here, it suffices to consider an infinite binary tree where each node has two children, one labeled by H and the other by L, with each edge labeled by probability 0.5. Let σ be a finite sequence over $\{H, L\}$. Then the set of paths where σ occurs infinitely many times in the tree has measure 1. Hence, if we define a finite sequence σ over $\{H, L\}$ that guarantees termination, then termination is guaranteed with probability 1.

We thus superimpose on the previous planner a *probabilistic planner* that "decides" the outcome of a sequence of random draws. If we can show that when this sequence leads to the desired liveness, we can conclude that liveness is attained with probability 1. Moreover, since the random draws are (or should be) independent of the state of the system, we are at liberty to invoke our chosen random sequence at a state of our choosing. Note that the probabilistic planner is "tighter" than a non-probabilistic one, since it imposes an exact sequence of random draws, while the non-probabilistic planner does not impose exact sequencing. Another, and more meaningful difference, is that the justice-based planner can sometimes be derived automatically by trial and error, while the probabilistic planner requires a deeper understanding of the program at hand.

In the case of Program MIS, there are several simple probabilistic planners. The simplest one is $(L^{|V|}); H; (L^{|V|})$ that first segment forces $|V|$ consecutive draws to be L, guaranteeing an end to a round where there may be some winners (and some losers). The second and third segments guarantee a single winner in a round. While being simple, the convergence induced by this probabilistic planner may be rather slow, since this it allows for rounds where nobody wins, notably, where the number of players is smaller than $|V|$. A slightly more sophisticated planner can be activated when all playing nodes are in phase 0, and then, the first one to draw draws H while all others draw L. In other words, using this probabilistic planner, the body of the protocol for nodes v for which $phase[v] = 0$ is "determinized" to:

$$\left[\begin{array}{l} \textbf{await } \forall u \in V., [u] = playing \to phase[u] \in \{0, 1\} \\ \textbf{if } phase[v] = 0 \land \forall u.phase[u] = 0 \textbf{ then } val[v] := H \\ \textbf{elsif } phase[v] = 0 \land \exists u.phase[u] = 1 \textbf{ then } val[v] = L \\ phase[v] := 1 \end{array} \right]$$

This guarantees that the first process to draw wins, while all its neighbors lose. The processes not in the neighborhood remain in the game (playing) and proceed to the next round.

An even more sophisticated probabilistic planner will allow a process in phase 0, to draw H if its direct neighbors are also in phase 0, allowing for several winners to emerge in a round and thus allowing for faster termination. Note that the first planner is ignorant of the state of the system, while the other two are aware of it.

As to the scheduling planner for Program MIS, we can use $(\|_{v \in V} J_v)^{|V|}$, or refine it to $(\|_{v \in V \wedge state[v]=playing} J_v)^{|V|}$ where J_v requires a process to take a step.

We omit describing the invariants obtained by the composition of the protocol, non-probabilistic monitor, and probabilistic planner(s) for sanity's sake. The takeaway message is that the L2S method can be applied to probabilistic protocols, where liveness is with probability 1, by imposing a planner that determinizes the probabilistic draws.

5 Conclusion and Future Work

The work presented here is a generalization of several prior works. It is motivated by the renewed interest in S2L for distributed systems such as [SB05, DCG+16, PHL+18]. The planner, which is a generalization of a similar construct used for parameterized systems, is another methodology to replace liveness by safety. Just like the other methodologies, it works best if one understands the reason the given system satisfies liveness. Even without liveness, obtaining automatic invariants for infinite-state systems (even "just" parameterized ones) is often difficult and the resulting invariants are hard to understand. The invariants resulting from the S2L transformation with planners are bound to be even harder to understand, since automatically generated counter-examples combine elements that originate in the protocol to be shown live, with elements that are originate in the monitors (that uses the planners.)

It may seem that more "precise" planners (for example, the planner for leader election that schedules all the leaves, then progresses to up the tree) are better, it is not obvious that more precise planners result in easier to understand automated proofs, since they may lead to systems whose invariants require more expressive logics than their less precise counterparts.

We hope that this paper will encourage those who study S2L transformations to use a larger set of examples drawn from the more classical distributed computing literature.

Acknowledgement. The author would like to thank Kenneth McMillan for many fruitful discussions, and for Kedar Namjoshi for reading, and providing numerous useful comments, to earlier versions of this manuscript. The work was supported by the NSF (National Science Foundation) under Grant Nos. CCS-2140207 and SHF-1918429, by the DoD (Department of Defense) under Grant No. W911NF2010310, and by the Discovery Partners Institute of the Universities of Illinois (DPI). The views, opinions, and/or findings expressed are those of the author and should not be interpreted as representing the official views or policies of the U.S. Government, Department of Defense, or the DPI.

References

APZ03.   Arons, T., Pnueli, A., Zuck, L.D.: Parameterized verification by probabilistic abstraction. In: Foundations of Software Science and Computational Structures, 6th International Conference, FOSSACS 2003 Held as Part of the Joint European Conference on Theory and Practice of Software, ETAPS 2003, Warsaw, Poland, April 7–11, 2003, Proceedings, volume 2620 of Lecture Notes in Computer Science, pp. 87–102. Springer (2003). https://doi.org/10.1007/978-3-031-62362-2_30

BPSZ12.   Balaban, I., Pnueli, A., Sa'ar, Y., Zuck, L.D.: Verification of multi-linked heaps. J. Comput. Syst. Sci. **78**(3), 853–876 (2012)

BPZ06.   Balaban, I., Pnueli, A., Zuck, L.D.: Invisible safety of distributed protocols. In: Bugliesi, M., Preneel, B., Sassone, V., Wegener, I. (eds.) ICALP 2006. LNCS, vol. 4052, pp. 528–539. Springer, Heidelberg (2006). https://doi.org/10.1007/11787006_45

BPZ07.   Balaban, I., Pnueli, A., Zuck, L.D.: Shape analysis of single-parent heaps. In: Cook, B., Podelski, A. (eds.) VMCAI 2007. LNCS, vol. 4349, pp. 91–105. Springer, Heidelberg (2007). https://doi.org/10.1007/978-3-540-69738-1_7

CM89.   Chandy, K.M., Misra, J.: Parallel Program Design - A Foundation. Addison-Wesley (1989)

DCG+16.   Daniel, J., Cimatti, A., Griggio, A., Tonetta, S., Mover, S.: Infinite-state liveness-to-safety via implicit abstraction and well-founded relations. In: Chaudhuri, S., Farzan, A. (eds.) CAV 2016. LNCS, vol. 9779, pp. 271–291. Springer, Cham (2016). https://doi.org/10.1007/978-3-319-41528-4_15

FMPZ06.   Fang, Y., McMillan, K.L., Pnueli, A., Zuck, L.D.: Liveness by invisible invariants. In: Najm, E., Pradat-Peyre, J.-F., Donzeau-Gouge, V.V. (eds.) FORTE 2006. LNCS, vol. 4229, pp. 356–371. Springer, Heidelberg (2006). https://doi.org/10.1007/11888116_26

Lub86.   Luby, M.: A simple parallel algorithm for the maximal independent set problem. SIAM J. Comput. **15**(4), 1036–1053 (1986)

Lyn96.   Nancy, A.: Lynch. In: Distributed Algorithms. Morgan Kaufmann (1996)

Man03.   Manna, Z.: Mathematical Theory of Computation. Dover Publications (2003).

MP91.   Manna, Z., Pnueli, A.: Completing the temporal picture. Theor. Comput. Sci. **83**(1), 91–130 (1991)

PHL+18.   Padon, O., Hoenicke, J., Losa, G., Podelski, A., Sagiv, M., Shoham, S.: Reducing liveness to safety in first-order logic. Proc. ACM Program. Lang. **2**(POPL), 1–33 (2018)

SB05.   Schuppan, V., Biere, A.: Liveness checking as safety checking for infinite state spaces. In: Proceedings of the 7th International Workshop on Verification of Infinite-State Systems, INFINITY 2005, San Francisco, CA, USA, August 27, 2005, volume 149 of Electronic Notes in Theoretical Computer Science, pp. 79–96. Elsevier (2005)

SRW02.   Sagiv, S., Reps, T.W., Wilhelm, R.: Parametric shape analysis via 3-valued logic. ACM Trans. Program. Lang. Syst. **24**(3), 217–298 (2002)

On the Power of Temporal Prophecy

Jochen Hoenicke[1], Oded Padon[2], and Sharon Shoham[3(✉)]

[1] Certora GmbH, Munich, Germany
[2] Weizmann Institute of Science, Rehovot, Israel
[3] Tel Aviv University, Tel Aviv, Israel
sharon.shoham@gmail.com

Abstract. We consider a technique for liveness and termination proofs that reduces temporal proofs to verification conditions in uninterpreted first-order logic based on a suitable notion of a fair abstract lasso. It was previously shown that *temporal prophecy* makes the technique more powerful, essentially empowering it to prove termination of nested loops. In this paper we show that temporal prophecy is even more powerful than previously demonstrated: it can even prove termination of the Ackermann function, which is not primitive recursive, and essentially represents "infinitely-many" nested loops.

1 Introduction

Verification of liveness properties of infinite-state systems is provably harder than verification of safety properties. As a result, every sound liveness-to-safety reduction is bound to be incomplete. Still, such reductions are useful in practice. This paper considers the liveness-to-safety reduction introduced in [6] for verifying properties in First-Order Linear Temporal Logic (FO-LTL). The reduction is based on the observation that, given an abstraction function with a finite image, the absence of an *abstract* fair lasso implies that no infinite fair trace exists, where an abstract fair lasso consists of a finite trace followed by a fair abstract cycle—a trace segment that begins and ends in states whose abstractions are the same and where all the fairness constraints are met. Fixing a finite abstraction a-priori makes the approach extremely limited. Instead, [6] proposes to delay the choice of the abstraction function until a *freeze point*, where the abstraction is determined by the *footprint* of the trace up to the freeze point. As a result, different traces may use different abstractions. Intuitively, the footprint of a trace consists of all the elements "touched" by the transitions along the trace. This ensures that the footprint of a finite trace (the trace up to the freeze point) is finite. We can therefore define a finite abstraction by projecting states to the elements in the footprint.

The benefit of this liveness-to-safety reduction, as opposed to reductions based on ranking function or well-founded relations, is that the resulting safety property can be specified in uninterpreted first-order logic, for which many automated reasoning engines exist.

D. Dietsch et al. (Eds.): Podelski Festschrift, LNCS 14765, pp. 40–53, 2026.
https://doi.org/10.1007/978-3-032-13711-1_3

With the original liveness-to-safety reduction, absence of an abstract lasso entails an upper bound on the number of fair segments that can follow the freeze point. It is bounded by $exp(poly(n))$, where n is the size of the footprint at the time of the freeze point. That is because the number of abstract values is $O(exp(poly(n)))$. Already in [6] some examples were given that cannot be proven live because they require a form of nesting. For example, if there is a nested loop where the number of iterations of the inner loop is chosen arbitrarily at each iteration of the outer loop, then an abstract fair cycle exists. The solution proposed in [6] was called a nesting structure. A nesting structure essentially decomposes the termination proof into levels, and allows to apply the absence of an abstract lasso argument in a level, assuming that lower levels (inner loops) terminate. In [7] a more elegant solution was developed in the form of temporal prophecy, that essentially achieves the effect of *case splitting* on which loop iterates infinitely often, the inner one or the outer one. The fact that temporal prophecy can perform this case splitting leads to a cut elimination property of the induced proof system. The ability of temporal prophecy to increase the power of the liveness-to-safety reduction is demonstrated in [7] on several examples, where temporal prophecy splits the proof into *finitely many* cases.

In this paper we show that temporal prophecy is even more powerful than demonstrated by the examples in [7]. We show that with temporal prophecy, it is possible to apply the liveness-to-safety reduction to prove termination of the Ackermann function [2,3], which, as shown in [6], cannot be done with any nesting structure. The Ackermann function is a prominent example of a function that is total and computable but not primitive recursive. Its recursive definition is:

$$A(0, n) = n + 1$$
$$A(m + 1, 0) = A(m, 1)$$
$$A(m + 1, n + 1) = A(m, A(m + 1, n))$$

To prove termination of the Ackermann function, we need more than to split to a finite number of cases, or introduce a finite number of cuts in the proof. Proving that $A(0, n) = n + 1$ terminates is akin to proving termination of loop-free code. Proving termination of $A(1, n) = n + 2$ is akin to proving a single loop terminates. Proving termination of $A(2, n) = 2n + 3$ is akin to proving two nested loops terminate, and $A(3, n) = 2^{n+3} - 3$ is similar to three nested loops. In general, proving that $A(k, n)$ terminates for some $k \in \mathbb{N}$ can be done by splitting to $k + 1$ cases. However, proving $A(m, n)$ terminates for all m is akin to proving termination of a program with infinitely many nesting levels, and requires "infinite case splitting". The crux of what we show in this paper is that temporal prophecy defined in FO-LTL is powerful enough to provide the infinite case splitting. In essence, finite nesting or cut elimination requires only prophecy over closed formulas. However, by using temporal prophecy over formulas with free variables, we essentially get the effect of infinite case splitting. Our proof uses a prophecy of the form $(\Box\Diamond\phi(x))$, where the relevant values of x are between 0 and m.

Outline. The rest of the paper is organized as follows. Section 2 provides a brief background on first-order specifications of transition systems and on first-order linear temporal logic (FO-LTL). Section 3 recaps the liveness-to-safety reduction of [6,7]. The totality (termination) proof of the Ackermann function using the liveness-to-safety reduction with temporal prophecy is then presented in Sect. 4. Section 5 discusses related work and concludes the paper.

2   Preliminaries

2.1   First-Order Specification of Transition Systems

We use first order logic with equality to specify transition systems, where states are structures over a given vocabulary and sets of states or transitions are specified using first-order formulas. In practice, we consider many-sorted first-order logic, but for simplicity, we present here the unsorted case.

A vocabulary Σ consists of sets of constant symbols, function symbols and relation symbols. A *structure* of Σ is a pair $s = (\mathcal{D}, \mathcal{I})$, where $\mathcal{D}$ is a nonempty set of elements, called the *domain* of s, and $\mathcal{I}$ is an *interpretation*, mapping each function symbol resp. predicate symbol a in Σ of arity k to its interpretation $\mathcal{D}^k \to \mathcal{D}$ resp. $\mathcal{D}^k \to \{true, false\}$.

Later, we abstract first-order structures by *projecting* them to a finite subset of their domain. The *projection* $s|_D$ of a structure $s = (\mathcal{D}, \mathcal{I})$ to the subdomain $D \subseteq \mathcal{D}$ is the structure $(D \cup \{\bot\}, \mathcal{I}|_D)$ where $\bot \notin \mathcal{D}$ is a fresh value and the interpretation for predicate symbols p and function symbols f is defined as

$$\mathcal{I}|_D(p)(\overline{d}) = \begin{cases} \mathcal{I}(p)(\overline{d}) & \text{if } \overline{d} \in D^* \\ false & \text{otherwise} \end{cases} \qquad \mathcal{I}|_D(f)(\overline{d}) = \begin{cases} \mathcal{I}(f)(\overline{d}) & \text{if } \overline{d} \in D^* \text{ and} \\ & \mathcal{I}(f)(\overline{d}) \in D \\ \bot & \text{otherwise} \end{cases}$$

A transition system is a tuple $T = (\Sigma, \Gamma, \iota, \tau)$, where Σ is a first-order vocabulary, Γ is a *background theory* given as a *finite* set of closed formulas over Σ, such that the states of T are the structures of Σ that satisfy Γ, ι is a closed formula over Σ specifying the initial states, and τ is a *two-vocabulary* closed formula specifying the transition relation. That is, τ is a closed formula over $\Sigma \uplus \Sigma'$, where $\Sigma' = \{a' \mid a \in \Sigma\}$. A transition of T is a pair of states (s, s') such that $\mathcal{D}(s) = \mathcal{D}(s')$ and $(\mathcal{D}(s), \mathcal{I}'') \models \tau$, where $\mathcal{I}''$ maps each $a \in \Sigma$ to $\mathcal{I}(s)(a)$ and each $a' \in \Sigma'$ to $\mathcal{I}(s')(a)$. With abuse of notation, we sometimes write $(s, s') \models \tau$ to denote that (s, s') is a transition of T.

A trace of T is a sequence of states $s_0, s_1, \ldots$ such that $s_0 \models \iota$ and $(s_i, s_{i+1}) \models \tau$, for every $i \geq 0$. Note that all states in a trace have the same domain. The *reachable states* of T are defined in the usual way.

We sometimes augment a transition system with a finite set of fairness constraints, Φ, where each fairness constraint $\phi \in \Phi$ is a first-order formula over Σ (possibly with free variables). A trace $s_0, s_1, \ldots$ of T satisfies a fairness constraint $\phi(\overline{x}) \in \Phi$ if for every assignment $\sigma : \overline{x} \to \mathcal{D}(s_0)$, there exist infinitely many indices $i \geq 0$ s.t. $s_i, \sigma \models \phi(\overline{x})$. The trace is *fair* if it satisfies all fairness constraints in Φ.

2.2 First-Order Linear Temporal Logic

For simplicity of presentation, we consider only the "globally" ($\Box$) temporal operators. Given a first-order vocabulary Σ, FO-LTL formulas are defined by:

$$f ::= r(t_1, \ldots, t_n) \mid t_1 = t_2 \mid \neg f \mid f_1 \vee f_2 \mid \exists x.f \mid \Box f$$

where r is an n-ary relation symbol in Σ, x is a variable, each t_i is a term over Σ (defined as in first-order logic) and $\Box$ denotes the "globally" temporal operator. We also use the standard shorthand for the "eventually" temporal operator: $\Diamond f = \neg\Box\neg f$, and the usual shorthands for logical operators (e.g., $\forall x.f = \neg\exists x.\neg f$). FO-LTL formulas over Σ are interpreted over infinite sequences of states (first-order structures) over Σ, with the same domain $\mathcal{D}$. Atomic formulas are interpreted over states (which are first-order structures), the temporal operators are interpreted as in traditional LTL, and first-order quantifiers are interpreted over the shared domain $\mathcal{D}$. We say that a first-order transition system $(\Sigma, \Gamma, \iota, \tau)$ satisfies a closed FO-LTL formula φ over Σ if all of its traces satisfy φ (i.e., for every $\mathcal{D}$).

3 Liveness to Safety Reduction

To verify FO-LTL formulas, we use the liveness-to-safety reduction introduced in [6,7]. The reduction is a composition of two reductions. First, we use a standard, sound and complete, reduction of FO-LTL verification to fair termination. We then reduce fair termination to safety. The latter reduction is based on a notion of an abstract lasso, whose absence is a safety property that implies that the transition system has no fair traces. The reduction from fair termination to safety is sound but incomplete: a transition system may have abstract lassos even when it has no fair traces. To improve the completeness of the overall reduction, we revisit its first step, i.e., the reduction of FO-LTL to fair termination, which constructs a product system of the transition system to be verified and the tableau of the (negated) FO-LTL formula. We use two forms of temporal prophecy in this construction. The addition of temporal prophecy does not affect soundness or completeness of the reduction to fair termination (which is already sound and complete), but it results in a transition system that is more likely to be free of spurious abstract lassos, enhancing the power of the second reduction.

In the sequel, we first present the reduction from fair termination to safety (Sect. 3.1). We then explain the reduction of FO-LTL verification to fair termination, and the augmentation of temporal prophecy into it (Sect. 3.2). Finally, we show how to reduce the safety problem obtained from the composition of the reductions to a simple non-reachability problem of an error state by means of a monitor construction (Sect. 3.3).

3.1 Reduction from Fair Termination to Safety: Absence of Abstract Lassos

Let $T_W = (\Sigma_W, \Gamma_W, \iota_W, \tau_W, \Phi_W)$ be a transition system with fairness constraints (e.g., the transition system obtained by the reduction from FO-LTL verification to fair termination we present in Sect. 3.2). The definition of an abstract lasso in T_W is based on a dynamic abstraction that is fixed at some point along the trace, henceforth called the *freeze point*. The abstraction function projects a state (a first-order structure) into the subset of its domain defined by the *footprint* of the trace up to the freeze point. Intuitively, the footprint of a trace $s_0, \ldots, s_i$, denoted $fp(s_0, \ldots, s_i)$, accumulates all elements "exposed" in the states and transitions along the trace. These include the interpretations of constant symbols in $s_0, \ldots, s_i$, as well as the witness assignments to the existentially quantified variables in ι_W and τ_W. Importantly, the footprint of a finite trace always contains finitely many elements. As a result, the resulting abstraction function has a finite range.

The footprint is also used to define *fair segments* of a trace. For each fairness constraint there are potentially infinitely many assignments to its free variables for which it needs to hold infinitely often along a fair trace. For a fair segment we only consider the finitely many assignments where each variable takes a value from the footprint of the preceding states. We require that the segment visits for each fairness constraint and each such assignment at least one state where the constraint holds. The formal definition follows.

Definition 1 (Fair Segment). *Let $\pi = s_0, s_1, \ldots$ be a sequence of states over Σ_W. For $0 \leq i \leq j < |\pi|$, we say the segment $[i, j]$ is fair if for every formula $\phi(\overline{x}) \in \Phi_W$, and for every assignment σ where every variable is assigned to an element of $fp(s_0, \ldots, s_i)$, there exists $i \leq k \leq j$ s.t. $s_k, \sigma \models \phi(\overline{x})$.*

Definition 2 (Abstract Lasso). *A finite trace $s_0, \ldots, s_n$ of T_W is an abstract lasso if there are $0 \leq i \leq j < k \leq n$ s.t. the segments $[0, i]$ and $[j, k]$ are fair, and $s_j|_{fp(s_0, \ldots, s_i)} = s_k|_{fp(s_0, \ldots, s_i)}$.*

Intuitively, in the above definition, i is the *freeze point*, where the abstraction is fixed. The states s_j and s_k are the "repeating states" – states that are indistinguishable by the abstraction that projects them to the footprint $fp(s_0, \ldots, s_i)$. The segment between j and k, respectively, the segment between 0 and i, meet all the fairness constraints restricted to elements in $fp(s_0, \ldots, s_j)$, respectively, in $fp(s_0)$. Fairness of the segment $[0, i]$ is needed to prevent the freeze point from being chosen too early, thus creating spurious abstract lassos. Note that the absence of abstract lassos is a safety property.

Lemma 1 (Soundness). *If T_W has no abstract lassos then it also has no fair traces.*

Lemma 1 states the soundness of the reduction of fair termination to safety. The reduction is, however, incomplete: the transition system T_W may have *spurious* abstract lassos, namely abstract lassos that exist even though T_W has no fair traces. Incompleteness is inherent: a sound and complete reduction from fair termination to safety does not exist.

3.2 Reduction from FO-LTL Verification to Fair Termination with Temporal Prophecy

Next, we present the reduction from FO-LTL verification to fair termination, which together with the previous reduction results in a reduction from FO-LTL verification to safety. Unlike the reduction from fair termination to safety, which is sound but incomplete, the reduction from FO-LTL verification to fair termination is sound and complete. Interestingly, using temporal prophecy in the reduction from FO-LTL verification to fair termination improves the power of the reduction from fair termination to safety, and as a result improves the completeness of the overall reduction.

Typically, to verify an LTL property φ for a transition system T, an automaton is constructed that accepts exactly the traces satisfying $\neg\varphi$. The property $\varphi \models T$ holds if the cross product of T and this automaton has no fair traces. The automaton can be constructed as a tableau that tracks the truth value for the set A of all subformulas of $\neg\varphi$. For every subformula in A an atom is introduced and the automaton nondeterministically assigns a truth value to each atom, such that exactly those transitions are possible that are consistent with the meaning of the subformula.

This idea is naturally extended to FO-LTL by introducing for a subformula ψ with k free variables a new predicate symbol r_ψ of arity k that tracks the truth value of the subformula. As an optimization, the predicate symbols are only introduced for subformulas of the form $\Box\psi(\overline{x})$. The value of the introduced predicate $r_{\Box\psi}$ is assigned non-deterministically, predicting whether the formula $\Box\psi$ holds. The transition relation ensures that the assigned value was predicted correctly, e.g., ensuring that if $r_{\Box\psi}$ is false and ψ is true, then $r_{\Box\psi}$ is still false in the next state. Fairness constraints are used to disallow traces where $r_{\Box\psi}$ is always false and ψ is always true.

This already results in a sound and complete reduction. However, we augment the construction of the product transition system with two forms of temporal prophecy: (i) temporal formulas and (ii) temporal witnesses, which can be understood as "refining" the product system to eliminate spurious abstract lassos.

Prophecy Formulas. The first kind of prophecy that we consider is simply additional FO-LTL formulas, beyond $\neg\varphi$ and its subformulas, that are added to the states of the tableau. Namely, the tableau is constructed w.r.t a finite set A of FO-LTL formulas (that includes $\neg\varphi$. The additional formulas in A split the states of the tableau into more states in the product system according to the future temporal behavior of their outgoing traces, and increase the fairness constraints. Next, we present the tableau construction and the product system.

For an FO-LTL formula φ, we denote by $sub(\varphi)$ the set of subformulas of φ, defined in the usual way. We consider sets A of FO-LTL formulas that are closed under subformulas, i.e. for every $\varphi \in A$, $sub(\varphi) \subseteq A$. Note that A may contain formulas with free variables.

Definition 3 (Tableau vocabulary). *Given a finite set A as above over a first-order vocabulary Σ, the tableau vocabulary for A, denoted Σ_A, is obtained from Σ by adding a fresh relation symbol $r_{\Box\varphi}$ of arity k for every formula $\Box\varphi \in A$ with k free variables.*

The symbols added in Σ_A will be used to "label" states by temporal subformulas that are satisfied by all outgoing fair traces. The following definition translates temporal formulas over Σ to first-order formulas over Σ_A.

Definition 4. *For an FO-LTL formula $\varphi \in A$ (over Σ), its first-order representation, denoted $\mathrm{FO}\,[\varphi]$, is a first-order formula over Σ_A, defined inductively, as follows.*

$$\mathrm{FO}\,[\varphi] = \varphi \quad \text{if } \varphi = r(t_1, \ldots, t_n) \text{ or } \varphi = t_1 = t_2$$
$$\mathrm{FO}\,[\Box\psi(\overline{x})] = r_{\Box\psi(\overline{x})}(\overline{x})$$
$$\mathrm{FO}\,[\neg\psi] = \neg\mathrm{FO}\,[\psi]$$
$$\mathrm{FO}\,[\psi_1 \vee \psi_2] = \mathrm{FO}\,[\psi_1] \vee \mathrm{FO}\,[\psi_2]$$
$$\mathrm{FO}\,[\exists x.\psi] = \exists x.\mathrm{FO}\,[\psi]$$

Note that $\mathrm{FO}\,[\varphi]$ has the same free variables as φ. We can now define the tableau for A as a fair transition system specification in first-order logic.

Definition 5 (Tableau transition system). *The tableau transition system for A is the first-order fair transition system $T_A = (\Sigma_A, \Gamma_A, \iota_A, \tau_A, \Phi_A)$ where Σ_A is defined as above, and:*

$$\Gamma_A = \emptyset$$
$$\iota_A = true$$
$$\tau_A = \bigwedge_{\Box\varphi \in A} \forall\overline{x}.\ (r_{\Box\varphi}(\overline{x}) \leftrightarrow (\mathrm{FO}\,[\varphi(\overline{x})] \wedge r_{\Box\varphi}{}'(\overline{x})))$$
$$\Phi_A = \{\mathrm{FO}\,[\Box\varphi(\overline{x}) \vee \neg\varphi(\overline{x})] \mid \Box\varphi(\overline{x}) \in A\}$$

Note that the original symbols in Σ (and Σ') are not constrained by τ_A, and may change arbitrarily with each transition. However, the $r_{\Box\varphi}$ relations are updated in accordance with the property that $\pi, \sigma \models \Box\varphi$ iff $s_0, \sigma \models \varphi$ and $\pi^1, \sigma \models \Box\varphi$ (where $\pi = s_0, s_1, \ldots$ is a trace and φ is a first-order formula over Σ). The definition of the fairness constraints Φ_A ensures that in a fair trace, an eventuality cannot be postponed forever (note that $\Box\varphi(\overline{x}) \vee \neg\varphi(\overline{x})$, used above, is equivalent to $\Diamond\neg\varphi(\overline{x}) \rightarrow \neg\varphi(\overline{x})$).

Definition 6 (Product system). *Given a transition system $T = (\Sigma, \Gamma, \iota, \tau)$, a closed FO-LTL formula φ over Σ, a finite set A of FO-LTL formulas over Σ closed under subformulas such that $\neg\varphi \in A$, we define the product system of*

T and $\neg\varphi$ over A as the first-order transition system $T_P = (\Sigma_P, \Gamma_P, \iota_P, \tau_P, \Phi_P)$ given by:

$$\Sigma_P = \Sigma_A$$
$$\Gamma_P = \Gamma$$
$$\iota_P = \iota \wedge \mathrm{FO}\left[\neg\varphi\right]$$
$$\tau_P = \tau \wedge \tau_A$$
$$\Phi_P = \Phi_A$$

where $T_A = (\Sigma_A, \Gamma_A, \iota_A, \tau_A, \Phi_A)$ is the tableau for A.

Lemma 2 (Soundness and Completeness). *Let T_P be the product system of T and $\neg\varphi$ over A as defined in Definition 6. Then $T \models \varphi$ iff T_P has no fair traces.*

Intuitively, the product system augments the states of T with temporal formulas from A, splitting each state into many (often infinitely many) states according to the future behavior of its outgoing traces.

Lemma 2 holds already when $A = sub(\neg\varphi)$. However, taking a larger set A is useful for verifying φ via the liveness to safety reduction since it contributes to the elimination of spurious abstract lassos in T_P. This is done in three ways. First, the increase in Φ_P refines the definition of a fair segment and accordingly of an abstract lasso. Second, the increase of Φ_P postpones the freeze point, thus increasing the footprint up to the freeze point, and as a result, making the abstraction defined by it more precise. Third, the additional relations in $\Sigma_P = \Sigma_A$ are part of the state as considered by the reduction, and a difference in these relations (projected to the footprint up to the freeze point) is a valid difference that prevents a cycle.

Prophecy Witnesses. The second kind of prophecy is given by fresh constant symbols that serve as *prophecy witnesses* for existential temporal properties. For example, for a temporal formula $\psi(x)$, we may add a constant symbol c and require that if there exists an x such that $\psi(x)$ holds, the interpretation of c will be taken as such an x, making c a witness for $\psi(x)$. Otherwise, c will be allowed to take any value. In the notation of Hilbert's epsilon calculus, we are defining the constant c to be $\epsilon x\, \psi(x)$.

The addition of the witness constant symbols to the vocabulary increases the footprint of a trace, and accordingly increases the precision of the abstraction that underlies the definition of an abstract lasso.

Formally, given a set $B \subseteq A$, we construct a transition system augmented with witness constants $T_W = (\Sigma_W, \Gamma_W, \iota_W, \tau_W, \Phi_W)$ as follows. We extend Σ_P to Σ_W by adding fresh constant symbols $c_1^\psi, \ldots, c_n^\psi$ for every formula $\psi \in B$ with n free variables. We denote by C the set of new constants, i.e., $\Sigma_W = \Sigma_P \cup C$. We set $\Gamma_W = \Gamma_P$ and $\Phi_W = \Phi_P$. To ensure that the constants $c_1^\psi, \ldots, c_n^\psi$ serve as witnesses for $\psi(x_1, \ldots, x_n) \in B$, we update the initial states formula

48   J. Hoenicke et al.

to require that if $\psi(x_1, \ldots, x_n)$ holds in the initial state for some elements, then $\psi(c_1^\psi, \ldots, c_n^\psi)$ holds as well (otherwise, the witness constants may have an arbitrary interpretation). We further extend the transition relation formula to require that the interpretation of $c_1^\psi, \ldots, c_n^\psi$ remains unchanged along a trace. Namely, $\tau_W = \tau_P \wedge \bigwedge_{c \in C} c = c'$, and

$$\iota_W = \iota_P \wedge \bigwedge_{\psi(x_1,\ldots,x_n) \in B} \mathrm{FO}\left[(\exists x_1, \ldots, x_n.\psi(x_1, \ldots, x_n)) \rightarrow \psi(c_1, \ldots, c_n)\right]$$

Adding these fresh constants and their defining formulas is a conservative extension, in the sense that every fair trace of T_P can be extended to a fair trace of T_W, and every fair trace of T_W can be projected to a fair trace of T_P. As such we have the following:

Lemma 3 (Soundness and Completeness). *Let $T_P = (\Sigma_P, \Gamma_P, \iota_P, \tau_P, \Phi_P)$ and $T_W = (\Sigma_W, \Gamma_W, \iota_W, \tau_W, \Phi_W)$ be defined as above. Then, T_P has no fair traces iff T_W has no fair traces.*

Remark 1. The addition of temporal prophecy formulas and witnesses may be repeated, allowing for prophecy formulas and witnesses that depend on previously defined prophecy witnesses.

Corollary 1 (Soundness). *Consider a given first-order transition system T and a closed FO-LTL formula φ both over Σ, as well as a given set of temporal prophecy formulas A over Σ that contains $\neg\varphi$ and is closed under subformula, and a given set of temporal prophecy witness formulas $B \subseteq A$. Let T_W be defined as above. If T_W has no abstract lasso, then $T \models \varphi$.*

3.3 Absence of Abstract Lassos as a Non-reachability Problem

Absence of an abstract lasso is a temporal safety property—it is a property of traces. To facilitate the use of inductive invariants for its verification, we use a standard (sound and complete) reduction to a non-reachability problem. Namely, we augment the transition system T_W, in which we wish to verify absence of abstract lassos, with a *monitor* that observes the traces of the system and reaches an error state if an abstract lasso was recognized.

Roughly, the monitor collects the footprint of the trace in the background by adding for each action the existentially quantified values to the footprint. For this it uses a predicate symbol fp which is updated by each transition. The monitor waits for the initial fair segment of an abstract lasso, by first adding each fairness constraint with each combination of parameters in the initial footprint to a wait list and removing an element from the wait list when a corresponding state is visited. When the list is empty, it reaches the freeze point where it copies the footprint and uses it to fix the abstraction. After the freeze point, it non-deterministically decides where the cycle of the lasso begins and saves a copy of the state and again uses the footprint to initialize the wait list for the fairness constraints; it then continues to wait for the completion of a fair cycle (in the abstraction); if a fair cycle is detected, the monitor goes to an *error* state. We denote the monitored transition system T_M.

Lemma 4 (Soundness and Completeness). *Let T_W be a transition system and T_M the monitored transition system for T_W described above. Then T_W has no abstract lasso iff an error state is not reachable in T_M.*

4 Proving Termination of the Ackermann Function

In this section we show that temporal prophecy makes it possible to prove totality (termination) of the Ackermann function with the liveness-to-safety reduction. We model the Ackermann function as a transition system that uses an explicit stack to mimic the recursion (similar to Algorithm 1 in [3]). In our model, whose first-order specification is given in Fig. 1, the individuals m and n store the arguments for the inner-most call while the stack stores the first argument for each outer call. (In [3], m and n are also stored in the stack.) Each of the three cases in the recursive definition is modeled by a corresponding action. Table 1 shows the first few steps in the computation of $A(6,5)$ (where A is the Ackermann function) in both the recursive form and the stack-based transition-system form. In the first-order specification of the transition system we further include a "setup" action that initializes m and n, a "start" action that starts the actual computation and a "finish" action that signals termination.

Totality of the Ackermann function corresponds to termination of the transition system that computes it. Termination can be expressed in FO-LTL as $\Box((\exists m, n.\mathrm{start}(m, n)) \rightarrow \Diamond(\exists r.\mathrm{finish}(r)))$. As mentioned in the introduction, it was shown in [6] that the baseline termination to safety reduction cannot prove termination of the Ackermann function: even though all traces of the program are terminating, the corresponding transition system has abstract lassos.

Next we show that temporal prophecy remedies the situation. Namely, with a proper choice of temporal prophecy formulas and witnesses, we manage to eliminate all spurious abstract lassos. Furthermore, we are able to verify the absence of abstract lassos in first-order logic by specifying an inductive invariant that proves that an error state cannot be reached in the monitored transition system.

In the proof we use the following prophecy witnesses:

$$m_{\mathrm{start}} := \epsilon\, m.\exists n.\Diamond\mathrm{start}(m, n)$$
$$p := \epsilon\, y.y \leq m_{\mathrm{start}} \wedge (\Box\Diamond\mathrm{step1}(y)) \wedge$$
$$\forall x.x \leq m_{\mathrm{start}} \wedge (\Box\Diamond\mathrm{step1}(x)) \rightarrow x \leq y$$

and the following prophecy formulas in addition to the subformulas of the prophecy witnesses and the negation of the termination formula:

$$\Diamond\Box\forall x.x \leq m_{\mathrm{start}} \rightarrow \neg step1(x)$$
$$\Box\Diamond(step1(p) \wedge \forall x.p < x \leq m_{\mathrm{start}} \rightarrow \Box\neg step1(x))$$

The prophecy witness m_{start} gives us the initial m for which the Ackermann function is invoked. It is useful since it is an upper bound for all m used during

```
 1  # background theory
 2  sort nat
 3  individual zero: nat
 4  relation ≤ : nat, nat
 5  axiom Γ_total order[≤, zero]
 6
 7  # state
 8  relation stack : nat, nat
 9  relation started
10  individual len : nat
11  individual m : nat
12  individual n : nat
13
14  init len = zero
15  init ∀ I, M : nat.  stack(I,M) = false
16  init m = zero
17  init n = zero
18  init started = false
19
20  # set the input m, n
21  action setup {
22      assume ¬started;
23      if * { m := succ(m) };
24      if * { n := succ(n) };
25  }
26
27  # start the computation
28  action start(m_init, n_init) {
29      assume ¬started;
30      assume m = m_init;
31      assume n = n_init;
32      started := true;
33  }
34
35  # A(0, n) = n + 1, len = 0
36  # return n + 1
37  action finish(result) {
38      assume started;
39      assume m = zero;
40      assume len = zero;
41
42      assume result = succ(n);
43  }

44  # A(0, n) = n + 1, len ≠ 0
45  # pop m_pop from stack
46  # update m,n := m_pop, n + 1
47  action step1(m_pop) {
48      assume started;
49      assume m = zero;
50      assume len ≠ zero;
51      assume stack(pred(len), m_pop);
52
53      len := pred(len);
54      stack(len, m_pop) := false;
55      m := m_pop;
56      n := succ(n);
57  }
58
59  # A(m, 0) = A(m − 1, 1)
60  # update m,n := m − 1,1
61  action step2 {
62      assume started;
63      assume m ≠ zero;
64      assume n = zero;
65
66      m := pred(m);
67      n := succ(zero);
68  }
69
70  # A(m,n) = A(m − 1, A(m, n − 1))
71  # push m − 1 on the stack
72  # update m,n := m,n − 1
73  action step3 {
74      assume started;
75      assume m ≠ zero;
76      assume n ≠ zero;
77
78      stack(len, pred(m)) := true;
79      len := succ(len);
80      n := pred(n);
81  }
82
83
84
85  temporal property
86  □((∃m,n.start(m,n)) → ◊∃r.finish(r))
```

Fig. 1. First-order specification of an iterative computation of the Ackermann function.

the computation. The second prophecy witness p is the core of the termination argument: it is the maximum value for m which is infinitely often popped from the stack in a nonterminating run. The goal is to show that no such value exists and from some point no step1 operation is performed. In that case it is easy to show termination by observing that m or n are strictly decreasing. If a value p with the above property exists, we use the second prophecy formula to delay the freeze point until p is popped from the stack and no value greater than p is ever popped from the stack any more. Then we can argue that p cannot be pushed on the stack again (because we can prove $m \leq p$ holds after the freeze point), which implies that we cannot pop p from the stack infinitely.

In essence, the prophecy formulas $\Box\Diamond\text{step1}(x)$ have the effect of an "infinite" case-splitting, and the prophecy variable p lets us focus on the case that is needed for the termination proof.

Table 1. The first steps of the computation of A(6,5) by the transition system in Fig. 1. The transition system uses a stack to keep track of the first parameter of the outer applications and uses m, n to store the parameters of the inner-most application.

	Stack	m	n
$A(6,5)$	[]	6	5
$\downarrow$ step3			
$A(5, A(6,4))$	[5]	6	4
$\downarrow$ step3			
$A(5, A(5, A(6,3)))$	[5,5]	6	3
$\downarrow$ step3			
$A(5, A(5, A(5, A(6,2))))$	[5,5,5]	6	2
$\downarrow$ step3			
$A(5, A(5, A(5, A(5, A(6,1)))))$	[5,5,5,5]	6	1
$\downarrow$ step3			
$A(5, A(5, A(5, A(5, A(5, A(6,0))))))$	[5,5,5,5,5]	6	0
$\downarrow$ step2			
$A(5, A(5, A(5, A(5, A(5, A(5,1))))))$	[5,5,5,5,5]	5	1
$\downarrow$ step3			
$A(5, A(5, A(5, A(5, A(5, A(4, A(5,0)))))))$	[5,5,5,5,5,4]	5	0
$\downarrow$ step2			
$A(5, A(5, A(5, A(5, A(5, A(4, A(4,1)))))))$	[5,5,5,5,5,4]	4	1
$\downarrow$ step3			
$A(5, A(5, A(5, A(5, A(5, A(4, A(3, A(4,0))))))))$	[5,5,5,5,5,4,3]	4	0
$\downarrow$ step2			
$A(5, A(5, A(5, A(5, A(5, A(4, A(3, A(3,1))))))))$	[5,5,5,5,5,4,3]	3	1
$\downarrow$ step3			
$A(5, A(5, A(5, A(5, A(5, A(4, A(3, A(2, A(3,0)))))))))$	[5,5,5,5,5,4,3,2]	3	0
$\downarrow$ step2			
$A(5, A(5, A(5, A(5, A(5, A(4, A(3, A(2, A(2,1)))))))))$	[5,5,5,5,5,4,3,2]	2	1
$\downarrow$ step3			
$A(5, A(5, A(5, A(5, A(5, A(4, A(3, A(2, A(1, A(2,0))))))))))$	[5,5,5,5,5,4,3,2,1]	2	0
$\downarrow$ step2			
$A(5, A(5, A(5, A(5, A(5, A(4, A(3, A(2, A(1, A(1,1))))))))))$	[5,5,5,5,5,4,3,2,1]	1	1
$\downarrow$ step3			
$A(5, A(5, A(5, A(5, A(5, A(4, A(3, A(2, A(1, A(0, A(1,0)))))))))))$	[5,5,5,5,5,4,3,2,1,0]	1	0
$\downarrow$ step2			
$A(5, A(5, A(5, A(5, A(5, A(4, A(3, A(2, A(1, A(0, A(0,1)))))))))))$	[5,5,5,5,5,4,3,2,1,0]	0	1
$\downarrow$ step1(0)			
$A(5, A(5, A(5, A(5, A(5, A(4, A(3, A(2, A(1, A(0,2))))))))))$	[5,5,5,5,5,4,3,2,1]	0	2
$\downarrow$ step1(1)			
$A(5, A(5, A(5, A(5, A(5, A(4, A(3, A(2, A(1,3)))))))))$	[5,5,5,5,5,4,3,2]	1	3

We now explain how, using the temporal prophecy formulas and witnesses defined above, the intuitive termination argument from above is expressed in an inductive invariant in first-order logic that proves the absence of an abstract lasso. The invariant[1] handles several cases, showing in each one that the monitor cannot reach its error state (proving the absence of an abstract lasso, and therefore proving termination).

---

[1] The complete first-order model and the inductive invariant, specified and verified in Ivy [5], can be found in https://github.com/odedp/ivy/blob/b006fee/examples/liveness/ackermann_termination_proof.ivy.

Case 1: Finitely Many Step1's. The first case is characterized by the formula $\Diamond\Box\forall x.x \leq m_{\mathrm{start}} \rightarrow \neg\mathrm{step1}(x)$. In this case, at the freeze point, we have observed the fairness constraint of the above formula and therefore $\mathrm{step1}(x)$ is never executed after the freeze point. The footprint at the freeze point already contains all values up to m_{start} and n. The other actions *step2* and *step3* ensure that the current values of m, n are always in the abstraction (note that *succ(zero)* is in the abstraction if $m > 0$). After the freeze point each step either decreases m or m stays constant and n decreases. Therefore, there is no abstract lasso. The invariant formalizes this argument by asserting that after the freeze point, $\Box\forall x.x \leq m_{\mathrm{start}} \rightarrow \neg\mathrm{step1}(x)$ holds, and that the footprint and the abstraction are large enough to observe the decrease in m or n.

Case 2: Infinitely Many Step1(p) and Finitely Many Step1(x) for $x > p$. The second case utilizes p, and is the "main" case of the proof. It is characterized by the formula $\Box\Diamond(\mathrm{step1}(p) \wedge \forall x.p < x \leq m_{\mathrm{start}} \rightarrow \Box\neg\mathrm{step1}(x))$. In case this formula holds, we observe the formula $(\mathrm{step1}(p) \wedge \forall x.p < x \leq m_{\mathrm{start}} \rightarrow \Box\neg\mathrm{step1}(x))$ before the freeze point, and from that point on we will never see $\mathrm{step1}(x)$ for $x > p$ and we have $m \leq p$ as an invariant. (This is the reason we use the above formula in this case, rather than directly using the definition of p.) At the freeze point $stack(i, p)$ is false for all i that are not in the footprint and will stay false, since only step3 can change *stack* to true and $pred(m) < p$ holds after the freeze point. An abstract lasso executes $\mathrm{step1}(p)$ at least once, changing for one i the value of $\mathrm{stack}(i, p)$ from *true* to *false*. It can never be set back to true and i, p are in the abstraction. Therefore there is no abstract lasso.

Other Cases. The rest of the proof shows that there is no abstract lasso in the case where $\Box\Diamond\exists x.x \leq m_{\mathrm{start}} \wedge \mathrm{step1}(x)$ and $\Diamond\Box(\mathrm{step1}(p) \rightarrow \exists x.p < x \leq m_{\mathrm{start}} \wedge \Diamond\mathrm{step1}(x))$ hold (the negation of the formulas defining case 1 and case 2). First, from the negation of case 1 and the fact that m_{start} is finite, the proof shows that there is one $x \leq m_{\mathrm{start}}$ that does infinitely many step1's. (That is, the invariant shows that if $\Box\Diamond\exists x.x \leq m_{\mathrm{start}} \wedge \mathrm{step1}(x)$ holds but $\exists x.x \leq m_{\mathrm{start}} \wedge \Box\Diamond\mathrm{step1}(x)$ does not hold then there is no abstract lasso.) The proof then uses induction on m during the setup stage to show that if there is a value that does infinitely many step1's then there is also a maximal value that does so, and therefore p must be that maximal value. The remainder of the proof encodes rather rudimentary temporal reasoning to show that if p is the maximal value that does infinitely many step1's then the formula defining case 2 holds. (That is, the invariant shows that if p is the maximal value that does infinitely many step1's and the formula defining case 2 does not hold then there is no abstract lasso.)

5   Related Work and Conclusion

We have seen that first-order temporal prophecy and the liveness-to-safety reduction in first-order logic are powerful enough to prove termination of the computation of the Ackermann function [2].

The notion of temporal prophecy bares some similarity to the idea of *trace abstraction* [4], where a termination proof is split using temporal properties expressed using Büchi automata into simpler cases. For example, the termination proof of a nested loop can be split into the case where eventually the inner loop diverges and the case where the outer loop is executed infinitely often. Each case is expressed as a Büchi automaton and standard automata-theory algorithms are used to show that the cases cover all executions. Case splitting based on Büchi automata is similar to temporal prophecy, in the sense that they both case split based on different temporal behaviours of the trace. However, as this work shows, first-order temporal prophecy is more powerful since it can split into "infinitely-many" cases.

The liveness-to-safety reduction in first-order logic with temporal prophecy can be viewed as a proof system for FO-LTL. An interesting avenue for future research is analyzing its proof-theoretic power, in the spirit of [1]. From that perspective, the result of this paper shows that as a proof system it is more powerful than PRA (primitive recursive arithmetic) since PRA cannot prove totality of the Ackermann function. We conjecture that as a proof system it is as powerful as PA (Peano Arithmetic), but formally showing that is a topic of future work.

Another interesting topic for future work is to automatically synthesize the required temporal prophecy formulas and witnesses, and perhaps some inspiration can be taken from [4] where the Büchi automata used for case splitting are automatically constructed.

References

1. Abadi, M.: The power of temporal proofs. Theor. Comput. Sci. **65**(1), 35–83 (1989)
2. Ackermann, W.: Zum Hilbertschen Aufbau der reellen Zahlen. Math. Ann. **99**(1), 118–133 (1928)
3. Grossman, J.W., Zeitman, R.S.: An inherently iterative computation of Ackermanns's function. Theor. Comput. Sci. **57**, 327–330 (1988)
4. Heizmann, M., Hoenicke, J., Podelski, A.: Termination analysis by learning terminating programs. In: Biere, A., Bloem, R. (eds.) CAV 2014. LNCS, vol. 8559, pp. 797–813. Springer, Cham (2014). https://doi.org/10.1007/978-3-319-08867-9_53
5. McMillan, K.L., Padon, O.: Ivy: a multi-modal verification tool for distributed algorithms. In: Lahiri, S.K., Wang, C. (eds.) CAV 2020. LNCS, vol. 12225, pp. 190–202. Springer, Cham (2020). https://doi.org/10.1007/978-3-030-53291-8_12
6. Padon, O., Hoenicke, J., Losa, G., Podelski, A., Sagiv, M., Shoham, S.: Reducing liveness to safety in first-order logic. PACMPL **2**(POPL), 1–33 (2018)
7. Padon, O., Hoenicke, J., McMillan, K.L., Podelski, A., Sagiv, M., Shoham, S.: Temporal prophecy for proving temporal properties of infinite-state systems. Formal Methods Syst. Des. **57**(2), 246–269 (2021). https://doi.org/10.1007/s10703-021-00377-1

The Beauty of Predicate Automata

Azadeh Farzan[1] and Zachary Kincaid[2]

[1] University of Toronto, Toronto, Canada
`azadeh@cs.toronto.edu`
[2] Princeton University, Princeton, USA
`zkincaid@cs.princeton.edu`

Abstract. In [6], we introduced a class *data* automata, called *Predicate Automata*, which recognize languages over an alphabet $\Sigma \times \mathbb{N}$ where Σ is a finite alphabet. These automata were designed to capture the behaviour of parametrized programs, i.e. programs with an unbounded number of threads, and their correctness proofs. Since the focus of [6] was on the verification problem, the paper does not investigate the properties of these automata beyond the minimum which is necessary for the verification problem. In this paper, we study some of their key properties and relate them to other classes of data automata.

1 Introduction

For verification of concurrent and distributed programs, which consist of components executing simultaneously, the axiomatic approach to program reasoning was extended by Owicki/Gries [15] and Jones [10] to one that aims to construct a proof of correctness for the whole program out of proofs for individual components (a thread or a process) and some small glue that connects them together. This reasoning is based on the principle of non-interference: other threads/processes do not interfere with the functionality of the current one, and therefore do not have much impact on its proof of correctness.

Not all concurrent programs are designed with this principle in mind. For cooperative concurrency, in which processes work together to achieve some common goal, the notion of non-interference is not natural. Axiomatic proof systems have clever workarounds (e.g., ghost state) for these cases, but cleverness is an obstacle to automation: human verifiers are clever, but automated verifiers are not. In contrast, informal *operational arguments*, accommodate arbitrary global facts into proofs more naturally. Operational reasoning is very common among programmers as an informal way of reasoning about correctness of programs. One can think of it as a way of grouping similar program behaviours into a handful of *scenarios*, and arguing that the program behaves correctly in each *scenario*. One can think of doing operational reasoning using the following general proof rule:

$$\frac{P \subseteq \Pi, \ \Pi \text{ is correct by construction}}{P \text{ is correct}} \quad \text{(OR)}$$

D. Dietsch et al. (Eds.): Podelski Festschrift, LNCS 14765, pp. 54–74, 2026.
https://doi.org/10.1007/978-3-032-13711-1_4

where P stands for the set of behaviours of the program, and Π is a set of behaviours that are known to be correct by construction. The *subsumption* test $P \subseteq \Pi$ certifies P as correct.

In [6,7], we proposed algorithmic tools to implement the above proof rule as a sound and (in some sense) complete verification algorithm for parameterized programs. The thesis of our work is that operational arguments can be formalized using axiomatic proofs of a programs runs, which are sequences of instructions that are executed in order (without conditional branching, looping, etc.). The basic object of interest in such a proof system is a valid Hoare triple, $\{P\}\ \rho\ \{Q\}$, which consists of two assertions P and Q (called the pre-condition and post-condition of the triple, respectively), and a run ρ. Validity of the triple means that if ρ begins in a state that satisfies the pre-condition, it must end in a state that satisfies the post-condition. Hoare triples form the foundation of most axiomatic proof systems; the distinguishing feature of our notion of operational reasoning is that the program must be straight-line. This divergence reflects a difference of perspective: in, say, Hoare's proof system, we think of a program as a syntax tree, which is constructed from other syntax trees by certain formation rules (sequential composition, while loops, if-then-else statements, etc.). In an operational argument, we think of a program as a set of behaviours, corresponding to the possible paths of execution the program may take.

Any algorithmic implementation of Rule OR requires (1) an effective representation for Π and P, and (2) a way of constructing Π, and (3) a decidable subsumption test for $P \subseteq \Pi$. First, we briefly recall how we addressed (1) and (3) in [6] using a new model of infinite state automata, called *Predicate Automata* (PA). These two points inspired the design of this class of automata, whereas (2) is orthogonal to the investigation of this paper.

1.1   Proof Spaces

We proposed to construct a formal operational proof, like Π in Rule OR, around a finite set of valid Hoare triples H which can be associated with an infinite set of Hoare triples $S(H)$, comprised of Hoare triples that be obtained from H using the following three rules of inference:

- *Sequencing:* if $\{P_1\}\ \rho_1\ \{P_2\}$ and $\{P_2\}\ \rho_2\ \{P_3\}$ are valid triples, then so is $\{P_1\}\ \rho_1; \rho_2\ \{P_3\}^1$
- *Conjunction:* if $\{P_1\}\ \rho\ \{Q_1\}$ and $\{P_2\}\ \rho\ \{Q_2\}$ are valid, then so is $\{P_1 \wedge P_2\}\ \rho\ \{Q_1 \wedge Q_2\}$
- *Symmetry:* if $\{P\}\ \rho\ \{Q\}$ is a valid, then any triple $\{P'\}\ \rho'\ \{Q'\}$ that can be obtained by consistently renaming thread identifiers in all three components of the Hoare triple is also valid

---

[1] The sequencing rule in [6] also incorporates a weak form of the rule of consequence, which we omit here for brevity.

We call the set of Hoare triples $S(H)$ a **proof space**, and H a basis for $S(H)$. We say that a proof space proves that a set of runs $\mathcal{R}$ is correct with respect to a specification Pre/Post if for each run ρ in $\mathcal{R}$, the Hoare triple {Pre} ρ {Post} belongs to the proof space $S(H)$ generated by H; that is, there is a derivation of {Pre} ρ {Post} using the sequencing, conjunction, and symmetry rules, using the Hoare triples in H as axioms.

1.2   A Suitable Class of Automata

Let us now turn our attention to the subsumption test in the premise of Rule OR. A proof space is a proof for the program if and only if for every possible run of the program, there exists a valid Hoare triple proving its correctness in the proof space. If the proof space is represented by a finite basis, then this means that the Hoare triple for the run can be derived by the repeated application of the three rules (sequencing, conjunction, and symmetry).

We reduce the problem of deciding whether such a derivation exists for a given run to checking acceptance of the run (represented as a word) by a *Predicate Automaton* (PA). It is easy to see that the sequencing rule corresponds to the sequencing of transitions of an automaton. In this view, program statements are associated with letters of the alphabet of the automaton, and proof assertions with the states of the automaton. Predicate automata use the notion of *alternation* from Alternating Finite Automata (AFA) [3] to additionally accommodate the conjunction rule; this allows us to account for concurrent programs with a fixed number of threads. Finally, to accommodate also the symmetry rule (and account for concurrent programs with an unbounded number of threads), predicate automata make a shift from finite alphabets to alphabets indexed on natural numbers, in the spirit of *data* words [1].

1.3   Properties of Predicate Automata

In [6], we introduced predicate automata and briefly (i.e. within the confined limits of conference paper page limits) stated its core properties as relevant to the task of verification of parametrized systems. In this paper, we would like to take the opportunity to expand on our exposition of this simple yet powerful data automata model and its properties in connection to both verification and other automata models.

Specifically, in this paper:

- We establish that predicate automata are equivalent in expressive power to a variant of Alternating Register Automata (ARA) [1].
- We investigate properties of languages recognized by predicate automata, and in particular, we prove that they are not closed under reversal.
- We investigate the properties of the images of these languages under a homomorphism that forgets the *data* part of the alphabet, and in particular show that these languages are not necessarily context free.

- We give an alternative proof of decidability of verification of parameterized boolean programs, by giving a construction for a *most general proof* Π_{bool}, as a *monadic* predicate automaton, that subsumes *all* correct parametrized boolean programs over a fixed set of commands. This, combined by the results already presented in [6] that parametrized programs can also be modelled using *monadic* predicate automata and the subsumption test is decidable for monadic predicate automata, amounts to the new argument.

2   Predicate Automata

Predicate automata [6] are a class of infinite-state automata which recognize languages over an infinite alphabet of the form $\Sigma \times \mathbb{N}$.[2] We use the notation $a : \mathtt{i}$ or $\langle a : \mathtt{i} \rangle$ (with $a \in \Sigma$ and $\mathtt{i} \in \mathbb{N}$) to denote an element of this alphabet. A predicate automaton (PA) is equipped with a *vocabulary* $\langle Q, ar \rangle$ (in the usual sense of first-order logic) consisting of a finite set of predicate symbols Q and a function $ar : Q \to \mathbb{N}$ which maps each predicate symbol to its arity.

A state of a PA is a proposition $q(\mathtt{i}_1, ..., \mathtt{i}_{ar(q)})$ with $q \in Q$ and $\mathtt{i}_1, ..., \mathtt{i}_n \in \mathbb{N}$. The transition function maps such states to formulas in the vocabulary of the PA; disjunction corresponds to nondeterministic (existential) choice, and conjunction corresponds to universal choice. It is important to note that the symbols $q \in Q$ are "uninterpreted": they have no special semantics, and any subset of $\mathbb{N}^{ar(q)}$ is a valid interpretation of q.

For readers familiar with alternating finite automata (AFA) [3,4], a helpful analogy might be that predicate automata are to first-order logic what AFA are to propositional logic.

Given a vocabulary $\langle Q, ar \rangle$, let the set of *positive formulas* $\mathcal{F}(Q, ar)$ be the negation-free formulas over $\langle Q, ar \rangle$ where each atom is either (1) a proposition of the form $q(i_1, ..., i_n)$ (where $i_1, ..., i_n$ are natural number-typed variables), or (2) an equation $i = j$ (where i, j are variable symbols), or (3) a disequation $i \neq j$ (where i, j are variable symbols). A *ground* formula is defined similarly, except that natural numbers take the place of natural number-typed variables; the set of ground formulae over $\langle Q, ar \rangle$ is denoted $\underline{\mathcal{F}}(Q, ar)$. We adopt the convention that i, j, k range over natural number-typed variables, while $\mathtt{i}, \mathtt{j}, \mathtt{k}$ range over natural numbers. Predicate automata are defined as follows:

Definition 1 (Predicate automata [6]). *A predicate automaton (PA) is a 6-tuple $A = \langle Q, ar, \Sigma, \delta, \varphi_{\mathsf{start}}, F \rangle$ where*

- *$\langle Q, ar \rangle$ is a vocabulary*
- *Σ is a finite alphabet*
- *$\varphi_{\mathsf{start}} \in \mathcal{F}(Q, ar)$ is an initial formula with no free variables.*
- *$F \subseteq Q$ is a set of accepting predicate symbols*
- *$\delta : Q \times \Sigma \to \mathcal{F}(Q, ar)$ is a transition function which satisfies the property that for any $q \in Q$ and $\sigma \in \Sigma$, the free variables of $\delta(q, \sigma)$ are members of the set $\{i_0, ..., i_{ar(q)}\}$.* $\qquad\square$

---

[2] Such languages are commonly called *data languages* [14].

We can think of $\delta(q, \sigma)$ as a rewrite rule which instantiates the (implicit) formal parameters $i_1, ..., i_{ar(q)}$ of q to the actual parameters $\mathtt{i}_1, ..., \mathtt{i}_n$ and instantiates i_0 to $\mathtt{k}$ (the index of the letter being read). In light of this interpretation, we will often write δ in a form that makes the formal parameters explicit: for example, instead of

$$\delta(q, \sigma) = (i_0 \neq i_1 \wedge (q(i_0, i_1) \vee q(i_1, i_2))) \vee (i_0 = i_1 \wedge q(i_1, i_2) \wedge q(i_2, i_1))$$

we typically write

$$\delta(q(i, j), \langle \sigma : k \rangle) = (k \neq i \wedge (q(k, i) \vee q(i, j))) \vee (k = i \wedge q(i, j) \wedge q(j, i))$$

or more succinctly:

$$q(i, j) \xrightarrow{\sigma : k} (k \neq i \wedge (q(k, i) \vee q(i, j))) \vee (k = i \wedge q(i, j) \wedge q(j, i)) \ .$$

The arity of a PA is the a maximum arity among all of its predicate symbols. We call a PA *monadic* if this maximum arity is at most one.

In the following, we define the language accepted by a predicate automaton in two different (but equivalent) ways. The first is via an *extended transition relation*, which treats a PA as an deterministic automaton whose states are formulas, where each state is a ground positive formula over the vocabulary of the PA. This semantics is convenient (for instance) for relating predicate automata with Boolean programs (Sect. 5). The second definition treats a PA as an nondeterministic automaton whose states are conjunctive formulas. This is the semantics presented in [6], and is the basis of the decision procedure for checking of a monadic PA.

Deterministic Semantics. Let $A = \langle Q, ar, \Sigma, \delta, \varphi_{\mathsf{start}}, F \rangle$ be a predicate automaton. We may extend the transition relation δ to a function $\delta^* : \underline{\mathcal{F}}(Q, ar) \times (\Sigma \times \mathbb{N})^* \to \underline{\mathcal{F}}(Q, ar)$ as follows:

$$\delta^*(F \wedge G, w) \triangleq \delta^*(F, w) \wedge \delta^*(G, w)$$
$$\delta^*(F \vee G, w) \triangleq \delta^*(F, w) \vee \delta^*(G, w)$$
$$\delta^*(i = j, w) \triangleq i = j$$
$$\delta^*(i \neq j, w) \triangleq i \neq j$$
$$\delta^*(F, \epsilon) \triangleq F$$
$$\delta^*(q(\mathtt{j}_1, \ldots, \mathtt{j}_n), w\langle a : \mathtt{j} \rangle) \triangleq \delta^*(\delta(q, a)[i_0 \mapsto \mathtt{j}, i_1 \mapsto \mathtt{j}_1, \ldots, i_n \mapsto \mathtt{j}_n], w)$$

Note that the automaton reads the input word backwards (right-to-left).

The *accepting formulas* of A are defined as follows:

- $q(\mathtt{i}_1, \ldots, \mathtt{i}_n)$ is accepting iff $q \in F$
- $\mathtt{i} = \mathtt{i}$ is accepting
- $\mathtt{i} \neq \mathtt{j}$ (with $\mathtt{i}$ and $\mathtt{j}$ distinct) is accepting
- If F is accepting, then $F \vee G$ and $G \vee F$ are accepting for any G

– If F and G are accepting, so is $F \wedge G$

Finally, we say that a word w is accepted by a PA A if the formula $\delta^*(\varphi_{\text{start}}, w)$ is accepting, and define $\mathcal{L}(A)$ to be the set of all words accepted by A.

While checking emptiness of $\mathcal{L}(A)$ for a PA A is undecidable in general, it is decidable for *monadic* predicate automata [6]. The decision procedure is based on a *nondeterministic* semantics, which we describe in the following.

Nondeterministic Semantics. The high-level idea is that, rather than viewing a "state" of the automaton as a ground formula, we view it as a *conjunctive* formula which we call a *configuration*. For any configuration C and any indexed letter $\langle a : i \rangle$, C may nondeterministically transition to any of $C_1, \ldots, C_n$, where $C_1 \vee \cdots \vee C_n$ is the disjunctive normal form of $\delta^*(C, a : i)$. Formally,

Definition 2 (Configuration). *Let* $A = \langle Q, ar, \Sigma, \delta, \varphi_{\text{start}}, F \rangle$ *be a PA. A configuration* C *of A is finite set of ground propositions of the form* $q(i_1, ..., i_{ar(q)})$, *where* $q \in Q$ *and* $i_1, ..., i_{ar(q)} \in \mathbb{N}$. *We may identify a configuration* C *with the conjunctive formula* $\bigwedge_{q(i_1, ..., i_{ar(q)}) \in C} q(i_1, ..., i_{ar(q)})$.

A PA $A = \langle Q, ar, \Sigma, \delta, \varphi_{\text{start}}, F \rangle$ induces a transition relation on configurations as follows: $C \xrightarrow{\sigma:\text{k}} C'$ if C' is a clause in the DNF of the ground formula

$$\bigwedge_{q(\text{i}_1, ..., \text{i}_{ar(q)}) \in C} \delta(q, \sigma)[i_0 \mapsto \text{k}, i_1 \mapsto \text{i}_1, ..., i_{ar(q)} \mapsto \text{i}_{ar(q)}]$$

Note also that the formula above may contain equalities and disequalities, but since they are ground (have no free variables), they are equivalent to either *true* or *false*, and thus can be simplified.

A configuration is *initial* if it is a cube of the DNF of φ_{start}. A configuration is *accepting* if for all $q(\text{i}_1, ..., \text{i}_{ar(q)}) \in C$, we have $q \in F$; otherwise, it is *rejecting*. Finally, a word $w = \langle \sigma_1 : \text{i}_1 \rangle \cdots \langle \sigma_n : \text{i}_n \rangle$ is accepted by A if there is a sequence of configurations $C_{n+1}, ..., C_0$ such that:

1. C_{n+1} is initial
2. for each $r < n$, $C_{r+1} \xrightarrow{\sigma_r : \text{i}_r} C_r$
3. C_0 is accepting

It is straightforward to see that the deterministic and nondeterministic semantics of a predicate automaton define the same language.

The key observation of regarding the nondeterministic semantics is that we can define a covering relation $\preceq$ on configurations such that the transition relation is downwards-compatible with $\preceq$: if a configuration C' has a w-labeled path to an accepting configuration and $C \preceq C'$, then C must have a w'-labeled path to an accepting configuration for some relabeling w' of w. Formally,

Definition 3 (Covering). *Given a PA* $A = \langle Q, ar, \Sigma, \delta, \varphi_{\text{init}}, F \rangle$, *we define the covering pre-order on the configurations of A as follows: if C and C' are configurations of A, then* $C \preceq C'$ *("C covers C'") if there is a permutation* $\pi : \mathbb{N} \to \mathbb{N}$ *such that for all* $q \in Q$ *and all* $q(i_1, \ldots, i_{ar(q)}) \in C$, *we have* $q(\pi(i_1), \ldots, \pi(i_{ar(q)}))$.

Lemma 1 (Downwards compatibility [6]**).** *Let* $A = \langle Q, ar, \Sigma, \delta, \varphi_{\text{start}}, F \rangle$ *be a PA, and let* $\mathcal{C}, \mathcal{C}'$ *be configurations of* A *such that* $\mathcal{C} \preceq \mathcal{C}'$. *Then we have the following:*

1. *If* $\mathcal{C}'$ *is accepting, then* $\mathcal{C}$ *is accepting.*
2. *For any* $\langle \sigma : j \rangle \in \Sigma \times \mathbb{N}$, *if we have*

$$\mathcal{C}' \xrightarrow{\sigma : j} \overline{\mathcal{C}}'$$

then there exists a configuration $\overline{\mathcal{C}}$ *and an index* $k \in \mathbb{N}$ *such that*

$$\mathcal{C} \xrightarrow{\sigma : k} \overline{\mathcal{C}}$$

and $\overline{\mathcal{C}} \preceq \overline{\mathcal{C}}'$. $\qquad\qquad\square$

If we imagine an emptiness checking algorithm as searching the reachable states of a PA for an accepting configuration, then the significance of downwards compatibility is that we may prune from the search space any configuration that is covered by another. Thus pruning is sufficient to make the search space finite for *monadic* predicate automata, for which $\preceq$ is a well-quasi order (i.e., for any infinite sequence of configurations $\mathcal{C}_1, \mathcal{C}_2, \ldots$, there is some $i < j$ such that $\mathcal{C}_i \preceq \mathcal{C}_j$) [6].[3]

Theorem 1 ([6])**.** *Checking emptiness of monadic PAs is decidable.*

2.1   Predicate Automata with ϵ-Transitions

In many classes of automata, for example nondeterministic finite automata (NFA) or nondeterministic pushdown automata, the addition of epsilon transitions does not change the expressive power of the model. This is also true for predicate automata.

Definition 4 (ϵ-Predicate Automata). *An ϵ-Predicate Automaton (ϵ-PA) is a 7-tuple* $A = \langle Q, ar, \Sigma, \delta, \varphi_{\text{start}}, F, \epsilon \rangle$ *where* $\langle Q, ar, \Sigma, \delta, \varphi_{\text{start}}, F \rangle$ *is a predicate automaton and* $\epsilon : Q \to \mathcal{F}(Q, ar)$ *is a ϵ-transition function which satisfies the property that for any* $q \in Q$, *the free variables of* $\delta(q, \sigma)$ *are members of the set* $\{i_1, \ldots, i_{ar(q)}\}$.

The nondeterministic semantics of PA can be extended to ϵ-PA as follows. Define a labeled transition relation $\to^*$ on configurations to be the least relation such that

- If $\mathcal{C}'$ is cube of the DNF of $\epsilon(q)[i_1 \mapsto \mathbf{i}_1, \ldots, i_{ar(q)} \mapsto \mathbf{i}_{ar(q)}]$, then

$$\mathcal{C} \wedge q(\mathbf{i}_1, \ldots, \mathbf{i}_{ar(q)}) \xrightarrow{\epsilon}^* \mathcal{C} \wedge \mathcal{C}'$$

---

[3] That is, monadic predicate automata are well-structured transition systems [9].

- If C' is cube of the DNF of $\delta^*(C, \langle a : i \rangle)$, then $C \xrightarrow{\langle a:i \rangle}_* C'$
- If $C \xrightarrow{u} C'$ and $C' \xrightarrow{v} C''$, then $C \xrightarrow{uv}_* C''$

Finally, define $\mathcal{L}(A)$ to be the set of words w such that there exists an initial configuration C and an accepting configuration C' such that $C \xrightarrow{w^R}_* C'$.

Lemma 2 (ϵ-elimination). *Let A be an ϵ-PA. Then we can construct a predicate automaton B from A such that $\mathcal{L}(A) = \mathcal{L}(B)$.*

Proof. Let $A = \langle Q, ar, \Sigma, \delta, \varphi_{\mathsf{start}}, F, \epsilon \rangle$ be an ϵ-PA. We show that we can construct a function $\bar{\epsilon}$ such that $B = \langle Q, ar, \Sigma, \bar{\epsilon} \circ \delta, \bar{\epsilon}(\varphi_{\mathsf{start}}), F \rangle$ accepts the same language as A. Define a sequence of functions $\epsilon_0, \epsilon_1, \ldots$ mapping $\mathcal{F}(Q, ar)$ to $\mathcal{F}(Q, ar)$ as follows.

$$\epsilon_0 \text{ is the identity function}$$
$$\epsilon_{i+1}(F) = \epsilon_i(F) \vee \hat{\epsilon}(\epsilon_i(F))$$

where $\hat{\epsilon}$ is defined as

$$\hat{\epsilon}(q(\mathtt{i}_1, \ldots, \mathtt{i}_{ar(q)})) \triangleq \epsilon(q)[i_1 \mapsto \mathtt{i}_1, \ldots, i_{ar(q)} \mapsto \mathtt{i}_{ar(q)}]$$
$$\hat{\epsilon}(F \wedge G) \triangleq (\hat{\epsilon}(F) \wedge G) \vee (F \wedge \hat{\epsilon}(G))$$
$$\hat{\epsilon}(F \vee G) \triangleq (\hat{\epsilon}(F) \vee \hat{\epsilon}(G))$$

Due to the free variable restriction of ϵ, all free variables of $\epsilon_i(F)$ are also free in F. Since there are only finitely many formulas in $\mathcal{F}(Q, ar)$ with a fixed set of free variables (up to logical equivalence), the ascending chain $\epsilon_0(F) \models \epsilon_1(F) \models \epsilon_2(F) \ldots$ must stabilize: there is some k such that $\epsilon_k(F) \equiv \epsilon_{k+1}(F) \equiv \ldots$. Define $\bar{\epsilon}(F)$ to this stabilization point $\epsilon_k(F)$.

Observe that for any configuration C, we have $C \xrightarrow{\epsilon}_* C'$ if and only if C' is a cube of the DNF of $\bar{\epsilon}(C)$. One may thus show (by induction on length) that for any word w, have a w-labelled path from C to C' in A iff there is a w-labelled path from C to C' in B, and thus the language accepted by B is exactly that of A. $\square$

3 Languages of Predicate Automata

This section studies the class of languages that can be accepted by a PA.

Example 1 (from [6]). Let us illustrate how the language of runs in a parameterized program P can be defined as a predicate automaton. A parameterized program is one in which any number of threads may execute the same *thread template* in parallel. A thread template $T = \langle \mathsf{Loc}, E, \ell_{\mathsf{init}}, \ell_{\mathsf{err}}, \mathsf{src}, \mathsf{tgt} \rangle$ is a 6-tuple in which Loc is a finite set of control locations, E is a finite set of edges, $\ell_{\mathsf{init}} \in \mathsf{Loc}$ is an initial location $\ell_{\mathsf{err}} \in \mathsf{Loc}$ is an error location, and $\mathsf{src}, \mathsf{tgt} : E \to \mathsf{Loc}$ map each edges to their source and target. The idea is that a thread template is equipped with a distinguished error location ℓ_{err} (for example, marking an assertion violation) and we want to capture the language of all (syntactic) runs of the program that reach it. To use this model in verification, it suffices to show that all these runs are infeasible and as such establish that the program admits no feasible erroneous execution. In fact, the automaton will recognize the reversal of all these runs, namely, the runs that start at an error location and follow the control flow of the program back to a start state.

We define $A_P = \langle Q, ar, \Sigma, \delta, \varphi_{\mathsf{start}}, F \rangle$, where

- $Q = \{\mathsf{loc}, \mathsf{err}\} \cup \mathsf{Loc}$, where err is a distinguished symbol which intuitively represents "some thread is at the error location", and loc is a distinguished symbol which intuitively represents "every thread is at some location."
- $ar(\mathsf{loc}) = ar(\mathsf{err}) = 0$ and for all $\ell \in \mathsf{Loc}$, $ar(\ell) = 1$
- For $\sigma \in \Sigma$, and $\ell \in \mathsf{Loc}$, we define

$$\delta(\ell(i), \langle \sigma : j \rangle) \triangleq \begin{cases} (i = j \wedge \ell'(i)) \vee (i \neq j \wedge \ell(i)) & \text{if } \mathsf{tgt}(\sigma) = \ell \\ i \neq j \wedge \ell(i) & \text{otherwise} \end{cases}$$

where ℓ' denotes $\mathsf{src}(\sigma)$. The transition rule for loc is given by

$$\delta(\mathsf{loc}, \langle \sigma : i \rangle) = \mathsf{loc} \wedge \ell'(i)$$

where $\sigma \in \Sigma$ and ℓ' denotes $\mathsf{src}(\sigma)$. The transition rule for err is given by

$$\delta(\mathsf{err}, \langle \sigma : i \rangle) = \begin{cases} \ell'(i) & \text{if } \mathsf{tgt}(\sigma) = \ell_{\mathsf{err}} \\ \mathsf{err} & \text{otherwise} \end{cases}$$

where ℓ' denotes $\mathsf{src}(\sigma)$.
- $\varphi_{\mathsf{start}} = \mathsf{loc} \wedge \mathsf{err}$
- $F = \{\ell_{\mathsf{init}}, \mathsf{loc}\}$ $\qquad\qquad\qquad\qquad\qquad\qquad\qquad\qquad\qquad$ $\square$

The structure of A_P fairly closely mirrors the (reversed) control structure of T. The predicate loc deserves further discussion: loc ensures that for every reachable configuration $\mathcal{C}$, every $\sigma \in \Sigma$ and every $\mathtt{i} \in \mathbb{N}$, we have that if $\mathcal{C} \xrightarrow{\sigma:\mathtt{i}} \mathcal{C}'$, then $\ell'(\mathtt{i}) \in \mathcal{C}'$, where $\ell' = \mathsf{src}(\sigma)$.

Note that it is essential to recognize this language in the reverse order: we begin in state where *some* thread is at the error location, and work backwards to a state where *all* threads are in their initial location. The acceptance condition of predicate automata (*all* predicates in a configuration are accepting) can be used to encode the initial state of the program. To capture the initial condition of the program in the *initial* condition of the PA (rather than its accepting condition) would require universal quantification, which PA do not have (though note that such an extension was introduced in [7]).

In [6], we proved the following closure properties of the class of languages recognized by predicate automata, which are essential to their use in algorithmic verification:

Proposition 1 ([6]). *Predicate automata languages, denoted by* PAL, *are closed under intersection and complement.*

Remark 1. All constructions that prove the closure properties in Proposition 1 preserve the arity of the PA. Hence, languages recognized by monadic PAs are closed under all boolean operations (union, intersection, and complementation).

In this section, we explore more properties of this class of languages (PAL) an also the class of languages which are images of these languages under a homomorphism that forgets the natural number part of the alphabet symbols, and hence are just languages over Σ^* (PAFL, for predicate automata finite languages).

3.1 Data Languages of Predicate Automata

For any $\pi : \mathbb{N} \to \mathbb{N}$ and any $w \in (\Sigma \times \mathbb{N})^*$ define:

$$\pi(w) \triangleq \begin{cases} \epsilon & \text{if } w = \epsilon \\ \langle a : \pi(k) \rangle \pi(u) & \text{if } w = \langle a : k \rangle u \end{cases}$$

Proposition 2 (Symmetry). *Every language recognized by a PA A is symmetric, in the sense that for all $w \in \mathcal{L}(A)$, and any bijection $\pi : \mathbb{N} \to \mathbb{N}$, we have $\pi(w) \in \mathcal{L}(A)$.*

Proposition 2 provides a light tool to formally argue why certain languages, i.e. non-symmetric ones, are not recognized by any PA. In the spirit of a pumping lemma, the following proposition, provides another such tool.

Lemma 3 (Characterization). *Let $L \subseteq (\Sigma \times \mathbb{N})^*$ be a language recognized by a monadic PA. Let $u_1, u_2, \ldots$ and $v_1, v_2, \ldots$ be infinite sequences of words in $(\Sigma \times \mathbb{N})^*$ such that for each i, $u_i v_i \in L$. Then there exists $i < j$ and some permutation $\pi : \mathbb{N} \to \mathbb{N}$ such that $\pi(u_j) v_i \in L$.*

Proof. Let $\langle Q, ar, \Sigma, \delta, \varphi_{\mathsf{start}}, F \rangle$ be a PA that recognizes L. By assumption, A recognizes $u_i v_i$ for each i. It follows that there are configurations $\mathcal{C}_{i,0}$, $\mathcal{C}_{i,1}$, and $\mathcal{C}_{i,2}$ such that

1. $\mathcal{C}_{i,0} \models \varphi_{\mathsf{init}}$
2. $\mathcal{C}_{i,0} \xrightarrow{v_i^R} \mathcal{C}_{i,1} \xrightarrow{u_i^R} \mathcal{C}_{i,2}$
3. $\mathcal{C}_{i,2}$ is accepting.

Accordingly, consider the infinite sequence of (blue) configurations induced by the original sequences of the words from the assumption:

$$
\begin{array}{ccccccccc}
\mathcal{C}_{1,0} & \mathcal{C}_{2,0} & \cdots & \mathcal{C}_{i,0} & \cdots & \mathcal{C}_{j,0} & \cdots \\
\downarrow v_1^R & \downarrow v_2^R & & \downarrow v_i^R & & \downarrow v_j^R & \\
\mathcal{C}_{1,1} & \mathcal{C}_{2,1} & \cdots & \mathcal{C}_{i,1} & \cdots & \mathcal{C}_{j,1} & \cdots \\
\downarrow u_1^R & \downarrow u_2^R & & \downarrow u_i^R & & \downarrow u_j^R & \\
\mathcal{C}_{1,2} & \mathcal{C}_{2,2} & \cdots & \mathcal{C}_{i,2} & \cdots & \mathcal{C}_{j,2} & \cdots
\end{array}
$$

Since $\preceq$ is a well-quasi order on configurations, there exists $i < j$ such that $\mathcal{C}_{i,1} \preceq \mathcal{C}_{j,1}$. By downwards compatibility (Lemma 1), there exists a configuration $\mathcal{C}'_{i,2}$ and a permutation $\pi : \mathbb{N} \to \mathbb{N}$ such that $\mathcal{C}_{i,1} \xrightarrow{\pi(u_j^R)} \mathcal{C}'_{i,2}$ and $\mathcal{C}'_{i,2} \preceq \mathcal{C}_{j,2}$, and furthermore (since $\mathcal{C}_{j,2}$ is accepting by assumption), $\mathcal{C}'_{i,2}$ is accepting. It follows that A has an accepting path $\mathcal{C}_{i,0} \xrightarrow{v_i^R} \mathcal{C}_{i,1} \xrightarrow{\pi(u_j^R)} \mathcal{C}'_{i,2}$ and thus accepts $\pi(u_j)v_i$.

Example 2. Let L be the language consisting of all data words w that can be obtained by shuffling n words $w_1, \ldots, w_n$ where each w_i is either $\langle a : j_i \rangle \langle b : j_i \rangle$ or $\langle b : j_i \rangle$ for some j, and each j_i is distinct. Using Lemma 3, we can observe that L cannot be recognized by a PA. Consider the sequences $u_1, u_2, \ldots$ and $v_1, v_2, \ldots$ where

$$u_i \triangleq \langle a : 1 \rangle \langle a : 2 \rangle \ldots \langle a : i \rangle$$
$$v_i \triangleq \langle b : 1 \rangle \langle b : 2 \rangle \ldots \langle b : i \rangle$$

Then for each i we have $u_i v_i \in L$. For a contradiction, suppose that L is recognized by PA. By Lemma 3, there is some $i < j$ and some permutation $\pi : \mathbb{N} \to \mathbb{N}$ such that $\pi(u_j)v_i \in L$. However, $\pi(u_j)v_i$ contains strictly more occurrences of a than b, which is not possible for a word in L.

Lemma 3 leads to the observation that PAL is not closed under reversal (justifying the necessity of the reversed order in Example 1):

Proposition 3. *Languages recognized by monadic predicate automata are not closed under reversal.*

Proof. Let L be the language from Example 2, which is not recognizable by a PA. We show that its reversal is accepted by a PA.

Define a PA $A = \langle \{q_0, q_a, q_b\}, ar, \Sigma, \delta, q_0, \{q_0, q_b\} \rangle$ as follows. The vocabulary consists of one nullary predicate q_0 along with two unary predicates q_a and q_b. The intuition is that $q_a(i)$ indicates that thread i has read a (and is obligated to read b), while $q_b(i)$ indicates that thread i may not read any more letters. The predicates q_0 and q_b are accepting, while q_a is not. The transition relation is

$$q_0 \xrightarrow{a:i} q_a(i) \qquad\qquad q_0 \xrightarrow{b:i} q_b(i)$$
$$q_a(i) \xrightarrow{a:j} i \neq j \wedge q_a(i) \qquad q_a(i) \xrightarrow{b:j} (i = j \wedge q_b(i)) \vee (i \neq j \wedge q_a(i))$$
$$q_b(i) \xrightarrow{a:j} i \neq j \wedge q_b(i) \qquad\qquad q_b(i) \xrightarrow{b:j} i \neq j \wedge q_b(i)$$

3.2   Finite Alphabets Languages of Predicate Automata

This section compares predicate automata with classical automata that operate on finite alphabets.

One mechanism for understanding PA languages over a finite alphabet is to restrict the alphabet $\Sigma \times \mathbb{N}$ to a finite number of threads $[n] = \{1, \ldots, n\}$. Any language over a finite alphabet like this recognized by a PA is *regular*. This can be argued easily once one observes that the PA in this case is syntactically nearly identical to an alternating finite automaton. One simply renames every ground instance of a predicate $q(\mathtt{i}_1, \ldots, \mathtt{i}_k)$ from the set of states of A as a fresh proposition $q_{(\mathtt{i}_1, \ldots, \mathtt{i}_k)}$ and the rest follows by definition.

Remark 2. For any language $L \subseteq (\Sigma \times \mathbb{N})^*$ recognized by a predicate automaton, $L \cap (\Sigma \times [n])^*$ is regular.

Besides restriction, another way to finitize the alphabet of a predicate automaton is by considering the image of PA language under a homomorphism mapping $(\Sigma \times \mathbb{N})^*$ to Σ^*. We define two such homomorphisms (by their action on the generators $(\Sigma \times \mathbb{N})$, extending to words and languages in the natural way):

- π_Σ forgets the natural number component of each letter: $\pi_\Sigma(a : \mathtt{i}) \triangleq a$

- $\pi_\mathtt{i}$ forgets all letters except those of $\mathtt{i}$: $\pi_\mathtt{i}(a : \mathtt{j}) \triangleq \begin{cases} a & \text{if } \mathtt{i} = \mathtt{j} \\ \epsilon & \text{otherwise} \end{cases}$

An immediate question jumping to mind is where PAFL fits in the Chomsky-Schützenberger hierarchy.

Proposition 4 (Inverse Images of Regular Languages). *Let $L \subseteq \Sigma^*$ be a regular language. Then the language $\{w \in (\Sigma \times \mathbb{N})^* : \pi_\Sigma(w) \in L\}$ is recognizable by a nullary predicate automaton.*

Proof. Since L is regular, its reversal is recognizable by an NFA $A = \langle Q, \Sigma, \Delta, s, F \rangle$. Construct the PA as follows. The set of predicates is exactly Q, the accepting predicates are F, and the arity of each is zero. For each $q \in Q$ and $a \in \Sigma$, we define $\delta(q, a : \mathtt{i}) \triangleq \bigvee_{\langle q, a, q' \rangle \in \Delta} q'()$. Finally, the initial formula is $s()$.

Proposition 4 implies that PAFL includes all regular languages. The proposition below then indicates that PAFL can include strictly context-sensitive languages.

Proposition 5. *There is language L, recognized by a monadic PA, such that $\pi_\Sigma(L) = \{a^i b^j c^k : i \geq j \geq k\}$*

Proof. Define a PA $A = \langle Q, ar, \Sigma, \delta, s_c, F \rangle$ as follows. The vocabulary consists of three nullary predicates s_c, s_b, s_a along with three unary predicates q_b, q_a, and q_ϵ; the alphabet Σ is $\langle a, b, c \rangle$; the final predicates are s_a, s_c, and q_ϵ. Intuitively, s_c, s_b, and s_a track whether the automaton is currently reading a sequence of c's, b's, or a's; $q_b(i)$ indicates an obligation to read $b : i$, $q_a(i)$ indicates an obligation to read $a : i$, and $q_\epsilon(i)$ indicates an obligation to read no more letters with index i. The transition relation is defined as follows:

$$s_c \xrightarrow{c:i} (s_c \vee s_b) \wedge q_b(i) \quad s_b \xrightarrow{c:i} \mathit{false} \qquad\qquad s_a \xrightarrow{c:i} \mathit{false}$$
$$s_c \xrightarrow{b:i} \mathit{false} \qquad\qquad s_b \xrightarrow{b:i} (s_b \vee s_a) \wedge q_a(i) \quad s_a \xrightarrow{b:i} \mathit{false}$$
$$s_c \xrightarrow{a:i} \mathit{false} \qquad\qquad s_b \xrightarrow{a:i} \mathit{false} \qquad\qquad s_a \xrightarrow{a:i} s_a \wedge q_\epsilon(i)$$

$$q_b(i) \xrightarrow{c:j} \mathit{false} \qquad\qquad q_a(i) \xrightarrow{c:j} \mathit{false} \qquad\qquad q_\epsilon \xrightarrow{c:j} \mathit{false}$$
$$q_b(i) \xrightarrow{b:j} i = j \vee (i \neq j \wedge q_b(i)) \quad q_a(i) \xrightarrow{b:j} \mathit{false} \qquad q_\epsilon \xrightarrow{b:j} \mathit{false}$$
$$q_b(i) \xrightarrow{a:j} \mathit{false} \qquad\qquad q_a(i) \xrightarrow{a:j} i = j \vee (i \neq j \wedge q_a(i)) \quad q_\epsilon \xrightarrow{c:j} i \neq j$$

Observe that

$$\mathcal{L}(A) = \{w \in (\Sigma \times \mathbb{N})^* : \pi_\Sigma(w) \in a^*b^*c^* \wedge \forall i \in \mathbb{N}.\pi_i(w) = \{\epsilon, a, ab, abc\}\}$$

and so $\pi_\Sigma(\mathcal{L}(A)) = \{a^i b^j c^k : i \geq j \geq k\}$.

Finally, let us turn our attention to the images of PA languages under π_i homomorphisms. It is tempting to believe that restricted to a single index, the language of a PA would turn into a regular language. The following proposition refutes that notion.

Proposition 6. *There exists a language L recognized by a monadic PA such that $\pi_1(L)$ is not context-free.*

Proof. For a contradiction, suppose that for any language L recognized by a monadic PA, $\pi_1(L)$ is regular. Clearly, the language $L_1 \triangleq \bigcup_{i \in \mathbb{N}} (d : i)^*(e : i)^*(f : i)^*$ is recognizable by a monadic PA. By Proposition 5, there is a PA-recognizable language L_2 such that $\pi_\Sigma(L_2) = \{a^i b^j c^k : i \geq j \geq k\}$. Then we have that $L_1 \times L_2$ is PA-recognizable by Lemma 4 (below). By Proposition 4, the set of all words w such that $\pi_\Sigma(w) \in (da)^*(eb)^*(fc)^*$ is recognizable by a monadic PA, and so $L_3 \triangleq \{w \in L_1 \times L_2 : \pi_\Sigma(w) \in (da)^*(eb)^*(fc)^*\}$ is recognizable by a monadic PA. By assumption, $\pi_1(L_3)$ is context-free. Let $h : \{a, b, c, d, e, f\}^* \to \{d, e, f\}^*$ be the homomorphism mapping a, b, and c to ϵ and which is the identity on d, e, and f. Since context-free languages are closed under homomorphism,

$$h(\pi_1(L_3)) = \{d^i e^j c^k : i \geq j \geq k\}$$

is context-free, a contradiction.

The proof relies on the following lemma:

Lemma 4. *Let L and L' be PA-recognizable languages. The language*

$$L_1 \times L_2 \triangleq \{(a_1 : i_1)(a_1' : i_1') \ldots (a_n : i_n)(a_n' : i_n') :$$
$$(a_1 : i_1) \ldots (a_n : i_n) \in L, (a_1' : i_1') \ldots (a_n' : i_n') \in L'\}$$

is PA-recognizable.

Proof. Let $A = \langle Q, ar, \Sigma, \delta, \varphi_{\mathsf{start}}, F \rangle$ and $A' = \langle Q', ar', \Sigma, \delta', \varphi'_{\mathsf{start}}, F' \rangle$ be PA that recognize L and L' respectively. Without loss of generality, suppose Q and Q' are disjoint. Construct a PA as follows:

- For each $q \in Q \cup Q'$ there are two predicates q_0 and q_1, with the same arity as q. For any formula $F \in \mathcal{F}(Q, ar)$, we use $F|_0$ to denote the result of replacing each $q \in Q$ with q_0, and $F|_1$ to denote the result of replacing each $q \in Q$ with q_1; similarly for formulas in $\mathcal{F}(Q', ar)$. Intuitively, we construct an automaton that simulates A on the odd positions and A' on the even positions of an input word.
- The initial formula is $\varphi_{\mathsf{init}}|_0 \wedge \varphi'_{\mathsf{init}}|_0$.
- For each $q \in Q$, the transition function $\hat{\delta}$ is defined

$$\hat{\delta}(q_0(i_1, \ldots, i_n), a : j) \triangleq \delta(q(i_1, \ldots, i_n), a : j)|_1$$
$$\hat{\delta}(q_1(i_1, \ldots, i_n), a : j) \triangleq q_0(i_1, \ldots, i_n)$$

- For each $q' \in Q'$, the transition function $\hat{\delta}$ is defined

$$\hat{\delta}(q'_0(i_1, \ldots, i_n), a : j) \triangleq q'_1(i_1, \ldots, i_n)$$
$$\hat{\delta}(q'_1(i_1, \ldots, i_n), a : j) \triangleq \delta'(q'(i_1, \ldots, i_n), a : j)|_0$$

- Finally, the final predicates are $\{q_1 : q \in F\} \cup \{q'_1 : q' \in F'\}$.

4   Comparison with Register Automata

Register automata are a class of automata that, like predicate automata, recognize languages of data words. A register automaton is equipped with finitely many registers, each of which may store data values (which for our purposes are natural numbers). The transition relation of a register automaton may test equality between values stored in registers and the data component of the input letter and may assign new data to registers. There is an apparent gap in the operational descriptions of predicate automata and register automata; predicate automata are declarative whereas register automata are imperative. Nonetheless, predicate automata have the same expressive power as a variant of register automata with ϵ transitions and alternation. Intuitively, one can think of a ground predicate $p(\mathtt{i}_1, \ldots, \mathtt{i}_n)$ of a predicate automaton to be analogous to a configuration of a register automaton with n registers holding data values $\mathtt{i}_1, \ldots, \mathtt{i}_n$. The fact that the only operations on registers are equality tests and assignment corresponds to the fact that PA treat thread identifiers symmetrically. For instance, a transition $q \xrightarrow{a:\mathtt{k}} q'$ of a two-register automaton that stores the value $\mathtt{k}$ to the second register on the condition that both registers store the same value corresponds to the PA transition $q(i, j) \xrightarrow{a:k} i = j \wedge q'(i, k)$.

There are several different definitions of (alternating) register automata in the literature [1,5,8,12]. The model of [12] is strictly more expressive than predicate automata, because it permits starting from an initial sate that does not have to be symmetric. The one in [8] is a variation that restricts this choice symmetric states and therefore is similar to predicate automata, but is only defined for a single register.

We choose the model of [1] to illustrate the equality of the two models and extend it with ϵ-transitions (which appear in some other models in the form of "non-moving" transitions [5,8]). This model is closer to predicate automata in that it eschews imperative register operations in favor of an abstract transition relation satisfying a *semantic equivariance* condition that enforces data symmetry (in the same way threads are treated symmetrically by predicate automata).

Definition 5 (Alternating register automaton). *An **alternating register automaton** (ARA) is an 8-tuple $A = \langle Q_\forall, Q_\exists, R, \Sigma, \Delta, \Delta_\epsilon, q_0, F \rangle$ where Σ is a finite alphabet and*

- *$Q \triangleq Q_\forall \cup Q_\exists$ is set of states, partitioned into a set of universal ($Q_\forall$) and existential ($Q_\exists$) states; $q_0 \in Q$ is an initial state and $F \subseteq Q$ is a set of final states.*
- *R is a finite set of register names.*
- *$\Delta \subseteq Q \times (\mathbb{N} \cup \{\perp\})^R \times \Sigma \times \mathbb{N} \times Q \times (\mathbb{N} \cup \{\perp\})^R$ is a transition relation. Δ is required to be **equivariant** in the sense that for any permutation $\pi : \mathbb{N} \to \mathbb{N}$ and any transition $\langle q, v, a, i, q', v' \rangle \in \Delta$, we have $(q, \pi_\perp \circ v, a, \pi(i), q', \pi_\perp \circ v') \in \Delta$, where $\pi_\perp : \mathbb{N} \cup \{\perp\} \to \mathbb{N} \cup \{\perp\}$ is the extension of π that maps $\perp \mapsto \perp$.*
- *$\Delta_\epsilon \subseteq Q \times (\mathbb{N} \cup \{\perp\})^R \times Q \times (\mathbb{N} \cup \{\perp\})^R$ is an ϵ-transition relation. Δ_ϵ is similarly required to be equivariant.*

*A is **non-guessing** if (1) for each transition $(q, v, a, i, q', v') \in \Delta$, for each register r, $v'(r)$ is either i or in the range of v, and (2) for each transition $(q, v, q', v') \in \Delta_\epsilon$, for each register r, $v'(r)$ is in the range of v.*

A **configuration** of an alternating register automaton is a set of states, where each state belongs to $Q \times (\mathbb{N} \cup \{\perp\})^R$. We say that a configuration C is **accepting** if for all $\langle q, v \rangle \in C$, we have $q \in F$. The **initial** configuration is $\{\langle q_0, \perp^R \rangle\}$. For configurations C, C', a letter $a \in \Sigma$, and a thread identifier $i \in \mathbb{N}$, write $C \xrightarrow{a:i} C'$ iff

- For each $\langle q, v \rangle \in C$ such that $q \in Q_\exists$, there is some $(q', v') \in C'$ such that $(q, v, a_j, i_j, q', v') \in \Delta$
- For each $\langle q, v \rangle \in C$ such that $q \in Q_\forall$, for all $q' \in Q$ and $v' \in (\mathbb{N} \cup \{\perp\})^R$ such that there is some $\langle q, v, a_j, i_j, q', v' \rangle \in \Delta$, we have $\langle q', v' \rangle \in C'$.

For configurations C and C', we write $C \xrightarrow{\epsilon} C'$ if there is some $\langle q, v \rangle \in C$ such that

- $q \in Q_\exists$ and there is some $(q, v, q', v') \in \Delta_\epsilon$ such that $C' = (C \setminus \{(q, v)\}) \cup \{(q', v')\}$
- $q \in Q_\forall$ and $C' \setminus (C \setminus \{(q, v)\}) = \{(q', v') : (q, v, q', v') \in \Delta_\epsilon\}$.

We say that an alternating register automaton accepts a word w if there is a sequence $C_0 \xrightarrow{w_1} C_1 \xrightarrow{w_2} \ldots \xrightarrow{w_n} C_n$ such that $w = w_1 \ldots w_n$, C_0 is initial, and C_n is accepting.

Proposition 7. *For any language L recognized by a k-register ϵ-ARA, L^R, the language of the words of L in reverse, is recognized by a PA with arity k.*

Proof. We prove the case with one register. Let $A = \langle Q_\forall, Q_\exists, R, \Sigma, \Delta, \Delta_\epsilon, q_0, F \rangle$ be an non-guessing 1-register ϵ-ARA. Define an ϵ-PA $\widehat{A} = \langle \widehat{Q}, ar, \Sigma, \delta, \varphi_{\mathsf{start}}, \widehat{F}, \epsilon \rangle$ that recognizes the reverse of the language recognized by A as follows.

The set of predicates $\widehat{Q}$ contains one unary predicate q and one nullary predicate $q_\perp$ for each $q \in Q$; intuitively, the predicate $q_\perp()$ corresponds the ARA state $\langle q, \perp \rangle$, and the predicate $q(i)$ corresponds to the ARA state $\langle q, i \rangle$. Define the initial formula to be $q_{0,\perp}$, and the accepting predicates $\widehat{F}$ to be $F \cup \{q_\perp : q \in F\}$. Finally, we define the transition relation. Observe that since Δ is equivariant, it is a finite union of *transition orbits* [1], of the form

$$\{(q, \pi_\perp \circ v, a, \pi(i), q', \pi_\perp \circ v') : \pi \text{ is a permutation } \mathbb{N} \to \mathbb{N}\}$$

for some $\langle q, v, a, i, q', v' \rangle$. Since A is non-guessing, each orbit can be classified as one of the following seven types $\mathcal{O}_1 - \mathcal{O}_7$, each of which can be associated with an $\mathcal{F}(\widehat{Q}, ar)$-formula $F_1 - F_7$:

Transition orbit	Corresponding formula
$\mathcal{O}_1(q, a, q') \triangleq \{(q, i, a, j, q', j) : i \neq j \in \mathbb{N}\}$	$F_1(q') \triangleq i_0 \neq i_1 \wedge q'(i_1)$
$\mathcal{O}_2(q, a, q') \triangleq \{(q, i, a, j, q', i) : i \neq j \in \mathbb{N}\}$	$F_2(q') \triangleq i_0 \neq i_1 \wedge q'(i_0)$
$\mathcal{O}_3(q, a, q') \triangleq \{(q, i, a, i, q', i) : i \in \mathbb{N}\}$	$F_3(q') \triangleq i_0 = i_1 \wedge q'(i_1)$
$\mathcal{O}_4(q, a, q') \triangleq \{(q, i, a, j, q', \perp) : i \neq j \in \mathbb{N}\}$	$F_4(q') \triangleq i_0 \neq i_1 \wedge q'_\perp()$
$\mathcal{O}_5(q, a, q') \triangleq \{(q, i, a, i, q', \perp) : i \in \mathbb{N}\}$	$F_5(q') \triangleq i_0 = i_1 \wedge q'_\perp()$
$\mathcal{O}_6(q, a, q') \triangleq \{(q, \perp, a, i, q', \perp) : i \in \mathbb{N}\}$	$F_6(q') \triangleq q'_\perp()$
$\mathcal{O}_7(q, a, q') \triangleq \{(q, \perp, a, i, q', i) : i \in \mathbb{N}\}$	$F_7(q') \triangleq q'(i)$

For any $q \in Q$ and $a \in \Sigma$, define the transition relation as follows:

$$\delta(q, a) \triangleq \begin{cases} \bigvee \{F_k(q') : q' \in Q, 1 \leq k \leq 5, \mathcal{O}_k(q, a, q') \subseteq \Delta\} & q \in Q_\exists \\ \bigwedge \{F_k(q') : q' \in Q, 1 \leq k \leq 5, \mathcal{O}_k(q, a, q') \subseteq \Delta\} & q \in Q_\forall \end{cases}$$

$$\delta(q_\perp, a) \triangleq \begin{cases} \bigvee \{F_k(q') : q' \in Q, k \in \{6, 7\}, \mathcal{O}_k(q, a, q') \subseteq \Delta\} & q \in Q_\exists \\ \bigwedge \{F_k(q') : q' \in Q, k \in \{6, 7\}, \mathcal{O}_k(q, a, q') \subseteq \Delta\} & q \in Q_\forall \end{cases}$$

The construction of the ϵ transition function from Δ_ϵ is similar. Finally, we may find a PA equivalent to the ϵ-PA A via the ϵ-elimination lemma (Lemma 2).

The construction for k registers is similar.

Proposition 8. *For any language L recognized by a PA with arity k, L^R is recognized by a $(k+1)$-register non-guessing ϵ-ARA.*

Proof. The essential obstacle in translating PA to ARA is that PA transitions involve arbitrary combinations of conjunctions and disjunctions, whereas each state in an ARA may have *only* conjunctive (universal) or disjunctive (existential) transitions.

Without loss of generality, suppose that for each state predicate $q \in Q$ and each letter $a \in \Sigma$, $\delta(q, a) = \bigvee_{i=1}^{N_{q,a}} C_{q,a,i}$, where $C_{q,a,i}$ is a conjunctive formula. Construct an alternating register automaton with one existential state p_q for each $q \in Q$, one universal state $p_{q,a,i}$ for each $q \in Q$, $a \in \Sigma$, and $1 \leq i \leq N_{q,a}$, one rejecting existential state *sink*, and registers $r_0, \ldots, r_k$ (where k is the maximum arity of any predicate in Q). The transition relation stores the read thread index i of the input into the register r_0 and transitions to *some* state $p_{q,a,j}$ (corresponding a cube of the formula $\delta(q, a)$):

$$\Delta \triangleq \left\{ \langle p_q, v, a, i, p_{q,a,j}, v[r_0 \leftarrow i] \rangle : q \in Q, a \in \Sigma, v \in (\mathbb{N} \cup \{\bot\})^R \right\}$$

The ϵ-transitions are responsible for transitioning from states of the form $p_{q,a,j}$ to *all* states described by $C_{q,a,i}$.

$$\Delta_\epsilon \triangleq \left\{ (p_{q,a,i}, v, p', v') : (p', v') \in At(C_{q,a,i}, v) \right\}$$

where

$$At(i_j = i_k, v) = \begin{cases} \emptyset & \text{if } v(r_j) = v(r_k) \\ (sink, v) & \text{otherwise} \end{cases}$$

$$At(i_j \neq i_k, v) = \begin{cases} \emptyset & \text{if } v(r_j) \neq v(r_k) \\ (sink, v) & \text{otherwise} \end{cases}$$

$$At(q'(i_{j_1}, \ldots, i_{j_n}), v) = \{(p_{q'}, (\bot, v(i_{j_1}), \ldots, v(i_{j_n}), \bot, \ldots, \bot))\}$$

$$At(F \wedge G, v) = At(F, v) \cup At(G, v)$$

5 Verification of Parameterized Boolean Programs

Here, we discuss how one can use predicate automata as a decision procedure for verification of parameterized boolean programs. We give a construction for a *universal* language of all infeasible runs, made of commands from a finite predetermined set Σ (that of some program). Then this serves as a proof Π_B for any Boolean program P whose commands belong to Σ. Since we limit the set of commands, without loss of generality, to assume statements and assign statements, the set Σ is determined by the set of local and global variables of the program.

A boolean program is defined by a set of variables $X = X_L \uplus X_G$, partitioned into a set of local boolean variables X_L and global boolean variables X_G, a thread template $T = \langle \mathsf{Loc}, E, \ell_{\mathsf{init}}, \ell_{\mathsf{err}}, \mathsf{src}, \mathsf{tgt} \rangle$, and a function $C : E \to Cmd$ that maps each edge to a *command* in the language defined below

$$x, y, z \in X$$
$$F, G \in \text{\textit{Formula}} ::= x \mid \neg x \mid F \wedge G \mid F \vee G$$
$$c \in \text{\textit{Cmd}} ::= \texttt{assume}(F)$$
$$\mid x := F$$

v_0 is a designated entry location, and v_{err} is designated error location. Note that formulas are in negation normal form. For a formula F, we use $\neg F$ to denote the negation-normal formula obtained from the negation of F by application of De Morgan's laws.

A formula in the above syntax can be thought of as a *thread state predicate*, in the sense that it can be interpreted from the perspective of any one thread. To express predicates over many threads, we extend formulas to **indexed formulas** as follows

$$F, G \in \text{\textit{IndexedFormula}} ::= x(\texttt{i}) \mid \neg x(\texttt{i}) \qquad x \in X_L, \texttt{i} \in \mathbb{N}$$
$$\mid y \mid \neg y \qquad y \in X_G$$
$$\mid F \wedge G \mid F \vee G$$

For instance $(x(0) \wedge \neg x(1)) \vee (\neg x(0) \wedge x(1))$ expresses that exactly one of threads 0 and 1 have their local variable x set to *true*. For any formula F and any natural number $\texttt{i}$, we use $F(\texttt{i})$ to denote the result of replacing each local variable x appearing in F with $x(\texttt{i})$. We can define a weakest precondition operator on indexed formulas and indexed commands as usual:

$$wp(x := F : \texttt{j}, G) \triangleq G[x(\texttt{j}) \mapsto F(\texttt{j})]$$
$$wp(\texttt{assume}(F) : \texttt{j}, G) \triangleq G \vee \neg F(\texttt{j})$$
$$wp(wc, G) \triangleq wp(w, wp(c, G))$$

Let Σ denote a finite subset of *Cmd*. We construct an automaton Π_B that recognizes exactly the set of *infeasible* paths over Σ (assuming each variable is initialized to *false*) as follows. The vocabulary Q consists of

- One nullary predicate *contra*, indicating a contradiction.
- Two nullary predicates q_z and $q_{\overline{z}}$ for each $z \in X_G$.
- Two unary predicates q_x and $q_{\overline{x}}$ for each $x \in X_L$.

For any variable symbol i, define a function $h_i : \text{\textit{Formula}} \to \mathcal{F}(Q, ar)$ by

$$h_i(F \wedge G) = h_i(F) \wedge h_i(G)$$
$$h_i(F \vee G) = h_i(F) \vee h_i(G)$$
$$h_i(x) = \begin{cases} q_x(i) & \text{if } x \in X_L \\ q_x() & \text{otherwise} \end{cases}$$
$$h_i(\neg x) = \begin{cases} q_{\overline{x}}(i) & \text{if } x \in X_L \\ q_{\overline{x}}() & \text{otherwise} \end{cases}$$

The transition relation of the automaton mimics the weakest precondition operator:

$$\delta(contra(), \texttt{assume(F)} : j) = h_j(\neg F) \vee contra()$$
$$\delta(contra(), x := F : j) = contra()$$
$$\delta(q_x(i), x := F : j) = (i \neq j \wedge q_x(i)) \vee (i = j \wedge h_i(F))$$
$$\delta(q_{\overline{x}}(i), x := F : j) = (i \neq j \wedge q_{\overline{x}}(i)) \vee (i = j \wedge h(\neg F))$$
$$\delta(q_z(), z := F : j) = h_j(F)$$
$$\delta(q_{\overline{z}}(), z := F : j) = h_j(\neg F)$$
$$\delta(q_x(i), y := F : j) = q_x(i) \qquad\qquad x \neq y$$
$$\delta(q_{\overline{x}}(i), y := F : j) = q_{\overline{x}}(i) \qquad\qquad x \neq y$$
$$\delta(q_z(), y := F : j) = q_z() \qquad\qquad y \neq z$$
$$\delta(q_{\overline{z}}(), y := F : j) = q_{\overline{z}}() \qquad\qquad y \neq z$$
$$\delta(q_x(i), \texttt{assume(F)} : j) = q_x(i)$$
$$\delta(q_{\overline{x}}(i), \texttt{assume(F)} : j) = q_{\overline{x}}(i)$$

The accepting predicates for Π_B are $\{q_{\overline{x}} : x \in X\}$, and the initial formula is $contra()$.

Theorem 2. *Let Σ be a finite alphabet of commands, and let Π_B be the predicate automaton as constructed above. For any sequence $w \in (\Sigma \times \mathbb{N})^*$, we have $w \in \mathcal{L}(\Pi_B)$ iff w is infeasible starting from a state where all variables are false.*

Proof. For any formula $F \in \mathcal{F}(Q, ar)$, let $\underline{F}$ denote the indexed formula obtained by replacing each $q_x(\texttt{i})$ with $x(\texttt{i})$, each $q_{\overline{x}}(\texttt{i})$ with $\neg x(\texttt{i})$, each $q_y()$ with y, each $q_{\overline{y}}()$ with $\neg y$, and $contra()$ with *false*.

One may show (by induction on length) that for any word w we have that $wp(w, false) \equiv \underline{\delta^*(contra(), w)}$, by induction on w. Finally, observe that a formula $F \in \mathcal{F}(Q, ar)$ is accepting exactly when $\underline{F}$ is satisfied by the state where all variables are *false*.

The construction of Π_B, as a monadic predicate automaton, yields a decision procedure for reachability of parameterized boolean programs. Example 1 gives a construction, as a monadic predicate automaton, of the language of error runs of the program. Theorem 1 and Proposition 1 imply that checking the subsumption of the set of program error runs by $\mathcal{L}(\Pi_B)$ is decidable.

6   Related Work

Automata on Infinite Alphabets. The automata theory community has developed generalizations of automata to infinite alphabets; the most relevant to our work is *(alternating) register automata (ARA)*.

Register automata were first introduced in [12]. Universality for register automata was shown to be undecidable in [14], which implies alternating register automata emptiness is undecidable in the general case. However, the emptiness problem for alternating register automata with 1 register (cf. monadic predicate automata) was proved to be decidable in [5] by reduction to reachability for lossy counter machines; and a direct proof based on well-structured transition systems was later presented in [8].

It is noteworthy that the models of register automata used in the aforementioned papers are all different, and they are different from the one from [1] that we use in Sect. 4. In particular, the models from [1,5] recognize symmetric languages, like predicate automata, however, the one from [12] recognizes non-symmetric languages. The model from [5] is closed under union, intersection, and complementation, while the one from [12] is not closed under complementation.

The model from [8] is an extension of the one from [5], which is also not closed under complementation. In both models, most transitions are *non-moving*; that is, the transition does not proceed forward when it reads an input symbol, similar to a classic ϵ-transition. There is a specific type of transition that moves the head to the next position to the right.

Predicate automata have alternation built-in. To relate them to alternating register automata, we opted for the definition in [1], except we added ϵ-transitions to the model. The similarity between the notion of *equivariance* in the definition of alternating register automata in [1] and the notion of symmetry in predicate automata is extremely helpful in producing elegant reductions between the two models. We added ϵ-transitions to the model in [1] to make the model as expressive as the one in [5] and proved equivalence of the model to predicate automata.

In [1] relations between weaker models of register automata (namely, nondeterministic and deterministic ones) and *Data Automata* and *Nominal Automata* is discussed. At the high level, it is understood that data automata are a slight generalization of nondeterministic register automata, and alternation strictly adds expressive power.

Parameterized Boolean Programs. There has been a great deal of work in the area of automated verification and analysis of concurrent programs where the number of threads is unbounded but the threads are finite-state [2,11,13,16]. This paper provides an alternative proof for the known result that verification of parameterized boolean programs is decidable.

References

1. Bojanczyk, M.: Slightly infinite sets. https://www.mimuw.edu.pl/~bojan/upload/main-10.pdf
2. Bouajjani, A., Jonsson, B., Nilsson, M., Touili, T.: Regular model checking. In: CAV, pp. 403–418 (2000)
3. Brzozowski, J., Leiss, E.: On equations for regular languages, finite automata, and sequential networks. Theoret. Comput. Sci. **10**(1), 19–35 (1980)
4. Chandra, A.K., Kozen, D.C., Stockmeyer, L.J.: Alternation. J. ACM **28**(1), 114–133 (1981)

5. Demri, S., Lazić, R.: LTL with the freeze quantifier and register automata. ACM Trans. Comput. Logic **10**(3), 16:1–16:30 (2009)
6. Farzan, A., Kincaid, Z., Podelski, A.: Proof spaces for unbounded parallelism. In: Rajamani, S.K., Walker, D. (eds.) Proceedings of the 42nd Annual ACM SIGPLAN-SIGACT Symposium on Principles of Programming Languages, POPL 2015, Mumbai, India, January 15–17, 2015, pp. 407–420. ACM (2015). https://doi.org/10.1145/2676726.2677012
7. Farzan, A., Kincaid, Z., Podelski, A.: Proving liveness of parameterized programs. In: Grohe, M., Koskinen, E., Shankar, N. (eds.) Proceedings of the 31st Annual ACM/IEEE Symposium on Logic in Computer Science, LICS 2016, New York, NY, USA, July 5–8, 2016, pp. 185–196. ACM (2016). https://doi.org/10.1145/2933575.2935310
8. Figueira, D.: Alternating register automata on finite words and trees. Logical Methods Comput. Sci. (1) (2012)
9. Finkel, A., Schnoebelen, P.: Well-structured transition systems everywhere! Theoret. Comput. Sci. **256**(1), 63–92 (2001)
10. Jones, C.B.: Tentative steps toward a development method for interfering programs. ACM Trans. Program. Lang. Syst. **5**(4), 596–619 (1983). https://doi.org/10.1145/69575.69577
11. Kaiser, A., Kroening, D., Wahl, T.: Dynamic cutoff detection in parameterized concurrent programs. In: CAV, pp. 645–659 (2010)
12. Kaminski, M., Francez, N.: Finite-memory automata. Theor. Comput. Sci. **134**(2), 329–363 (1994)
13. Namjoshi, K.S.: Symmetry and completeness in the analysis of parameterized systems. In: VMCAI, pp. 299–313 (2007)
14. Neven, F., Schwentick, T., Vianu, V.: Finite state machines for strings over infinite alphabets. ACM Trans. Comput. Logic **5**(3), 403–435 (2004)
15. Owicki, S.S., Gries, D.: An axiomatic proof technique for parallel programs I. Acta Informatica **6**, 319–340 (1976). https://doi.org/10.1007/BF00268134
16. Pnueli, A., Ruah, S., Zuck, L.D.: Automatic deductive verification with invisible invariants. In: TACAS, pp. 82–97 (2001)

Find, Use, and Conserve
Tools for Formal Methods

Dirk Beyer

LMU Munich, Munich, Germany

Abstract. The research area of formal methods has made enormous progress in the last 20 years, and many tools exist to apply formal methods to practical problems. Unfortunately, many of these tools are difficult to find and install, and often they are not executable due to missing installation requirements. The findability and wide adoption of tools, and the reproducibility of research results, could be improved if all major tools for formal methods were conserved and documented in a central repository of tools for formal methods (cf. FAIR principles).

This paper describes a solution to this problem: Collect and maintain essential data about tools for formal methods in a central repository, called FM-Tools, available at `https://gitlab.com/sosy-lab/benchmarking/fm-tools`. The repository contains metadata, such as which tools are available, which versions are advertized for each tool, and what command-line arguments to use for default usage. The actual tool executables are stored in tool archives at Zenodo, and for technically deep documentation, references point to archived publications or project web sites. Two communities, which are concerned with software verification and testing, already adopted the FM-Tools repository for their comparative evaluations. Andreas Podelski and his research group, with their Ultimate family of tools for software verification, are among the early adopters of this strategy, and the Ultimate tools are included in the repository from its beginning.

Keywords: FAIR · Formal Methods · Long-Term Archiving · Reuse · Conservation · Reproducibility · Competitions · Software Tools · FM-Tools

1 Introduction

The research community of formal methods, especially formal verification of medium and large software systems, has seen a lot of progress in the past 20 years. As a result, there are many tool implementations available, and a recent survey [1], co-authored by Andreas Podelski, gives an overview of the milestones in the history of software model checking and the available tools for verification of C and Java programs. Those tools are mature in their performance and quality, as witnessed and regularly measured by comparative evaluations of the tools [2]. There are several competitions available in this research area of formal methods, for example, the competitions on satisfiability (SAT-COMP [3]), theorem proving (TPTP [4]), SMT solving (SMT-COMP [5]), software verification (SV-COMP [2], RERS [6] and VerifyThis [7]), software testing (Test-Comp [8]), and

© The Author(s), 2026

D. Dietsch et al. (Eds.), *On the Pursuit of Insight and Elegance*, LNCS 14765, pp. 75–91, 2026.

https://doi.org/10.1007/978-3-032-13711-1_5

termination checking (termCOMP [9]). More competitions in the area of formal methods are explained in the TOOLympics 2019 report [10].

Besides all this great progress, and many success stories with formal verification of software in industry [11, 12, 13, 14, 15, 16, 17], users still have reasons to complain that the tools are difficult to find and install, and often they are not executable due to missing requirements [18, 19]. This hinders the wide application of these tools; often it is not possible to reproduce results reported in research publications. There is no standard way to find or conserve tools and components in this research area. Such tools, and metadata for the tools, should follow the FAIR principles (findable, accessible, interoperable, and reusable) [20, 21].

We propose a solution to this problem, by designing a data repository in which metadata about tools for formal methods are collected and maintained. The goal is to conserve a definition of how to execute each tool and what their requirements are. This central repository of tools for formal methods is hosted on GitLab at `https://gitlab.com/sosy-lab/benchmarking/fm-tools` and freely accessible, since all information is licensed under the Creative Commons license CC-BY 4.0.

The repository is already actively used to store metadata about the tools, their archive ids, their versions, and their documentation. Currently the two competitions on software verification (SV-COMP) and testing (Test-Comp) use the repository to track the participation in their comparative evaluations. For this use case, the repository specifies which tool version to execute for the competition and with which command-line options. Furthermore, the data contain information about whom to contact and who from the development team of the tool represents the team in the competition jury. The actual tool archives with the executables are stored at Zenodo and identified by DOIs. The data repository also provides pointers to documentation, archived in digital libraries or project web sites.

This topic fits well for this Festschrift, because Andreas Podelski, together with his team, participates since 2013 in the competition on software verification. The Ultimate family of tools for software verification and the development team participate in the community service around the competition and achieve top results, witnessed by the many medals that the team won. They are also concerned with making their tools available to others via an easy-to-use web interface. Often, such an excellent infrastructure can be offered only by large and strong development teams. This paper proposes to make *all* tools available via a web service.

The goal of this paper is to describe the above-mentioned data repository, outline how to make all tools available to users and machines via an easy-to-use web interface as well as command-line interface, and how to achieve a central store of (meta) information about tools for formal methods.

Contributions. This paper makes the following contributions:

- the repository FM-TOOLS as solution to the problem of collecting and maintaining data about tools for formal methods,
- a description of the repository's structure and its integration with the tools COVERITEAM, COVERITEAM-SERVICE, and FM-WECK, and
- an artifact to try out executing a conserved tool.

Related Work. The web site YAHODA [22, 23] was created in 2002 to provide unified information about verification tools and to allow the developers of the tools to maintain the data about their tools. The last available version is from 2011 and contains 67 tool entries. The dataset ProVerB [24, 25] is also concerned with collecting information about tools for formal methods. The dataset contains a classification of tools and describes roughly the input and output of the tools, as well as some techniques that the tools support. The data set contains information about 384 tools, based on a systematic search, starting with the proceedings of the conferences CAV and TACAS. Maintaining the information is the main challenge in both cases: The web server for YAHODA is not reachable anymore, but thanks to the Internet Archive, the information is still available. The repository and web site of ProVerB was not touched since more than a year, but the data are also long-term archived at Zenodo. Our approach is to connect the maintenance of the data in the FM-Tools collection to regular comparative evaluations of the performance of tools (research competitions), and regularly publish FM-Tools snapshots in long-term archives at Zenodo [26].

This is not the first attempt to see formal-methods tools as components (cf. [27, 28, 29, 30]) or to provide them via a central web service [31, 32, 33, 34, 35]. Also, some tool projects provide specialized web services with their tools (e.g., Ultimate, CPAchecker). CoVeriTeam-Service [36] is more general: it provides a web service for almost all tools in the FM-Tools repository. The FM-Tools format (version 2) for describing tools can be seen as an extension of CoVeriTeam's format (version 1) for defining atomic actors [37, Listing 2]. With FM-Tools, we now add a lot more important information about the tools, in particular, it serves as the central location to announce the execution environment for a tool in form of container images in OCI image format and Ubuntu packages.

So far, no existing approach addresses the issue of conserving the tools and ensuring the tools' execution in the future.

2 The FM-Tools Repository

The current version of the FM-Tools repository `https://gitlab.com/sosy-lab/benchmarking/fm-tools` consists of the following directories (suffix '/') and files:

presentations/ Contains presentations that describe the tools (see below).

data/ Contains the main data about tools (see below).

ci/ Contains scripts that ensure the consistency of the data. The scripts are executed by the continuous-integration (CI) pipelines of the GitLab repository.

scripts/ Contains the contents of another repository as submodule. These scripts are used by the CI pipelines.

CODEOWNERS Contains a specification of which file in the repository may be changed by which set of users. The file follows the GitLab format and is derived from the metadata for the tools.

LICENSE.md Contains the license of all files in this repository.

README.md Contains a description of the repository.

```
1   name: UAutomizer
2   input_languages:
3     - C
4   project_url: https://ultimate-pa.org
5   repository_url: https://github.com/ultimate-pa/ultimate
6   spdx_license_identifier: LGPL-3.0-or-later
7   benchexec_toolinfo_module: ultimateautomizer.py
8   fmtools_format_version: "2.0"
9   fmtools_entry_maintainers:
10    - danieldietsch
```

Fig. 1: Data file for Ultimate Automizer — tool data

The directory **presentations/** contains presentations about tools described in **data/**. An entry consists of two files: `presentations/<tool-id>_<event-id>.pdf` and `presentations/<tool-id>_<event-id>.pdf.license`, where `<tool-id>` matches one of the file names `data/<tool-id>.yml` and `<event-id>` identifies the event where the presentation was given. The file with extension `.pdf` contains a presentation in PDF/A format; the file with extension `.license` contains an SPDX identifier of the license (for example, `SPDX-License-Identifier: CC-BY-4.0`).

In the following subsections, we focus on the directory **data/**. This directory contains the special file **schema.yml**, which defines the format of all other files in the directory: the tool descriptions. The names of the tool-description files are of the form `<tool-id>.yml`, where `tool-id` is an identifier that consists of lowercase letters, digits, and hyphens. In the following we define the contents of the tool-description files. For illustration, we use the example file **uautomizer.yml** for the tool Ultimate Automizer [38], one of Andreas Podelski's tools.

2.1   Tool Description

Figure 1 shows an example of the tool-data section of the file. The tool description starts with the key `name`, whose value is the (stylized) name of the tool. The YAML key `input_languages` has a list of languages as value, specifying which input formats the tool supports. The keys `project_url` and `repository_url` specify the project's web site and the source-code repository, respectively. The key `spdx_license_identifier` specifies the license of the tool in the standard SPDX format (`https://spdx.org/licenses/`). The key `benchexec_toolinfo_module` specifies the BenchExec [39] tool-info module that is necessary to assemble the command line for the tool's execution and to interpret the tool's output. The YAML key `fmtools_format_version` specifies the version of the tool-description format, currently 2.0. The key `fmtools_entry_maintainers` specifies a list of maintainers of this tool description. The list elements must be valid GitLab user names, and those accounts will end up in the file `CODEOWNERS` in the top-level directory, in order to manage who can make changes to the data and approve merge requests.

```
1  maintainers:
2    - orcid: 0000-0003-4252-3558
3      name: Matthias Heizmann
4      institution: University of Freiburg
5      country: Germany
6      url: https://swt.informatik.uni-freiburg.de/staff/heizmann
7    - orcid: 0000-0003-4885-0728
8      name: Dominik Klumpp
9      institution: University of Freiburg
10     country: Germany
11     url: https://swt.informatik.uni-freiburg.de/staff/klumpp
12   - orcid: 0000-0002-5656-306X
13     name: "Frank Schüssele"
14     institution: University of Freiburg
15     country: Germany
16     url: https://swt.informatik.uni-freiburg.de/staff/schuessele
17   - orcid: 0000-0002-8947-5373
18     name: Daniel Dietsch
19     institution: University of Freiburg
20     country: Germany
21     url: https://swt.informatik.uni-freiburg.de/staff/dietsch
```

Fig. 2: Data file for ULTIMATE AUTOMIZER — tool maintainers

2.2   Maintainers

Figure 2 shows an example of the tool maintainers. The key `maintainers` has a list of dictionaries as value. Each dictionary specifies one maintainer, by the keys `orcid`, `name`, `institution`, `country`, and homepage `url`.

2.3   Tool Versions

Figure 3 shows an example of the tool versions (we list only those from 2024 here). The key `versions` has a list of dictionaries as value. Each dictionary specifies one tool version, by the following keys: The key `version` is an identifier for a specific version of the tool, to be referred to, for example, for the definition which version participated in a competition. The key `doi` defines the tool archive. The DOI points to a specific version of the tool archives on Zenodo. The key `benchexec_toolinfo_options` specifies the command-line options that the developers define to be used to obtain optimal functionality. The key `required_ubuntu_packages` defines a list of Ubuntu packages that are required to be installed for the tool to work properly. The key `base_container_images` identifies a list of a container images in OCI image format (as used by Docker and Podman) in which the tool can be correctly executed *after installing* the packages defined under `required_ubuntu_packages`. The key `full_container_-images` identifies a list of a container images in OCI image format in which the tool can be correctly executed *without* further installation of any packages. For example, ULTIMATE AUTOMIZER can be executed with the container image `registry.gitlab.com/sosy-lab/benchmarking/competition-scripts/user:2024` from the given domain and path without installing any package.

```yaml
versions:
  - version: svcomp24-correctness-post-deadline-yaml-wrapper-fix
    doi: 10.5281/zenodo.10223333
    benchexec_toolinfo_options:
      [--full-output, --witness-type, correctness_witness]
    required_ubuntu_packages:
      - openjdk-11-jre-headless
    base_container_images:
      - docker.io/ubuntu:22.04
    full_container_images:
      - registry.gitlab.com/sosy-lab/benchmarking/...-scripts/user:2024
  - version: svcomp24
    doi: 10.5281/zenodo.10203545
    benchexec_toolinfo_options: [--full-output]
    required_ubuntu_packages:
      - openjdk-11-jre-headless
    base_container_images:
      - docker.io/ubuntu:22.04
    full_container_images:
      - registry.gitlab.com/sosy-lab/benchmarking/...-scripts/user:2024
  - version: svcomp24-correctness
    doi: 10.5281/zenodo.10203545
    benchexec_toolinfo_options:
      [--full-output, --witness-type, correctness_witness]
    required_ubuntu_packages:
      - openjdk-11-jre-headless
    base_container_images:
      - docker.io/ubuntu:22.04
    full_container_images:
      - registry.gitlab.com/sosy-lab/benchmarking/...-scripts/user:2024
  - version: svcomp24-violation
    doi: 10.5281/zenodo.10203545
    benchexec_toolinfo_options:
      [--full-output, --witness-type, violation_witness]
    required_ubuntu_packages:
      - openjdk-11-jre-headless
    base_container_images:
      - docker.io/ubuntu:22.04
    full_container_images:
      - registry.gitlab.com/sosy-lab/benchmarking/...-scripts/user:2024
```

Fig. 3: Data file for ULTIMATE AUTOMIZER — tool versions (the identifier
`registry.gitlab.com/sosy-lab/benchmarking/competition-scripts/user:2024` is
abbreviated using ...)

2.4 Competition Participation

Figure 4 shows an example of the tool's participation declaration in the competition on software verification SV-COMP 2024 [2]. The corresponding YAML key `competition_participations` has a list of dictionaries as value. The key `competition` and `track` have as value the name of the competition and the name of the competition track for which this participation is meant, respectively. The key `tool_version` refers to a version of the tool that is defined under the key `versions` above. The key `jury_member` has a dictionary as value and defines the team member who represents this tool in the competition jury. The dictionary consists of entries with the keys `orcid`, `name`, `institution`, `country`, and `url`, where the URL refers to the person's home page. The declaration of the specific

```
 1  competition_participations:
 2    - competition: SV-COMP 2024
 3      track: Verification
 4      tool_version: svcomp24
 5      jury_member:
 6        orcid: 0000-0003-4252-3558
 7        name: Matthias Heizmann
 8        institution: University of Freiburg
 9        country: Germany
10        url: https://swt.informatik.uni-freiburg.de/staff/heizmann
11    - competition: SV-COMP 2024
12      track: Validation of Correctness Witnesses 1.0
13      tool_version: svcomp24-correctness
14      jury_member:
15        orcid: 0000-0003-4252-3558
16        name: Matthias Heizmann
17        institution: University of Freiburg
18        country: Germany
19        url: https://swt.informatik.uni-freiburg.de/staff/heizmann
20    - competition: SV-COMP 2024
21      track: Validation of Correctness Witnesses 2.0
22      tool_version: svcomp24-correctness-post-deadline-yaml-wrapper-fix
23      jury_member:
24        orcid: 0000-0003-4252-3558
25        name: Matthias Heizmann
26        institution: University of Freiburg
27        country: Germany
28        url: https://swt.informatik.uni-freiburg.de/staff/heizmann
29    - competition: SV-COMP 2024
30      track: Validation of Violation Witnesses 1.0
31      tool_version: svcomp24-violation
32      jury_member:
33        orcid: 0000-0003-4252-3558
34        name: Matthias Heizmann
35        institution: University of Freiburg
36        country: Germany
37        url: https://swt.informatik.uni-freiburg.de/staff/heizmann
```

Fig. 4: Data file for ULTIMATE AUTOMIZER — tool's competition participation

version, in particular via the DOI, together with the command-line options and the execution environment (container and packages) make it possible to execute this tool at any time, and reproduce the results obtained in the competition.

2.5   Documentation

Figure 5 shows an example of the documentation of the tool. The key `techniques` has a list of keywords as value, where each keyword refers to an established technique in software model checking. The key `literature` has a list of dictionaries as value. Each literature dictionary has the keys `doi` to identify the literature document (documents without DOI can be mentioned on the project web site), `title` to mention the title of the document, and `year` to mention the year of publication (the last two values are implied by the DOI, but are mentioned here to have the data human readable, consistency should be ensure via CI).

```
 1  techniques:
 2    - CEGAR
 3    - Predicate Abstraction
 4    - Bit-Precise Analysis
 5    - Lazy Abstraction
 6    - Interpolation
 7    - Automata-Based Analysis
 8    - Concurrency Support
 9    - Ranking Functions
10    - Algorithm Selection
11    - Portfolio
12
13  literature:
14    - doi: 10.1007/978-3-642-39799-8_2
15      title: "Software Model Checking for People Who Love Automata"
16      year: 2013
17    - doi: 10.1007/978-3-031-30820-8_39
18      title: "Ultimate Automizer 2023 (Competition Contribution)"
19      year: 2023
```

Fig. 5: Data file for ULTIMATE AUTOMIZER — tool documentation

2.6   FAIR Principles of the FM-TOOLS Repository

At the time of writing, FM-TOOLS describes and captures metadata of 91 tools from the formal-methods research community. The repository is hosted at GitLab. FM-TOOLS is an open-source data repository that follows the FAIR principles [20, 21] (findable, accessible, interoperable, reusable).

F: The repository FM-TOOLS is searchable on the public internet, and mirrored by the software archive Software Heritage. A human readable web site with the most important information is continuously generated from the repository.

A: All files of FM-TOOLS are retrievable using the HTTP protocol via the GitLab web service. Authentication is not necessary for reading the data (change requests require a GitLab account). If GitLab should become unavailable, the snapshots at Zenodo and the mirror at Software Heritage are still available.

I: The format of the tool entries in FM-TOOLS is defined using a YAML schema, and continuous-integration pipelines check the syntax and context conditions. The tool archives are identified using DOIs (pointing to the archives' landing page at Zenodo) and the researchers are identified using ORCIDs (pointing to the researchers' profiles at ORCID).

R: The license of the FM-TOOLS data is CC-BY 4.0. The data represented in FM-TOOLS meet the community standards of the competitions SV-COMP (`https://sv-comp.sosy-lab.org`) and Test-Comp (`https://test-comp.sosy-lab.org`). It is under the researchers' control how much they reveal about themselves on ORCID, and under which license the tool is available on Zenodo.

3   Integration of the FM-TOOLS Repository with CoVeriTeam and FM-Weck

The data in the FM-TOOLS repository can be used to conveniently execute tools for formal methods, without the need to install them or to take measures such as containers to ensure isolated execution without security risks on the user machine.

3.1   Tool Execution via CoVeriTeam Service

CoVeriTeam [37] is a tool that, among other things, automates the download, installation, and execution of tools in safe and secure environments based on BenchExec [39]. CoVeriTeam-Service [36] is a service that offers the features of CoVeriTeam as a web service, that is, the input files are sent to a remote server, the tool is executed on the remote server, and results are fetched from the remote server and delivered back to the user. Since CoVeriTeam Service executes formal-methods tools remotely without locally installing them, this way of execution is ideal for continuous integration, because the actual automated-reasoning work is offloaded to a remote compute server.

In the following we assume that the repository for CoVeriTeam is cloned using

```
git clone --recurse-submodules \
  git@gitlab.com:sosy-lab/software/coveriteam.git
```

and that the current directory is the main directory of that checkout. A full command line to execute ULTIMATE AUTOMIZER remotely, using the specific version svcomp24 of the tool, the specification no-overflow, and the particular program AdditionIntMax.i would look as follows:

```
bin/verify --remote -t uautomizer -v svcomp24 --spec no-overflow \
  examples/test-data/c/AdditionIntMax.i
```

This command is executed on the remote server (by default, CoVeriTeam Service uses the server coveriteam-service.sosy-lab.org), which downloads, installs, and executes the tool ULTIMATE AUTOMIZER in version svcomp24, and returns the result to the user. The verdict from ULTIMATE AUTOMIZER is reported as false(no-overflow), that is, an overflow of a variable of type signed integer happens. More detailed information can be found in the CoVeriTeam output folder cvt-output/, in particular, the execution trace with measurements of consumed resources (such as CPU time, wall time, and memory), the complete log of the tool's output to stdout, and possibly a verification witness.

3.2   Tool Execution via FM-Weck

FM-Weck [40] provides support for conveniently running tools from the FM-TOOLS repository in their designated OCI containers: it downloads the tool and its container, and executes the tool in its container (in isolation). The tool has two modes: (i) FM-Weck takes a base container image specified as a value in the list for key `base_container_images` of the version dictionary in the `versions` section, installs the packages listed in the key `required_ubuntu_packages`, and executes the tool available in the archive specified by the value for key `doi`. (ii) FM-Weck takes a full container image specified as a value in the list for key `full_container_images` of the version dictionary in the `versions` section, and executes the tool available in the archive specified by the value for key `doi`, without installing any packages.

FM-Weck enables all users to take advantage of the conserved tools as defined in the FM-Tools repository. This approach makes it possible to execute the formal-methods tools hopefully after many years, when a machine with the required operating system and packages cannot be found anymore. The container images will still be available, and thus, the tools still be executable. Currently, it is an open challenge for the formal-methods community to achieve reproducibility of any experimental results obtained with tools and published articles. Full reproducibility is not yet achieved up to now, partially because tools are not easy to execute, which is the concern that FM-Weck tries to address.

We now explain how to execute UAutomizer via FM-Weck. We assume in the following a GNU/Linux machine with a working Podman installation. First, we install FM-Weck via pip:

```
pip install fm-weck
```

Assuming that `AdditionIntMax.i` and `no-overflow.prp` are in the current directory, the following command line downloads and executes UAutomizer in version `svcomp24` in a container specified under `full_container_images` in the FM-Tools record for version `svcomp24`:

```
fm-weck run uautomizer:svcomp24 \
  --property no-overflow.prp --data-model LP64 AdditionIntMax.i
```

The output of UAutomizer is the same as above. The command-line arguments and input files to UAutomizer can be adjusted using the option -m for FM-Weck.

4 Overview Web Site Generated from the Data

The community suffers from the situation that there is no central point of information that brings together all information necessary to understand which tools for what purpose are available. Thanks to the FM-Tools repository, we are able to generate a web site that lists the tools, and for each tool an information section displaying all interesting data, such as contact developers, documentation, supported techniques, where to find the tool archives, and which competitions used the tool to provide comparative results on effectivity and efficiency of the tool. The web site generated from the FM-Tools repository is available at `https://fm-tools.sosy-lab.org`.

For example, if we are interested in learning which tools use the technique CEGAR, then we can visit the above web site, select 'Techniques' from the menu and 'CEGAR' from the table of contents, to receive an overview of this technique and the tools supporting it. The overview starts with a short description of the technique CEGAR,

> "CounterExample-Guided Abstraction Refinement is a model-checking technique that iteratively refines the abstract model of the transition system by analyzing spurious counterexamples and learning a more precise abstraction."

followed by a list of literature references [41, 42, 43] and a list of tools using the technique CEGAR: BRICK [44], CoVeriTeam-Verifier-AlgoSelection [37, 45], CoVeriTeam-Verifier-ParallelPortfolio [37, 45], CoVeriTest [46, 47], CPA-BAM-BnB [48, 49], CPAchecker [50, 51], CPALockator [52, 53], Gazer-Theta [54, 55], Graves-CPA [56], HybridTiger [57, 58], JayHorn [59, 60], PeSCo-CPA [61, 62], PIChecker [63], Theta [64, 65], UAutomizer [38, 66], UGemCutter [67, 68], UKojak [69, 70], UTaipan [71, 72], UTestGen [73], VeriAbs [74, 75], and VeriAbsL [76].

5 Conclusion

This article defines a standard format for the collection and maintenance of important information about tools for formal methods. The goal is to address challenges with regards to findability, reusability, reproducibility, and conservation. (i) Findability is addressed by having a standard format that is used by a significant amount of users. Currently the repository contains over 90 tools for formal methods, mainly from the research communities in the area of software verification and testing, around the competitions SV-COMP and Test-Comp. (ii) Reusability is addressed by having contact information, data about various versions, and documentation available. (iii) Reproducibility is addressed by having authoritative archives with tool executables identified via DOIs, providing developer-recommended command-line parameters to be used with the tool, and the tool archives are long-term published at Zenodo. (iv) Conservation is addressed by capturing the execution environment, which consists of a defined list of container images in OCI image format and a list of required packages.

We hope that the ideas in this paper help towards addressing the grand challenge of reproducibility of experimental results that are obtained with formal-methods tools and published in the formal-methods proceedings and journals. We congratulate Andreas Podelski to his 65th birthday and especially to the many tools that were developed under his guidance — we are happy that we can contribute to conserving such excellent research products for future generations.

Data-Availability Statement. The FM-TOOLS repository is available open access (CC-BY 4.0) at https://gitlab.com/sosy-lab/benchmarking/fm-tools. Important versions of the FM-TOOLS repository are archived at Zenodo [26] (current version is 2.0). The repository is also mirrored at Software Heritage. The generated web site https://fm-tools.sosy-lab.org/ is also mirrored at the Internet Archive. The artifact supporting this paper is available at Zenodo [77] and contains a snapshot of the COVERITEAM repository in version 1.2.3 (such that CoVeriTeam Service can be executed) and a snapshot of the FM-Tools repository in version 2.0 as submodule (such that all data can be inspected).

Funding Statement. FM-Weck was supported by Deutsche Forschungsgemeinschaft (DFG) – 378803395 (ConVeY). CoVeriTeam and CoVeriTeam Service were supported by Deutsche Forschungsgemeinschaft (DFG) – 418257054 (Coop) and 378803395 (ConVeY).

Acknowledgements. We thank Sudeep Kanav and Henrik Wachowitz for the joint work on CoVeriTeam [37], CoVeriTeam Service [36], and FM-Weck [40].

References

1. Beyer, D., Podelski, A.: Software model checking: 20 years and beyond. In: Principles of Systems Design. pp. 554–582. LNCS 13660, Springer (2022). https://doi.org/10.1007/978-3-031-22337-2_27
2. Beyer, D.: State of the art in software verification and witness validation: SV-COMP 2024. In: Proc. TACAS (3). pp. 299–329. LNCS 14572, Springer (2024). https://doi.org/10.1007/978-3-031-57256-2_15
3. Järvisalo, M., Berre, D.L., Roussel, O., Simon, L.: The international SAT solver competitions. AI Magazine **33**(1) (2012). https://doi.org/10.1609/aimag.v33i1.2395
4. Sutcliffe, G.: The CADE ATP system competition: CASC. AI Magazine **37**(2), 99–101 (2016). https://doi.org/10.1609/aimag.v37i2.2620
5. Weber, T., Conchon, S., Déharbe, D., Heizmann, M., Niemetz, A., Reger, G.: The SMT competition 2015-2018. J. Satisf. Boolean Model. Comput. **11**(1), 221–259 (2019). https://doi.org/10.3233/SAT190123
6. Howar, F., Isberner, M., Merten, M., Steffen, B., Beyer, D., Păsăreanu, C.S.: Rigorous examination of reactive systems. The RERS challenges 2012 and 2013. Int. J. Softw. Tools Technol. Transfer **16**(5), 457–464 (2014). https://doi.org/10.1007/s10009-014-0337-y
7. Ernst, G., Huisman, M., Mostowski, W., Ulbrich, M.: VerifyThis: Verification competition with a human factor. In: Proc. TACAS. pp. 176–195. LNCS 11429, Springer (2019). https://doi.org/10.1007/978-3-030-17502-3_12
8. Beyer, D.: Software testing: 5th comparative evaluation: Test-Comp 2023. In: Proc. FASE. pp. 309–323. LNCS 13991, Springer (2023). https://doi.org/10.1007/978-3-031-30826-0_17
9. Giesl, J., Mesnard, F., Rubio, A., Thiemann, R., Waldmann, J.: Termination competition (termCOMP 2015). In: Proc. CADE. pp. 105–108. LNCS 9195, Springer (2015). https://doi.org/10.1007/978-3-319-21401-6_6
10. Bartocci, E., Beyer, D., Black, P.E., Fedyukovich, G., Garavel, H., Hartmanns, A., Huisman, M., Kordon, F., Nagele, J., Sighireanu, M., Steffen, B., Suda, M., Sutcliffe, G., Weber, T., Yamada, A.: TOOLympics 2019: An overview of competitions in formal methods. In: Proc. TACAS (3). pp. 3–24. LNCS 11429, Springer (2019). https://doi.org/10.1007/978-3-030-17502-3_1
11. Ball, T., Levin, V., Rajamani, S.K.: A decade of software model checking with Slam. Commun. ACM **54**(7), 68–76 (2011). https://doi.org/10.1145/1965724.1965743
12. Ball, T., Cook, B., Levin, V., Rajamani, S.K.: Slam and Static Driver Verifier: Technology transfer of formal methods inside Microsoft. In: Proc. IFM. pp. 1–20. LNCS 2999, Springer (2004). https://doi.org/10.1007/978-3-540-24756-2_1

13. Khoroshilov, A.V., Mutilin, V.S., Petrenko, A.K., Zakharov, V.: Establishing Linux driver verification process. In: Proc. Ershov Memorial Conference. pp. 165–176. LNCS 5947, Springer (2009). https://doi.org/10.1007/978-3-642-11486-1_14

14. Calcagno, C., Distefano, D., Dubreil, J., Gabi, D., Hooimeijer, P., Luca, M., O'Hearn, P., Papakonstantinou, I., Purbrick, J., Rodriguez, D.: Moving fast with software verification. In: Proc. NFM. pp. 3–11. LNCS 9058, Springer (2015). https://doi.org/10.1007/978-3-319-17524-9_1

15. Cook, B.: Formal reasoning about the security of Amazon web services. In: Proc. CAV (2). pp. 38–47. LNCS 10981, Springer (2018). https://doi.org/10.1007/978-3-319-96145-3_3

16. Chong, N., Cook, B., Kallas, K., Khazem, K., Monteiro, F.R., Schwartz-Narbonne, D., Tasiran, S., Tautschnig, M., Tuttle, M.R.: Code-level model checking in the software development workflow. In: Proc. ICSE. pp. 11–20. ICSE-SEIP '20, ACM (2020). https://doi.org/10.1145/3377813.3381347

17. Darke, P., Metta, R., Medicherla, R.K., Venkatesh, R.: Impactful research and tooling for program correctness. Commun. ACM **65**(11), 52–53 (October 2022). https://doi.org/10.1145/3551665

18. Alglave, J., Donaldson, A.F., Kröning, D., Tautschnig, M.: Making software verification tools really work. In: Proc. ATVA. pp. 28–42. LNCS 6996, Springer (2011). https://doi.org/10.1007/978-3-642-24372-1_3

19. Garavel, H., ter Beek, M.H., van de Pol, J.: The 2020 expert survey on formal methods. In: Proc. FMICS. pp. 3–69. LNCS 12327, Springer (2020). https://doi.org/10.1007/978-3-030-58298-2_1

20. Wilkinson, M.D., Dumontier, M., Aalbersberg, I.J., Appleton, G., Axton, M., Baak, A., Blomberg, N., Boiten, J.W., d. Silva Santos, L.B., Bourne, P.E., Bouwman, J., Brookes, A.J., Clark, T., Crosas, M., Dillo, I., Dumon, O., Edmunds, S., Evelo, C.T., Finkers, R., Gonzalez-Beltran, A., Gray, A.J.G., Groth, P., Goble, C., Grethe, J.S., Heringa, J., 't Hoen, P.A.C., Hooft, R., Kuhn, T., Kok, R., Kok, J., Lusher, S.J., Martone, M.E., Mons, A., Packer, A.L., Persson, B., Rocca-Serra, P., Roos, M., v. Schaik, R., Sansone, S.A., Schultes, E., Sengstag, T., Slater, T., Strawn, G., Swertz, M.A., Thompson, M., v. d. Lei, J., v. Mulligen, E., Velterop, J., Waagmeester, A., Wittenburg, P., Wolstencroft, K., Zhao, J., Mons, B.: The FAIR guiding principles for scientific data management and stewardship. Sci. Data **3** (2016). https://doi.org/10.1038/sdata.2016.18

21. Jacobsen, A., d. Miranda Azevedo, R., Juty, N.S., Batista, D., Coles, S.J., Cornet, R., Courtot, M., Crosas, M., Dumontier, M., Evelo, C.T.A., Goble, C.A., Guizzardi, G., Hansen, K.K., Hasnain, A., Hettne, K.M., Heringa, J., Hooft, R.W.W., Imming, M., Jeffery, K.G., Kaliyaperumal, R., Kersloot, M.G., Kirkpatrick, C.R., Kuhn, T., Labastida, I., Magagna, B., McQuilton, P., Meyers, N., Montesanti, A., v. Reisen, M., Rocca-Serra, P., Pergl, R., Sansone, S.A., d. Silva Santos, L.O.B., Schneider, J., Strawn, G.O., Thompson, M., Waagmeester, A., Weigel, T., Wilkinson, M.D., Willighagen, E.L., Wittenburg, P., Roos, M., Mons, B., Schultes, E.: FAIR principles: Interpretations and implementation considerations. Data Intell. **2**(1-2), 10–29 (2020). https://doi.org/10.1162/DINT_R_00024

22. Crhová, J., Krčál, P., Strejček, J., Šafránek, D., Šimeček, P.: YAHODA: Verification tools database. In: Proc. Tools Day. pp. 99–103. FI MU Report Series FIMU-RS-2002-05, Masaryk University (2002)

23. Crhová, J., Krcál, P., Strejček, J., Šafránek, D., Simecek, P.: YAHODA: Verification tools database. http://www.fi.muni.cz/yahoda/ (2002), [Available in the Inter-

net Archive at `https://web.archive.org/web/20111119200847/http://anna.fi.muni.cz/yahoda`]

24. Lathouwers, S., Zaytsev, V.: Modelling program-verification tools for software engineers. In: Proc. MODELS. pp. 98–108. ACM (2022). https://doi.org/10.1145/3550355.3552426

25. Lathouwers, S., Zaytsev, V.: Proverb: Dataset of tools and formats for program verification. Zenodo (2024). https://doi.org/10.5281/zenodo.10806218

26. Beyer, D.: FM-Tools releases. Zenodo. https://doi.org/10.5281/zenodo.10669734

27. Spector, A.Z.: Invited talk: Modular architectures for distributed and databases systems. In: Proc. PODS. pp. 217–224. ACM (1989). https://doi.org/10.1145/73721.73743

28. Giunchiglia, E., Narizzano, M., Tacchella, A., Vardi, M.Y.: Towards an efficient library for SAT: A manifesto. Electronic Notes in Discrete Mathematics **9**, 290–310 (2001). https://doi.org/10.1016/S1571-0653(04)00329-4

29. Shankar, N.: Little engines of proof. In: Proc. FME. pp. 1–20. LNCS 2391, Springer (2002). https://doi.org/10.1007/3-540-45614-7_1

30. Lampson, B.: Software components: Only the giants survive. In: Computer Systems. Monographs in Computer Science. pp. 137–145. Springer (2004). https://doi.org/10.1007/0-387-21821-1_21

31. Steffen, B., Margaria, T., Braun, V.: The Electronic Tool Integration platform: Concepts and design. STTT **1**(1-2), 9–30 (1997). https://doi.org/10.1007/s100090050003

32. Margaria, T., Nagel, R., Steffen, B.: jETI: A tool for remote tool integration. In: Proc. TACAS. pp. 557–562. LNCS 3440, Springer (2005). https://doi.org/10.1007/978-3-540-31980-1_38

33. Margaria, T., Nagel, R., Steffen, B.: Remote integration and coordination of verification tools in jETI. In: Proc. ECBS. pp. 431–436 (2005). https://doi.org/10.1109/ECBS.2005.59

34. Margaria, T.: Web services-based tool-integration in the ETI platform. Software and Systems Modeling **4**(2), 141–156 (2005). https://doi.org/10.1007/s10270-004-0072-z

35. Steffen, B.: The physics of software tools: SWOT analysis and vision. Int. J. Softw. Tools Technol. Transf. **19**(1), 1–7 (2017). https://doi.org/10.1007/s10009-016-0446-x

36. Beyer, D., Kanav, S., Wachowitz, H.: CoVeriTeam Service: Verification as a service. In: Proc. ICSE, companion. pp. 21–25. IEEE (2023). https://doi.org/10.1109/ICSE-Companion58688.2023.00017

37. Beyer, D., Kanav, S.: CoVeriTeam: On-demand composition of cooperative verification systems. In: Proc. TACAS. pp. 561–579. LNCS 13243, Springer (2022). https://doi.org/10.1007/978-3-030-99524-9_31

38. Heizmann, M., Hoenicke, J., Podelski, A.: Software model checking for people who love automata. In: Proc. CAV. pp. 36–52. LNCS 8044, Springer (2013). https://doi.org/10.1007/978-3-642-39799-8_2

39. Beyer, D., Löwe, S., Wendler, P.: Reliable benchmarking: Requirements and solutions. Int. J. Softw. Tools Technol. Transfer **21**(1), 1–29 (2019). https://doi.org/10.1007/s10009-017-0469-y

40. Beyer, D., Wachowitz, H.: FM-Weck: Containerized execution of formal-methods tools. In: Proc. FM. LNCS, Springer (2024)

41. Clarke, E.M., Grumberg, O., Jha, S., Lu, Y., Veith, H.: Counterexample-guided abstraction refinement. In: Proc. CAV. pp. 154–169. LNCS 1855, Springer (2000). https://doi.org/10.1007/10722167_15

42. Ball, T., Rajamani, S.K.: Boolean programs: A model and process for software analysis. Tech. Rep. MSR Tech. Rep. 2000-14, Microsoft Research (2000), `https://www.microsoft.com/en-us/research/wp-content/uploads/2016/02/tr-2000-14.pdf`

43. Clarke, E.M., Grumberg, O., Jha, S., Lu, Y., Veith, H.: Counterexample-guided abstraction refinement for symbolic model checking. J. ACM **50**(5), 752–794 (2003). https://doi.org/10.1145/876638.876643
44. Bu, L., Xie, Z., Lyu, L., Li, Y., Guo, X., Zhao, J., Li, X.: BRICK: Path enumeration-based bounded reachability checking of C programs (competition contribution). In: Proc. TACAS (2). pp. 408–412. LNCS 13244, Springer (2022). https://doi.org/10.1007/978-3-030-99527-0_22
45. Beyer, D., Kanav, S., Richter, C.: Construction of verifier combinations based on off-the-shelf verifiers. In: Proc. FASE. pp. 49–70. Springer (2022). https://doi.org/10.1007/978-3-030-99429-7_3
46. Jakobs, M.C., Richter, C.: CoVeriTest with adaptive time scheduling (competition contribution). In: Proc. FASE. pp. 358–362. LNCS 12649, Springer (2021). https://doi.org/10.1007/978-3-030-71500-7_18
47. Beyer, D., Jakobs, M.C.: CoVeriTest: Cooperative verifier-based testing. In: Proc. FASE. pp. 389–408. LNCS 11424, Springer (2019). https://doi.org/10.1007/978-3-030-16722-6_23
48. Andrianov, P., Friedberger, K., Mandrykin, M.U., Mutilin, V.S., Volkov, A.: CPA-BAM-BnB: Block-abstraction memoization and region-based memory models for predicate abstractions (competition contribution). In: Proc. TACAS. pp. 355–359. LNCS 10206, Springer (2017). https://doi.org/10.1007/978-3-662-54580-5_22
49. Volkov, A.R., Mandrykin, M.U.: Predicate abstractions memory modeling method with separation into disjoint regions. Proceedings of the Institute for System Programming (ISPRAS) **29**, 203–216 (2017). https://doi.org/10.15514/ISPRAS-2017-29(4)-13
50. Baier, D., Beyer, D., Chien, P.C., Jankola, M., Kettl, M., Lee, N.Z., Lemberger, T., Lingsch-Rosenfeld, M., Spiessl, M., Wachowitz, H., Wendler, P.: CPAchecker 2.3 with strategy selection (competition contribution). In: Proc. TACAS (3). pp. 359–364. LNCS 14572, Springer (2024). https://doi.org/10.1007/978-3-031-57256-2_21
51. Beyer, D., Keremoglu, M.E.: CPAchecker: A tool for configurable software verification. In: Proc. CAV. pp. 184–190. LNCS 6806, Springer (2011). https://doi.org/10.1007/978-3-642-22110-1_16
52. Andrianov, P., Mutilin, V., Khoroshilov, A.: CPALockator: Thread-modular approach with projections (competition contribution). In: Proc. TACAS (2). pp. 423–427. LNCS 12652, Springer (2021). https://doi.org/10.1007/978-3-030-72013-1_25
53. Andrianov, P.S.: Analysis of correct synchronization of operating system components. Program. Comput. Softw. **46**, 712–730 (2020). https://doi.org/10.1134/S0361768820080022
54. Ádám, Zs., Sallai, Gy., Hajdu, Á.: Gazer-Theta: LLVM-based verifier portfolio with BMC/CEGAR (competition contribution). In: Proc. TACAS (2). pp. 433–437. LNCS 12652, Springer (2021). https://doi.org/10.1007/978-3-030-72013-1_27
55. Hajdu, Á., Micskei, Z.: Efficient strategies for CEGAR-based model checking. J. Autom. Reasoning **64**(6), 1051–1091 (2020). https://doi.org/10.1007/s10817-019-09535-x
56. Leeson, W., Dwyer, M.: Graves-CPA: A graph-attention verifier selector (competition contribution). In: Proc. TACAS (2). pp. 440–445. LNCS 13244, Springer (2022). https://doi.org/10.1007/978-3-030-99527-0_28
57. Ruland, S., Lochau, M., Jakobs, M.C.: HybridTiger: Hybrid model checking and domination-based partitioning for efficient multi-goal test-suite generation (competition contribution). In: Proc. FASE. pp. 520–524. LNCS 12076, Springer (2020). https://doi.org/10.1007/978-3-030-45234-6_26

58. Bürdek, J., Lochau, M., Bauregger, S., Holzer, A., von Rhein, A., Apel, S., Beyer, D.: Facilitating reuse in multi-goal test-suite generation for software product lines. In: Proc. FASE. pp. 84–99. LNCS 9033, Springer (2015). https://doi.org/10.1007/978-3-662-46675-9_6

59. Shamakhi, A., Hojjat, H., Rümmer, P.: Towards string support in JayHorn (competition contribution). In: Proc. TACAS (2). pp. 443–447. LNCS 12652, Springer (2021). https://doi.org/10.1007/978-3-030-72013-1_29

60. Kahsai, T., Rümmer, P., Sanchez, H., Schäf, M.: JayHorn: A framework for verifying Java programs. In: Proc. CAV. pp. 352–358. LNCS 9779, Springer (2016). https://doi.org/10.1007/978-3-319-41528-4_19

61. Richter, C., Wehrheim, H.: PeSCo: Predicting sequential combinations of verifiers (competition contribution). In: Proc. TACAS (3). pp. 229–233. LNCS 11429, Springer (2019). https://doi.org/10.1007/978-3-030-17502-3_19

62. Richter, C., Hüllermeier, E., Jakobs, M.C., Wehrheim, H.: Algorithm selection for software validation based on graph kernels. Autom. Softw. Eng. **27**(1), 153–186 (2020). https://doi.org/10.1007/s10515-020-00270-x

63. Su, J., Yang, Z., Xing, H., Yang, J., Tian, C., Duan, Z.: PIChecker: A POR and interpolation-based verifier for concurrent programs (competition contribution). In: Proc. TACAS (2). pp. 571–576. LNCS 13994, Springer (2023). https://doi.org/10.1007/978-3-031-30820-8_38

64. Bajczi, L., Telbisz, C., Somorjai, M., Ádám, Z., Dobos-Kovács, M., Szekeres, D., Mondok, M., Molnár, V.: Theta: Abstraction based techniques for verifying concurrency (competition contribution). In: Proc. TACAS (3). pp. 412–417. LNCS 14572, Springer (2024). https://doi.org/10.1007/978-3-031-57256-2_30

65. Tóth, T., Hajdu, A., Vörös, A., Micskei, Z., Majzik, I.: Theta: A framework for abstraction refinement-based model checking. In: Proc. FMCAD. pp. 176–179 (2017). https://doi.org/10.23919/FMCAD.2017.8102257

66. Heizmann, M., Bentele, M., Dietsch, D., Jiang, X., Klumpp, D., Schüssele, F., Podelski, A.: Ultimate automizer and the abstraction of bitwise operations (competition contribution). In: Proc. TACAS (3). pp. 418–423. LNCS 14572, Springer (2024). https://doi.org/10.1007/978-3-031-57256-2_31

67. Klumpp, D., Dietsch, D., Heizmann, M., Schüssele, F., Ebbinghaus, M., Farzan, A., Podelski, A.: Ultimate GemCutter and the axes of generalization (competition contribution). In: Proc. TACAS (2). pp. 479–483. LNCS 13244, Springer (2022). https://doi.org/10.1007/978-3-030-99527-0_35

68. Farzan, A., Klumpp, D., Podelski, A.: Sound sequentialization for concurrent program verification. In: Proc. PLDI. pp. 506–521. ACM (2022). https://doi.org/10.1145/3519939.3523727

69. Nutz, A., Dietsch, D., Mohamed, M.M., Podelski, A.: Ultimate Kojak with memory safety checks (competition contribution). In: Proc. TACAS. pp. 458–460. LNCS 9035, Springer (2015). https://doi.org/10.1007/978-3-662-46681-0_44

70. Ermis, E., Hoenicke, J., Podelski, A.: Splitting via interpolants. In: Proc. VMCAI. pp. 186–201. LNCS 7148, Springer (2012). https://doi.org/10.1007/978-3-642-27940-9_13

71. Dietsch, D., Heizmann, M., Klumpp, D., Schüssele, F., Podelski, A.: Ultimate Taipan 2023 (competition contribution). In: Proc. TACAS (2). pp. 582–587. LNCS 13994, Springer (2023). https://doi.org/10.1007/978-3-031-30820-8_40

72. Greitschus, M., Dietsch, D., Podelski, A.: Loop invariants from counterexamples. In: Proc. SAS. pp. 128–147. LNCS 10422, Springer (2017). https://doi.org/10.1007/978-3-319-66706-5_7

73. Barth, M., Dietsch, D., Heizmann, M., Jakobs, M.C.: ULTIMATE TESTGEN: Test case generation with automata-based software model checking (competition contribution). In: Proc. FASE. pp. 326–330. LNCS 14573, Springer (2024). https://doi.org/10.1007/978-3-031-57259-3_20
74. Darke, P., Agrawal, S., Venkatesh, R.: VERIABS: A tool for scalable verification by abstraction (competition contribution). In: Proc. TACAS (2). pp. 458–462. LNCS 12652, Springer (2021). https://doi.org/10.1007/978-3-030-72013-1_32
75. Afzal, M., Asia, A., Chauhan, A., Chimdyalwar, B., Darke, P., Datar, A., Kumar, S., Venkatesh, R.: VERIABS: Verification by abstraction and test generation. In: Proc. ASE. pp. 1138–1141. IEEE (2019). https://doi.org/10.1109/ASE.2019.00121
76. Darke, P., Chimdyalwar, B., Agrawal, S., Venkatesh, R., Chakraborty, S., Kumar, S.: VERIABSL: Scalable verification by abstraction and strategy prediction (competition contribution). In: Proc. TACAS (2). pp. 588–593. LNCS 13994, Springer (2023). https://doi.org/10.1007/978-3-031-30820-8_41
77. Beyer, D., Wachowitz, H.: COVERITEAM release 1.2.3 (with FM-TOOLS 2.0). Zenodo (2024). https://doi.org/10.5281/zenodo.11193820

On the Design of Program Logics

Patrick Cousot$^{(\boxtimes)}$ (iD)

Courant Institute of Mathematical Sciences, New York University, New York, USA
pcousot@cims.nyu.edu
https://cs.nyu.edu/pcousot/

Abstract. We illustrate the sound and complete construction of program logics by abstraction of a relational semantics into the theory of the logic followed by the formal derivation of the proof system. We consider Hoare logic, O'Hearn incorrectness logic and Hoare incorrectness logic formalizing debugging.

Keywords: Hoare logic · reverse Hoare logic · incorrectness logic · Hoare incorrectness logic · debugging · abstract interpretation

1 Introduction

We have recently proposed a methodology [6] to construct sound and complete Hoare'style (or transformational) program logics by defining the structural relational semantics of the programming language, which is abstracted into the theory of the logic (specifying the true formulas of the logic) and then expressed as an equivalent proof system using Peter Aczel correspondence between set-theoretic fixpoints and deductive rules as well as fixpoint induction principles to handle iteration. The construction of the logic consists in

1. Defining the relational semantics $[\![S]\!]$ of the programming language (in structural fixpoint form);
2. Defining the theory of the logics as an abstraction $\alpha(\{[\![S]\!]\})$ of the collecting semantics $\{[\![S]\!]\}$ (which is the strongest (hyper) property of statement S);
3. Calculating the theory $\alpha(\{[\![S]\!]\})$ in structural fixpoint form by fixpoint abstraction;
4. Calculating the proof system by fixpoint induction and Aczel correspondence [1] between fixpoints and deductive systems.

2 The Structural Natural Relational Semantics

We consider an imperative language $\mathbb{S}$ with assignments, sequential composition, conditionals, and conditional iteration. The syntax is $S \in \mathbb{S} ::= x = A \mid skip \mid S;S \mid if (B) S else S \mid while (B) S$. States $\sigma \in \Sigma \triangleq X \to V$ (also called environments) map variables $x \in X$ to their values $\sigma(x)$ in V. We deliberately

D. Dietsch et al. (Eds.): Podelski Festschrift, LNCS 14765, pp. 92–106, 2026.
https://doi.org/10.1007/978-3-032-13711-1_6

leave unspecified the syntax and semantics of arithmetic expressions $\mathcal{A}[\![A]\!] \in \Sigma \to \mathbb{V}$ and Boolean expressions $\mathcal{B}[\![B]\!] \in \wp(\Sigma) \simeq \Sigma \to \{\mathsf{true}, \mathsf{false}\}$. The only assumption on expressions is the absence of side effects. The natural (or angelic) semantics $[\![S]\!] \in \wp(\Sigma \times \Sigma)$ ignores nontermination [14]. We use judgements $\sigma \vdash S \Rightarrow \sigma'$ for $\langle \sigma, \sigma' \rangle \in [\![S]\!]$. In addition we write $\sigma \vdash \mathtt{while}\ (B)\ S \overset{i}{\Rightarrow} \sigma'$ to mean that if σ is a state before executing $\mathtt{while}\ (B)\ S$, then σ' is reachable after 0 or more iterations of the loop body (so $\sigma = \sigma'$ for 0 iterations, before entering the loop in case (1.a)). The semantics of iteration $W = \mathtt{while}\ (B)\ S$ is

$$\text{(a)}\ \sigma \vdash W \overset{i}{\Rightarrow} \sigma \quad \text{(b)}\ \frac{\sigma \vdash W \overset{i}{\Rightarrow} \sigma',\ \mathcal{B}[\![B]\!]\sigma',\ \sigma' \vdash S \Rightarrow \sigma''}{\sigma \vdash W \overset{i}{\Rightarrow} \sigma''} \quad \text{(c)}\ \frac{\sigma \vdash W \overset{i}{\Rightarrow} \sigma',\ \mathcal{B}[\![\neg B]\!]\sigma'}{\sigma \vdash W \Rightarrow \sigma'} \quad (1)$$

Aczel correspondence between deductive systems and set-theoretic fixpoints [1] allows us to derive an equivalent fixpoint definition of the semantics.

$$F(X) \triangleq \mathsf{id} \cup (X \, \mathring{,} \, [\![B]\!] \, \mathring{,} \, [\![S]\!]), \quad X \in \wp(\Sigma \times \Sigma) \tag{2}$$

$$[\![\mathtt{while}\ (B)\ S]\!] \triangleq \mathsf{lfp}^{\subseteq} F \, \mathring{,} \, [\![\neg B]\!] \tag{3}$$

where id is the identity relation and $\mathring{,}$ is the composition of relations. The transformer F are defined on the complete lattice $\langle \wp(\Sigma \times \Sigma), \subseteq, \emptyset, \Sigma \times \Sigma, \cup, \cap \rangle$ and is $\subseteq$-increasing, so $\mathsf{lfp}^{\subseteq} F$ does exist [19].

3 Aczel Correspondence Between Deductive Systems and Fixpoints

Rules $\frac{P}{c}$ on a universe $\mathcal{U}$ have a premise $P \in \wp(\mathcal{U})$ and a conclusion $c \in \mathcal{U}$. The premise $P = \emptyset$ is empty for axioms. A deductive system is a set of rules $R = \{\frac{P_i}{c_i} \mid i \in \Delta\} \in \wp(\wp(\mathcal{U}) \times \mathcal{U})$. The semantics of $\{\!|R|\!\}$ is the subset of the universe $\mathcal{U}$ defined by the rules.

The traditional proof-theoretic semantics of deductive systems is the set of provable terms (called theorems). Therefore $\{\!|R|\!\}^p = \{t_n \in \mathcal{U} \mid \exists t_1, \ldots, t_{n-1} \in \mathcal{U} \, . \, \forall k \in [1, n] \, . \, \exists \frac{P}{c} \in R \, . \, P \subseteq \{t_1, \ldots, t_{k-1}\} \wedge t_k = c\}$ (such finite proofs require the premiss P to be finite but transfinite proofs are also possible [15, Chapter 11], [1, Definition 1.4.1]). The model-theoretic semantics of deductive systems is the least fixpoint $\{\!|R|\!\}^m = \mathsf{lfp}^{\subseteq} F_R$ where the consequence operator $F_R(X) \triangleq \{c \mid \exists \frac{P}{c} \in R \, . \, P \subseteq X\}$ is increasing. Peter Aczel [1] proves that $\{\!|R|\!\}^m = \{\!|R|\!\}^p$. In the case of finite premisses, the idea is that the n-th iterates of F_R from $\emptyset$ is the set of all proofs of length n (hence the axioms for the first iterates). Conversely, any set-theoretic fixpoint $\mathsf{lfp}^{\subseteq} F$ of an increasing operator F (continuous for finite premisses) on the powerset $\wp(\mathcal{U})$ of a set $\mathcal{U}$ is the semantics $\{\!|R_F|\!\}^m = \{\!|R_F|\!\}^p$ of a deductive system $R_F = \{\frac{P}{c} \mid P \in \wp(\mathcal{U}) \wedge c \in F(P)\}$ (or $\{\frac{P}{c} \mid P \in \wp(\mathcal{U}) \wedge c \in F(P) \wedge \forall P' \in \wp(\mathcal{U}) \, . \, c \in F(P') \Rightarrow P \subseteq P'\}$ to eliminate redundant rules). Given the fixpoint characterization of the theory of a logic, obtained by abstraction $\alpha(\{[\![S]\!]\})$ of the fixpoint semantics $[\![S]\!]$, we can derive the proof system of the logic using this correspondence between fixpoints and rules.

4   Abstractions

Since the strongest property $\{[\![S]\!]\}$ of (the semantics $[\![S]\!]$ of) a statement S is an hyperproperty, it must be abstracted into an execution property $\alpha_C(\{[\![S]\!]\}) = [\![S]\!]$ where $\alpha_C(P) \triangleq \bigcup P$ is surjective and $\gamma_C(S) \triangleq \wp(S)$ is injective and is a Galois retraction $\langle \wp(\wp(\mathcal{D})), \subseteq \rangle \xleftrightarrow[\alpha_C]{\gamma_C} \langle \wp(\mathcal{D}), \subseteq \rangle$ [5, Chapter 11]. So $[\![S]\!]$ is the strongest property of executions of S.

Then program logics check reachability from preconditions or accessibility of postconditions which can be formalized by the post-image isomorphism $\mathsf{post}([\![S]\!])$ of the relational semantics where $\mathsf{post}(r)X \triangleq \{y \mid \exists x \in X \,.\, \langle x, y \rangle \in r\}$ maps a relation $r \in \wp(\mathcal{X} \times \mathcal{Y})$ to its union-preserving right-image $\mathsf{post}(r)$ so that $\langle \wp(\mathcal{X}), \subseteq \rangle \xleftrightarrow[\mathsf{post}(r)]{\widetilde{\mathsf{pre}}(r)} \langle \wp(\mathcal{Y}), \subseteq \rangle$ is a Galois connection with $\widetilde{\mathsf{pre}}(r)Q = \neg\mathsf{post}(r^{-1})\neg Q = \{x \mid \forall y \,.\, \langle x, y \rangle \in r \Rightarrow y \in Q\}$.

Contrary to predicate transformers, program logics are not functions but relations between predicates. Since a function $f \in \mathcal{X} \to \mathcal{Y}$ is isomorphic to its graph $\alpha_G(f) = \{\langle x, f(x) \rangle \mid x \in \mathcal{X}\}$, we can abstract a predicate transformer into a functional relation, which is a Galois isomorphism $\langle \mathcal{X} \to \mathcal{Y}, = \rangle \xleftrightarrow[\alpha_G]{\gamma_G} \langle \wp_{\mathsf{fun}}(\mathcal{X} \times \mathcal{Y}), = \rangle$ where $\gamma_G(r) \triangleq \lambda x \cdot (y \text{ such that } \langle x, y \rangle \in r)$ is uniquely well-defined since r is a functional relation.

5   The Strongest Postcondition Logic Theory

We can now define the strongest postcondition logic theory of a statement S as

$$\mathcal{T}[\![S]\!] = \alpha_G \circ \mathsf{post} \circ \alpha_C(\{[\![S]\!]\}) = \{\langle P, \mathsf{post}[\![S]\!]P \rangle \mid P \in \wp(\Sigma)\} \qquad (4)$$

The next step is to express this theory in fixpoint form. The main result from [9] is that the abstraction of a fixpoint is a fixpoint.

Theorem 1 (Fixpoint abstraction [9]). *If $\langle C, \sqsubseteq \rangle \xleftrightarrow[\alpha]{\gamma} \langle A, \preceq \rangle$ is a Galois connection between complete lattices $\langle C, \sqsubseteq \rangle$ and $\langle A, \preceq \rangle$, $f \in C \xrightarrow{i} C$ and $\bar{f} \in A \xrightarrow{i} A$ are increasing and commuting, that is, $\alpha \circ f = \bar{f} \circ \alpha$, then $\alpha(\mathsf{lfp}^{\sqsubseteq} f) = \mathsf{lfp}^{\preceq} \bar{f}$ (while semi-commutation $\alpha \circ f \preceq \bar{f} \circ \alpha$ implies $\alpha(\mathsf{lfp}^{\sqsubseteq} f) \preceq \mathsf{lfp}^{\preceq} \bar{f}$).*

As a simple application, we have the following corollary (which will allows us to define the predicate transformer for an iteration as the least fixpoint of a predicate transformer, as opposed to a (predicate transformer) transformer).

Corollary 1 (Pointwise abstraction). *Let $\langle L, \sqsubseteq, \top, \sqcup \rangle$ and $\langle L', \sqsubseteq', \top', \sqcup' \rangle$ be complete lattices. Assume that $F \in (L \to L') \xrightarrow{i} (L \to L')$ is increasing and that for all $Q \in L$, $\bar{F}_Q \in L' \xrightarrow{i} L'$ is increasing. Assume $\forall Q \in L \,.\, \forall f \in L \to L' \,.\, F(f)Q = \bar{F}_Q(f(Q))$. Then $\forall Q \in L \,.\, (\mathsf{lfp}^{\sqsubseteq'} F)Q = \mathsf{lfp}^{\sqsubseteq'} \bar{F}_Q$.*

By calculational design we get a fixpoint definition of the theory of strongest postconditions logics (common to Hoare logic and incorrectness logic with no consequence rules at all). For the iteration $\mathtt{W} = \mathtt{while}\ (\mathtt{B})\ \mathtt{S}$, we get $\mathcal{T}[\![\mathtt{W}]\!] \triangleq \{\langle P, \mathsf{post}[\![\neg\mathtt{B}]\!](\mathsf{lfp}^{\subseteq} F'_P)\rangle \mid P \in \wp(\Sigma)\}$ where $F'_P(X) = P \cup \mathsf{post}([\![\mathtt{B}]\!]\,\mathring{,}\,[\![\mathtt{S}]\!])X$.

For the proof, we have the commutation

$$
\begin{aligned}
& \mathsf{post}(F(X))P \\
=\ & \mathsf{post}(\mathsf{id} \cup (X\,\mathring{,}\,[\![\mathtt{B}]\!]\,\mathring{,}\,[\![\mathtt{S}]\!]))P && \wr\text{def. (2) of } F\wr \\
=\ & \mathsf{post}(\mathsf{id})P \cup \mathsf{post}(X\,\mathring{,}\,[\![\mathtt{B}]\!]\,\mathring{,}\,[\![\mathtt{S}]\!])P && \wr\text{post preserves arbitrary set unions}\wr \\
=\ & P \cup \mathsf{post}([\![\mathtt{B}]\!]\,\mathring{,}\,[\![\mathtt{S}]\!])(\mathsf{post}(X)P) && \wr\text{def. post, } \mathsf{post}(X\,\mathring{,}\,Y) = \mathsf{post}(Y) \circ \mathsf{post}(X)\wr \\
=\ & F'_P(\mathsf{post}(X)P) && \wr\text{def. } F'_P \triangleq \lambda X \cdot P \cup \mathsf{post}([\![\mathtt{B}]\!]\,\mathring{,}\,[\![\mathtt{S}]\!])X,\ \text{Q.E.D.}\wr
\end{aligned}
$$

It follows that

$$
\begin{aligned}
& \mathsf{post}[\![\mathtt{W}]\!] \\
=\ & \lambda P \cdot \mathsf{post}(\mathsf{lfp}^{\subseteq} F\,\mathring{,}\,[\![\neg\mathtt{B}]\!])P && \wr\text{by (3) and Church } \lambda\text{-notation}\wr \\
=\ & \lambda P \cdot \mathsf{post}[\![\neg\mathtt{B}]\!](\mathsf{post}(\mathsf{lfp}^{\subseteq} F)P) && \wr\mathsf{post}(X\,\mathring{,}\,Y) = \mathsf{post}(Y) \circ \mathsf{post}(X)\wr \\
=\ & \mathsf{post}[\![\neg\mathtt{B}]\!](\mathsf{lfp}^{\subseteq} F'_P) && \wr\text{commutation and corollary 1, Q.E.D.}\wr && (5)
\end{aligned}
$$

The characterization $\mathcal{T}[\![\mathtt{S}]\!] = \alpha_{\mathrm{G}} \circ \mathsf{post} \circ \alpha_{\mathrm{C}}(\{[\![\mathtt{S}]\!]\}) = \alpha_{\mathrm{G}} \circ \mathsf{post}([\![\mathtt{S}]\!]) = \{\langle P, \mathsf{post}[\![\mathtt{S}]\!]P\rangle \mid P \in \wp(\Sigma)\}$ follows directly from the definitions of α_C and α_G.

6   Deduction as Approximation

Lacking a consequence rule, the strongest postcondition logic theory is very strong and would, e.g., require the use of the strongest invariant for iteration, which by experience [12,13,16,20] is inadequately constraining.

The consequence abstraction can be defined by the component wise approximation $\langle x', y'\rangle \sqsubseteq, \preceq \langle x, y\rangle \triangleq x' \sqsubseteq x \wedge y' \preceq y$. Then $\mathsf{post}(\supseteq, \subseteq) = \lambda R \cdot \{\langle P, Q\rangle \mid \exists\langle P', Q'\rangle \in R\,.\,P \subseteq P' \wedge Q' \subseteq Q\}$ adds an over approximating consequence rule to the strongest postcondition logic theory to get the theory of Hoare logic

$$\mathcal{T}_{\mathrm{HL}}[\![\mathtt{S}]\!] \triangleq \mathsf{post}(\supseteq, \subseteq)(\mathcal{T}[\![\mathtt{S}]\!]) = \{\langle P, Q\rangle \mid \mathsf{post}[\![\mathtt{S}]\!]P \subseteq Q\} \tag{6}$$

while the $\subseteq$-dual $\mathsf{post}(\subseteq, \supseteq) = \lambda R \cdot \{\langle P, Q\rangle \mid \exists\langle P', Q'\rangle \in R\,.\,P' \subseteq P \wedge Q \subseteq Q'\}$ adds an under approximating consequence rule to the strongest postcondition logic theory to get the theory of incorrectness logic.

$$\mathcal{T}_{\mathrm{IL}}[\![\mathtt{S}]\!] \triangleq \mathsf{post}(\subseteq, \supseteq)(\mathcal{T}[\![\mathtt{S}]\!]) = \{\langle P, Q\rangle \mid Q \subseteq \mathsf{post}[\![\mathtt{S}]\!]P\} \tag{7}$$

Proof (of (6) and (7)).

$$
\begin{aligned}
&\ \mathsf{post}(\supseteq, \subseteq)(\mathcal{T}[\![\mathtt{S}]\!]) \\
=\ & \{\langle P, Q\rangle \mid \exists\langle P', Q'\rangle \in \mathcal{T}[\![\mathtt{S}]\!]\,.\,\langle P', Q'\rangle \supseteq.\subseteq \langle P, Q\rangle\} && \wr\text{def. post}\wr \\
=\ & \{\langle P, Q\rangle \mid \exists\langle P', Q'\rangle \in \mathcal{T}[\![\mathtt{S}]\!]\,.\,P \subseteq P' \wedge Q' \subseteq Q\} \\
& && \wr\text{and component wise order } \supseteq.\subseteq\wr
\end{aligned}
$$

$$= \{\langle P, Q\rangle \mid \exists\langle P', Q'\rangle \in \{\langle P'', \mathsf{post}[\![S]\!]P''\rangle \mid P'' \in \wp(\Sigma)\} . P \subseteq P' \wedge Q' \subseteq Q\}$$
$$\qquad\qquad\qquad\qquad\qquad\qquad\qquad\qquad \wr\text{def. (4) of } \mathcal{T}[\![S]\!]\wr$$
$$= \{\langle P, Q\rangle \mid \exists P', Q', P'' . P' = P'' \wedge Q' = \mathsf{post}[\![S]\!]P'' \wedge P \subseteq P' \wedge Q' \subseteq Q\}$$
$$\qquad\qquad\qquad\qquad\qquad\qquad\qquad\qquad\qquad\qquad \wr\text{def. } \in\wr$$
$$= \{\langle P, Q\rangle \mid \exists P' . P \subseteq P' \wedge \mathsf{post}[\![S]\!]P' \subseteq Q\} \qquad\qquad\qquad \wr\text{def. } =\wr$$
$$= \{\langle P, Q\rangle \mid \mathsf{post}[\![S]\!](P) \subseteq Q\}$$
$$\qquad\qquad \wr(\Rightarrow) \, \mathsf{post}[\![S]\!] \text{ is increasing, } (\Leftarrow) \text{ taking } P' = P, \text{ proving (6)}\wr$$

— (7) follows from (6) by $\subseteq$-order duality. $\qquad\qquad\qquad\qquad\qquad\qquad\square$

At this point, we could use Aczel correspondence between fixpoints and rules to get sound and complete proof rules with common rules for statements and different consequence rules for Hoare and incorrectness logics.

This is not satisfactory since, for iteration, we can approximate the pre and postconditions by the consequence rules but not the loop invariant itself. Requiring the invariant to be the strongest would be too demanding. This is precisely the point of fixpoint induction, which enables the use of consequences for the loop invariant. Fixpoint induction differs for Hoare logic (which requires a fixpoint over approximation) and incorrectness logic (which requires a fixpoint under approximation).

7   Fixpoint Induction

A sound and complete least fixpoint over approximation method is provided by David Park [4,18].

Theorem 2 (Least fixpoint over approximation [18]). *Let $\langle L, \sqsubseteq, \bot, \top, \sqcup, \sqcap\rangle$ be a complete lattice, $f \in L \xrightarrow{i} L$ be increasing, and $p \in L$. Then $\mathsf{lfp}^{\sqsubseteq} f \sqsubseteq p$ if and only if $\exists i \in L . f(i) \sqsubseteq i \wedge i \sqsubseteq p$.*

where the inductive invariant i is an over approximation of the strongest invariant $\mathsf{lfp}^{\sqsubseteq} f$.

For under approximation of least fixpoints, we can use the generalization [4] of Scott-Kleene induction based on transfinite induction when continuity does not apply and follows directly from the constructive version of Tarski's fixpoint theorem [8].

Theorem 3 (Fixpoint Under Approximation by Transfinite Iterates). *Let $f \in L \xrightarrow{i} L$ be an increasing function on a CPO $\langle L, \sqsubseteq, \bot, \sqcup\rangle$ (i.e. every increasing chain in L has a least upper bound in L, including $\bot = \sqcup\emptyset$). $P \in L$ is a fixpoint under approximation, i.e. $P \sqsubseteq \mathsf{lfp}^{\sqsubseteq} f$, if and only if there exists an increasing transfinite sequence $\langle X^{\delta}, \delta \in \mathbb{O}\rangle$ such that $X^0 = \bot$, $X^{\delta+1} \sqsubseteq f(X^{\delta})$ for successor ordinals, $\bigsqcup_{\delta<\lambda} X^{\delta}$ exists for limit ordinals λ such that $X^{\lambda} \sqsubseteq \bigsqcup_{\delta<\lambda} X^{\delta}$, and $\exists\delta \in \mathbb{O} . P \sqsubseteq X^{\delta}$.*

Theorem 3 could have assumed the existence of a well-founded set $\langle W, \preccurlyeq \rangle \in$ $\mathfrak{Wf}$ to replace the ordinals $\langle \mathbb{O}, \leqslant \rangle$. If f is continuous then $\delta = \omega$ is the first infinite ordinal.

Finally, to propose an alternative axiomatization of incorrectness, we will use the following theorem.

Theorem 4 (Non empty intersection with abstraction of least fixpoint). *Assume that (1)* $\langle L, \sqsubseteq, \bot, \top, \sqcap, \sqcup \rangle$ *is an atomic complete lattice; (2)* $f \in L \to L$ *preserves nonempty joins* $\sqcup$*; (3)* $\langle L, \sqsubseteq \rangle \xleftarrow[\alpha]{\gamma} \langle \bar{L}, \preceq, \curlywedge \rangle$*; (4)* $\bar{Q} \in \bar{L} \setminus \{0\}$ *where* $0 \triangleq \alpha(\bot)$*; (5) There exists an inductive invariant* $I \in L$ *of* f *(i.e.* $f(I) \sqsubseteq I$*); (6)* $\langle W, \leqslant \rangle$ *is a well-founded set and* $\nu \in \mathsf{atoms}(I) \to W$ *is a (variant) function; (7) There exists a sequence* $\langle a_i \in \mathsf{atoms}(I), i \in [1, \infty] \rangle$ *that (7.a)* $a_1 \in f(\bot)$*, (7.b)* $\forall i \in [1, \infty] . a_{i+1} \in \mathsf{atoms}(f(a_i))$*, (7.c)* $\forall i \in [1, \infty] . (a_i \neq a_{i+1}) \Rightarrow (\nu(a_i) > \nu(a_{i+1}))$*, (7.d)* $\forall i \in [1, \infty] . (\nu(a_i) \not> \nu(a_{i+1}) \Rightarrow \alpha(a_i) \curlywedge \bar{Q} \neq 0$*; Then, hypotheses (1) to (7) imply* $\alpha(\mathsf{lfp}^{\sqsubseteq} f) \curlywedge \bar{Q} \neq 0$*. Conversely (1) to (4) and* $\mathsf{lfp}^{\sqsubseteq} f \sqcap \gamma(\bar{Q}) \neq \bot$ *imply (5) to (7).*

Notice that if $L = \wp(\Sigma)$ then $\mathsf{atoms}(L) = \{\{x\} \mid x \in L\}$ so that $I \in \wp(\Sigma)$ and ν can be chosen in $I \to W$ instead of $\{\{x\} \mid x \in I\} \to W$. The proof of theorems 3 and 4 is given in [7].

8   Calculational Design of Hoare Logic

The calculus is by structural induction i.e. on the program syntax. The only non-trivial case is iteration $\mathtt{W} = \mathtt{while}$ $(\mathtt{B})$ $\mathtt{S}$. The theory of Hoare logic for iteration is

$$\mathcal{T}_{\mathrm{HL}}(\mathtt{W}) \triangleq \mathsf{post}(\supseteq, \subseteq)(\mathcal{T}[\![\mathtt{W}]\!]) \tag{8}$$
$$= \{\langle P, Q \rangle \mid \exists I . P \subseteq I \wedge \langle I \cap \mathcal{B}[\![\mathtt{B}]\!], I \rangle \in \mathcal{T}_{\mathrm{HL}}(\mathtt{S}) \wedge (I \cap \neg \mathcal{B}[\![\mathtt{B}]\!]) \subseteq Q\}$$

Proof (of (8)).

$\qquad \mathcal{T}_{\mathrm{HL}}[\![\mathtt{W}]\!]$

$= \mathsf{post}(\supseteq.\subseteq)(\mathcal{T}[\![\mathtt{W}]\!])$ $\qquad\qquad\qquad\qquad\qquad\qquad$ $\wr$def. (6) of $\mathcal{T}_{\mathrm{HL}}\wr$

$= \{\langle P', Q' \rangle \mid \exists \langle P, Q \rangle \in \mathcal{T}[\![\mathtt{W}]\!] . \langle P, Q \rangle \supseteq, \subseteq \langle P', Q' \rangle\}$ $\qquad$ $\wr$def. $\mathsf{post}\wr$

$= \{\langle P', Q' \rangle \mid \exists \langle P, Q \rangle \in \mathcal{T}[\![\mathtt{W}]\!] . P' \subseteq P \wedge Q \subseteq Q'\}$ $\wr$component wise def. $\supseteq, \subseteq\wr$

$= \{\langle P', Q' \rangle \mid \exists P, Q . P' \subseteq P \wedge \mathsf{post}[\![\neg \mathtt{B}]\!](\mathsf{lfp}^{\subseteq} F_P') \subseteq Q \wedge Q \subseteq Q'\}$ $\qquad$ $\wr(5)\wr$

$= \{\langle P', Q' \rangle \mid \exists P . P' \subseteq P \wedge \mathsf{post}[\![\neg \mathtt{B}]\!](\mathsf{lfp}^{\subseteq} F_P') \subseteq Q'\}$

$\qquad\qquad \wr(\subseteq) \exists Q . \mathsf{post}[\![\neg \mathtt{B}]\!](\mathsf{lfp}^{\subseteq} F_P') \subseteq Q \wedge Q \subseteq Q'$ and transitivity;

$\qquad\qquad (\supseteq)$ take $Q = Q'\wr$

$= \{\langle P', Q' \rangle \mid \exists P, Q . P' \subseteq P \wedge \mathsf{lfp}^{\subseteq} F_P' \subseteq Q \wedge \mathsf{post}[\![\neg \mathtt{B}]\!](Q) \subseteq Q'\}$

$\qquad\qquad \wr(\subseteq)$ take $Q = \mathsf{lfp}^{\subseteq} F_P'$; $\quad (\supseteq) \mathsf{post}[\![\mathtt{B}]\!]P = P \cap \mathcal{B}[\![\mathtt{B}]\!]$ so $\mathsf{post}[\![\mathtt{B}]\!]$ is increasing$\wr$

$= \{\langle P', Q' \rangle \mid \exists P, Q, I . P' \subseteq P \wedge F_P'(I) \subseteq I \wedge I \subseteq Q \wedge \mathsf{post}[\![\neg \mathtt{B}]\!](Q) \subseteq Q'\}$

$\qquad\qquad\qquad\qquad\qquad\qquad\qquad\qquad\qquad\qquad\qquad$ $\wr$Park fixpoint induction Th. 2$\wr$

$$= \{\langle P', Q'\rangle \mid \exists Q, I \,.\, F'_{P'}(I) \subseteq I \wedge I \subseteq Q \wedge \mathsf{post}[\![\neg\mathsf{B}]\!](Q) \subseteq Q'\}$$

$\wr(\subseteq)$ union hence $F'_P(X) = P \cup \mathsf{post}([\![\mathsf{B}]\!] \, \mathring{,} \, [\![\mathsf{S}]\!])X$ is $\subseteq$-increasing in P so $P' \subseteq P$ implies $F'_{P'}(I) \subseteq F'_P(I) \subseteq I$. $(\supseteq)$ take $P = P' \wr$

$$= \{\langle P, Q'\rangle \mid \exists I \,.\, F'_P(I) \subseteq I \wedge \mathsf{post}[\![\neg\mathsf{B}]\!](I) \subseteq Q'\}$$

$\wr$Rename P' into P. $(\subseteq)$ $I \subseteq Q$ implies $\mathsf{post}[\![\neg\mathsf{B}]\!](I) \subseteq \mathsf{post}[\![\neg\mathsf{B}]\!](Q)$ since $\mathsf{post}[\![\neg\mathsf{B}]\!]$ is increasing hence $\mathsf{post}[\![\neg\mathsf{B}]\!](I) \subseteq Q'$ by transitivity; $(\supseteq)$ take $Q = I \wr$

$$= \{\langle P, Q\rangle \mid \exists I \,.\, P \cup \mathsf{post}([\![\mathsf{B}]\!] \, \mathring{,} \, [\![\mathsf{S}]\!])(I) \subseteq I \wedge \mathsf{post}[\![\neg\mathsf{B}]\!](I) \subseteq Q\}$$

$\wr$renaming Q' into Q, def. $F'_P \wr$

$$= \{\langle P, Q\rangle \mid \exists I \,.\, P \subseteq I \wedge \mathsf{post}([\![\mathsf{B}]\!] \, \mathring{,} \, [\![\mathsf{S}]\!])I \subseteq I \wedge \mathsf{post}[\![\neg\mathsf{B}]\!](I) \subseteq Q\} \wr \text{def. } \subseteq \text{ and } \cup \wr$$

$$= \{\langle P, Q\rangle \mid \exists I \,.\, P \subseteq I \wedge \mathsf{post}[\![\mathsf{S}]\!](\mathsf{post}[\![\mathsf{B}]\!]I) \subseteq I \wedge \mathsf{post}[\![\neg\mathsf{B}]\!](I) \subseteq Q\}$$

$\wr$composition $\mathsf{post}(X \, \mathring{,} \, Y) = \mathsf{post}(Y) \circ \mathsf{post}(X) \wr$

$$= \{\langle P, Q\rangle \mid \exists I \,.\, P \subseteq I \wedge \mathsf{post}[\![\mathsf{S}]\!](I \cap \mathcal{B}[\![\mathsf{B}]\!]) \subseteq I \wedge (I \cap \neg\mathcal{B}[\![\mathsf{B}]\!]) \subseteq Q\}$$

$\wr \mathsf{post}[\![\mathsf{B}]\!]P = P \cap \mathcal{B}[\![\mathsf{B}]\!] \wr$

$$= \{\langle P, Q\rangle \mid \exists I \,.\, P \subseteq I \wedge \langle I \cap \mathcal{B}[\![\mathsf{B}]\!], I\rangle \in \{\langle P, Q\rangle \mid \mathsf{post}[\![\mathsf{S}]\!]P \subseteq Q\} \wedge (I \cap \neg\mathcal{B}[\![\mathsf{B}]\!]) \subseteq Q\}$$

$\wr$def. $\in \wr$

$$= \{\langle P, Q\rangle \mid \exists I \,.\, P \subseteq I \wedge \langle I \cap \mathcal{B}[\![\mathsf{B}]\!], I\rangle \in \{\langle P, Q\rangle \mid \exists P', Q' \,.\, P \subseteq P' \wedge \mathsf{post}[\![\mathsf{S}]\!]P' \subseteq Q' \wedge Q' \subseteq Q\} \wedge (I \cap \neg\mathcal{B}[\![\mathsf{B}]\!]) \subseteq Q\}$$

$\wr(\Rightarrow)$ Take $P' = P$ and $Q' = Q$. $(\Leftarrow)$ $P \subseteq P' \wedge \mathsf{post}[\![\mathsf{S}]\!]P' \subseteq Q' \wedge Q' \subseteq Q$ implies $\mathsf{post}[\![\mathsf{S}]\!]P \subseteq Q$ by transitivity.$\wr$

$$= \{\langle P, Q\rangle \mid \exists I \,.\, P \subseteq I \wedge \langle I \cap \mathcal{B}[\![\mathsf{B}]\!], I\rangle \in \mathsf{post}(\supseteq.\subseteq) \circ \mathcal{T}[\![\mathsf{S}]\!] \wedge (I \cap \neg\mathcal{B}[\![\mathsf{B}]\!]) \subseteq Q\}$$

$\wr$def. post and $\mathcal{T}[\![\mathsf{S}]\!] \wr$

$$= \{\langle P, Q\rangle \mid \exists I \,.\, P \subseteq I \wedge \langle I \cap \mathcal{B}[\![\mathsf{B}]\!], I\rangle \in T_{\mathrm{HL}}(\mathsf{S}) \wedge (I \cap \neg\mathcal{B}[\![\mathsf{B}]\!]) \subseteq Q\}$$

$\wr$def. $T_{\mathrm{HL}} \wr \qquad \square$

Defining $\{P\}\,\mathsf{S}\,\{Q\} \triangleq \langle P, Q\rangle \in \mathcal{T}[\![\mathsf{S}]\!]$, we can now derive the Hoare rules. For conditional iteration, it is

$$\frac{P \subseteq I, \ \{I \cap \mathcal{B}[\![\mathsf{B}]\!]\}\,\mathsf{S}\,\{I\}, \ (I \cap \neg\mathcal{B}[\![\mathsf{B}]\!]) \subseteq Q}{\{P\}\,\texttt{while (B) S}\,\{Q\}} \tag{9}$$

Proof of (9)). By structural induction (S being a strict component of `while (B) S`), the rule sfor $\{P\}\,\mathsf{S}\,\{Q\}$ have already been defined. By Aczel method, the (constant) fixpoint $\mathsf{lfp}^{\subseteq} \lambda X \bullet S$ is defined by $\{\frac{\emptyset}{c} \mid c \in S\}$. So for `while (B) S` we have an axiom $\dfrac{\emptyset}{\{P\}\,\texttt{while (B) S}\,\{Q\}}$ with side condition $P \subseteq I$, $\{I \cap \mathcal{B}[\![\mathsf{B}]\!]\}\,\mathsf{S}\,\{I\}$, $(I \cap \neg\mathcal{B}[\![\mathsf{B}]\!]) \subseteq Q$. Traditionally, the side condition is written as a premiss, to get (9). $\qquad \square$

Notice that the proof system is semantically sound and complete by construction (while using e.g. a logic for predicates might cause inexpressivity of the iteration invariant [2,3]). The proof is machine checkable, if not machine checked!

As a last remark on the calculational design of Hoare logic, observe that post is increasing so that (8) is $\mathcal{T}_{\mathrm{HL}}(\mathsf{S}) = \mathsf{post}(=.\subseteq) \circ \mathcal{T}[\![\mathsf{S}]\!]$. This means that the consequence rule $\dfrac{\{P\}\,\mathsf{S}\,\{Q\},\ Q \subseteq Q'}{\{P\}\,\mathsf{S}\,\{Q'\}}$ is complete and the unique necessary use of the precondition under approximation is that $P \subseteq I$ of the invariant in the iteration rule (9).

9 Calculational Design of Incorrectness Logic

The incorrectness logic theory (7) is the $\subseteq$-order dual of the Hoare logic theory (6). So the rules for statements, but for iteration, are the same because all correspond to the strongest postcondition logic theory (4) together with consequence rule $\dfrac{P' \subseteq P,\ \{P\}\,\mathsf{S}\,\{Q\},\ Q \subseteq Q'}{\{P'\}\,\mathsf{S}\,\{Q'\}}$ for Hoare logic and the dual $\dfrac{P' \supseteq P,\ \{P\}\,\mathsf{S}\,\{Q\},\ Q \supseteq Q'}{\{P'\}\,\mathsf{S}\,\{Q'\}}$ for incorrectness logic. As for iteration, fixpoint induction is the over approximation theorem 2 for Hoare logic and under approximation theorem 3 for incorrectness logic.

For iteration $\mathsf{W} = \mathtt{while}\ (\mathsf{B})\ \mathsf{S}$, the theory of incorrectness logic is

$$\mathcal{T}_{\mathrm{IL}}[\![\mathsf{W}]\!] \triangleq \mathsf{post}(\subseteq.\supseteq)(\mathcal{T}[\![\mathsf{W}]\!]) \tag{10}$$
$$= \{\langle P,\, Q\rangle \mid \exists \langle J^n,\, n \in \mathbb{N}\rangle\ .\ J^0 = P \wedge \langle J^n \cap \mathcal{B}[\![\mathsf{B}]\!],\, J^{n+1}\rangle \in \mathcal{T}_{\mathrm{IL}}[\![\mathsf{S}]\!] \wedge$$
$$Q \subseteq (\textstyle\bigcup_{n\in\mathbb{N}} J^n) \cap \mathcal{B}[\![\neg\mathsf{B}]\!]\}$$

(which is similar to O'Hearn backward variant [17] since the consequence rule can also be separated).

Proof (of (10)). We let $\mathsf{W} = \mathtt{while}\ (\mathsf{B})\ \mathsf{S}$.

$\mathcal{T}_{\mathrm{IL}}[\![\mathsf{W}]\!]$

$= \mathsf{post}(\subseteq.\supseteq)(\mathcal{T}[\![\mathsf{W}]\!])$ $\qquad\qquad\qquad\qquad\qquad$ $\wr$def. (7) of $\mathcal{T}_{\mathrm{IL}}\wr$

$= \{\langle P,\, Q\rangle \mid \exists \langle P',\, Q'\rangle \in \mathcal{T}[\![\mathsf{W}]\!]\ .\ \langle P',\, Q'\rangle \subseteq.\supseteq \langle P,\, Q\rangle\}$ $\qquad$ $\wr$def. post$\wr$

$= \{\langle P,\, Q\rangle \mid \exists \langle P',\, Q'\rangle \in \mathcal{T}[\![\mathsf{W}]\!]\ .\ P' \subseteq P \wedge Q \subseteq Q'\}$ $\qquad$ $\wr$def. $\subseteq.\supseteq\wr$

$= \{\langle P,\, Q\rangle \mid \exists \langle P',\, Q'\rangle \in \{\langle P'',\ \mathsf{post}[\![\mathsf{W}]\!]P''\rangle \mid P'' \in \wp(\Sigma)\}\ .\ P' \subseteq P \wedge Q \subseteq Q'\}$

$\qquad\qquad\qquad\qquad\qquad\qquad\qquad\qquad\qquad$ $\wr$def. (4) of $\mathcal{T}[\![\mathsf{W}]\!]\wr$

$= \{\langle P,\, Q\rangle \mid \exists P', Q', P''\ .\ P' = P'' \wedge Q' = \mathsf{post}[\![\mathsf{W}]\!]P'' \wedge P' \subseteq P \wedge Q \subseteq Q'\}$

$\qquad\qquad\qquad\qquad\qquad\qquad\qquad\qquad\qquad\qquad\qquad$ $\wr$def. $\in\wr$

$= \{\langle P,\, Q\rangle \mid \exists P'\ .\ P' \subseteq P \wedge Q \subseteq \mathsf{post}[\![\mathsf{W}]\!]P'\}$ $\qquad\qquad\qquad$ $\wr$def. $=\wr$

$= \{\langle P,\, Q\rangle \mid Q \subseteq \mathsf{post}[\![\mathsf{W}]\!]P\}$

$\qquad$ $\wr(\subseteq)$ $\mathsf{post}[\![\mathsf{W}]\!]$ increasing and transitivity; $(\supseteq)$ take $P' = P$ and reflexivity$\wr$

$= \{\langle P,\, Q\rangle \mid Q \subseteq \mathsf{post}[\![\neg\mathsf{B}]\!](\mathsf{lfp}^{\subseteq} F'_P)\}$ $\quad$ $\wr(5)$ with $F'_P(X) \triangleq P \cup \mathsf{post}([\![\mathsf{B}]\!]\,\mathring{,}\,[\![\mathsf{S}]\!])X\wr$

$= \{\langle P,\, Q\rangle \mid \exists I\ .\ Q \subseteq \mathsf{post}[\![\neg\mathsf{B}]\!](I) \wedge I \subseteq \mathsf{lfp}^{\subseteq} F'_P\}$

$\qquad$ $\wr(\subseteq)$ $\quad$ Take $I = \mathsf{lfp}^{\subseteq} F'_P$ and reflexivity;

$\qquad\quad$ $(\supseteq)$ $\quad$ By Galois connection $\langle \wp(\mathcal{X}),\, \subseteq\rangle \xleftarrow[\mathsf{post}(r)]{\widetilde{\mathsf{pre}}(r)} \langle \wp(\mathcal{Y}),\, \subseteq\rangle$, $\mathsf{post}[\![\neg\mathsf{B}]\!]$ is increasing so $Q \subseteq \mathsf{post}[\![\neg\mathsf{B}]\!](I) \subseteq \mathsf{post}[\![\neg\mathsf{B}]\!](\mathsf{lfp}^{\subseteq} F'_P)$ and transitivity$\wr$

$$= \{\langle P, Q\rangle \mid \exists I \ . \ Q \subseteq \mathsf{post}[\![\neg \mathsf{B}]\!](I) \wedge \exists \langle J^n, n < \omega\rangle \ . \ J^0 = \emptyset \wedge J^{n+1} \subseteq F'_P(J^n) \wedge I \subseteq \bigcup_{n<\omega} J^n\} \qquad \wr \text{fixpoint under approximation Th. II.3.6} \wr$$

$$= \{\langle P, Q\rangle \mid \exists \langle J^n, n < \omega\rangle \ . \ J^0 = \emptyset \wedge J^{n+1} \subseteq F'_P(J^n) \wedge Q \subseteq \mathsf{post}[\![\neg \mathsf{B}]\!](\bigcup_{n<\omega} J^n)\}$$

$\wr(\subseteq)$ By Galois connection $\langle \wp(\mathcal{X}), \subseteq\rangle \xleftarrow{\widetilde{\mathsf{pre}}(r)} \xrightarrow{\mathsf{post}(r)} \langle \wp(\mathcal{Y}), \subseteq\rangle$ $\mathsf{post}[\![\neg \mathsf{B}]\!]$ is increasing so $Q \subseteq \mathsf{post}[\![\neg \mathsf{B}]\!](I) \subseteq \mathsf{post}[\![\neg \mathsf{B}]\!](\bigcup_{n<\omega} J^n)$ and transitivity; $(\supseteq)$ take $I = \bigcup_{n<\omega} J^n \wr$

$$= \{\langle P, Q\rangle \mid \exists \langle J^n, n < \omega\rangle \ . \ J^0 = \emptyset \wedge J^{n+1} \subseteq (P \cup \mathsf{post}([\![\mathsf{B}]\!] \fatsemi [\![\mathsf{S}]\!])(J^n)) \wedge Q \subseteq \mathsf{post}[\![\neg \mathsf{B}]\!](\bigcup_{n<\omega} J^n)\} \qquad \wr \text{def. } F'_P \wr$$

$$= \{\langle P, Q\rangle \mid \exists \langle J^n, 1 \leqslant n < \omega\rangle \ . \ J^1 = P \wedge J^{n+1} \subseteq \mathsf{post}([\![\mathsf{B}]\!] \fatsemi [\![\mathsf{S}]\!])(J^n) \wedge Q \subseteq \mathsf{post}[\![\neg \mathsf{B}]\!](\bigcup_{1\leqslant n<\omega} J^n)\} \qquad \wr \text{getting rid of } J^0 = \emptyset \wr$$

$$= \{\langle P, Q\rangle \mid \exists \langle J^n, n \in \mathbb{N}\rangle \ . \ J^0 = P \wedge J^{n+1} \subseteq \mathsf{post}([\![\mathsf{B}]\!] \fatsemi [\![\mathsf{S}]\!])(J^n) \wedge Q \subseteq \mathsf{post}[\![\neg \mathsf{B}]\!](\bigcup_{n\in\mathbb{N}} J^n)\} \qquad \wr \text{changing } n+1 \text{ to } n \wr$$

$$= \{\langle P, Q\rangle \mid \exists \langle J^n, n \in \mathbb{N}\rangle \ . \ J^0 = P \wedge J^{n+1} \subseteq \mathsf{post}[\![\mathsf{S}]\!](J^n \cap \mathcal{B}[\![\mathsf{B}]\!]) \wedge Q \subseteq (\bigcup_{n\in\mathbb{N}} J^n) \cap \mathcal{B}[\![\neg \mathsf{B}]\!]\} \qquad \wr \mathsf{post}[\![\mathsf{B}]\!]P = P \cap \mathcal{B}[\![\mathsf{B}]\!] \wr$$

$$= \{\langle P, Q\rangle \mid \exists \langle J^n, n \in \mathbb{N}\rangle \ . \ J^0 = P \wedge \langle J^n \cap \mathcal{B}[\![\mathsf{B}]\!], J^{n+1}\rangle \in \{\langle P', Q'\rangle \mid Q' \subseteq \mathsf{post}[\![\mathsf{S}]\!])P)\} \wedge Q \subseteq (\bigcup_{n\in\mathbb{N}} J^n) \cap \mathcal{B}[\![\neg \mathsf{B}]\!]\} \qquad \wr \text{def. } \in \wr$$

$$= \{\langle P, Q\rangle \mid \exists \langle J^n, n \in \mathbb{N}\rangle \ . \ J^0 = P \wedge \langle J^n \cap \mathcal{B}[\![\mathsf{B}]\!], J^{n+1}\rangle \in \mathcal{T}_{\mathrm{IL}}[\![\mathsf{S}]\!] \wedge Q \subseteq (\bigcup_{n\in\mathbb{N}} J^n) \cap \mathcal{B}[\![\neg \mathsf{B}]\!]\} \qquad \wr \text{def. } \mathcal{T}_{\mathrm{IL}} \wr \qquad \square$$

Defining $[P]\,\mathsf{S}\,[Q] \triangleq \langle P, Q\rangle \in \mathcal{T}_{\mathrm{IL}}[\![\mathsf{S}]\!]$, the calculational design of incorrectness logic rules is as follows

$$\frac{J^0 = P, \ [J^n \cap \mathcal{B}[\![\mathsf{B}]\!]]\,\mathsf{S}\,[J^{n+1}], \ Q \subseteq (\bigcup_{n\in\mathbb{N}} J^n) \cap \mathcal{B}[\![\neg \mathsf{B}]\!]}{[P]\,\mathtt{while\ (B)\ S}\,[Q]} \qquad (11)$$

Proof (of (11)). By structural induction (S being a strict component of $\mathtt{while}$ (B) S), the rule for $[P]\,\mathsf{S}\,[Q]$ have already been defined. By Aczel method, the (constant) fixpoint $\mathsf{lfp}^{\subseteq} \lambda X \cdot S$ is defined by $\{\frac{\emptyset}{c} \mid c \in S\}$. So for $\mathtt{while}$ (B) S we have an axiom $\dfrac{\emptyset}{\{P\}\,\mathtt{while\ (B)\ S}\,\{Q\}}$ with side condition $J^0 = P$, $[J^n \cap \mathcal{B}[\![\mathsf{B}]\!]]\,\mathsf{S}\,[J^{n+1}]$, $Q \subseteq (\bigcup_{n\in\mathbb{N}} J^n) \cap \mathcal{B}[\![\neg \mathsf{B}]\!]$; Traditionally, the side condition is written as a premiss, to get (11). $\square$

10   On Hoare Incorrectness

Incorrectness logic, a variant of reverse Hoare logic [21] was introduced by [17] as a counterpoint of Hoare logic *"When reasoning informally about a program, people make abstract inferences about what might go wrong, as well as about what must go right. [. . .] We explore our hypothesis by defining incorrectness logic, a formalism that is similar to Hoare's logic of program correctness [13], except that it is oriented to proving incorrectness rather than correctness."* However, incorrectness logic is not Hoare incorrectness logic. It is sufficient but not necessary. Assuming $Q \neq \Sigma$, we have

$$\neg(\{P\}\, \mathsf{S}\, \{Q\}) \overset{\not\Leftarrow}{\Leftarrow} [P]\, \mathsf{S}\, [\neg Q] \tag{12}$$
$$\Leftrightarrow \exists R \in \wp(\Sigma)\,.\, [P]\, \mathsf{S}\, [R] \wedge R \cap \neg Q \neq \emptyset$$
$$\Leftrightarrow \exists \sigma \in \Sigma\,.\, [P]\, \mathsf{S}\, [\{\sigma\}] \wedge \sigma \notin Q$$

The incompleteness of incorrectness logic $[P]\, \mathsf{S}\, [\neg Q]$ to prove Hoare incorrectness $\neg(\{P\}\, \mathsf{S}\, \{Q\})$ comes from the fact that we may have $\{P\}\, \mathsf{S}\, \{Q'\}$ for some $Q' \subseteq Q$. Therefore we have to select $R = \neg Q \setminus Q'$ to ensure completeness. However, the formula $\exists R \in \wp(\Sigma)\,.\, [P]\, \mathsf{S}\, [R] \wedge R \cap \neg Q \neq \emptyset$ is not a formula of the incorrectness logic. Moreover, R can be reduced to a single state $\{\sigma\}$ since a single counter example is sufficient to prove Hoare incorrectness. This leads to Hoare incorrectness logic.

Proof (of (12)).

— $[P]\, \mathsf{S}\, [\neg Q]$

$\Leftrightarrow \langle P, \neg Q \rangle \in \mathcal{T}_{\mathrm{IL}}[\![\mathsf{S}]\!]$ ⎰incorrectness triple definition⎱

$\Leftrightarrow \neg Q \subseteq \mathsf{post}[\![\mathsf{S}]\!]P$ ⎰def. (7) of $\mathcal{T}_{\mathrm{IL}}[\![\mathsf{S}]\!]$⎱

$\Rightarrow \mathsf{post}[\![\mathsf{S}]\!]P \cap (\neg Q) \neq \emptyset$ ⎰assuming $Q \neq \Sigma$ so $(\neg Q) \neq \emptyset$⎱

$\Leftrightarrow \neg(\mathsf{post}[\![\mathsf{S}]\!]P \subseteq Q)$ ⎰def. $\subseteq$⎱

$\Leftrightarrow \neg(\langle P, Q \rangle \in \{\langle P, Q \rangle \mid \mathsf{post}[\![\mathsf{S}]\!]P \subseteq Q\})$ ⎰def. $\in$⎱

$\Leftrightarrow \neg(\langle P, Q \rangle \in \mathcal{T}_{\mathrm{HL}}[\![\mathsf{S}]\!])$ ⎰def. (6) of $\mathcal{T}_{\mathrm{HL}}[\![\mathsf{S}]\!]$⎱

$\Leftrightarrow \neg(\{P\}\, \mathsf{S}\, \{Q\})$ ⎰Hoare triple definition, Q.E.D.⎱

□

The converse is not true, as shown by the counter example $\neg(\{\mathsf{true}\}\, \mathtt{x}\ =\ \mathtt{0}\{x \neq 0 \wedge x \neq 1\})$ holds but not $[\mathsf{true}]\, \mathtt{x}\ =\ \mathtt{0}[x = 0 \vee x = 1]$.

— $\neg(\{P\}\, \mathsf{S}\, \{Q\})$ ⎰def. incorrect Hoare triple⎱

$\Leftrightarrow \neg(\langle P, Q \rangle \in \mathcal{T}_{\mathrm{HL}}[\![\mathsf{S}]\!])$ ⎰def. Hoare triple⎱

$\Leftrightarrow \neg(\langle P, Q \rangle \in \{\langle P, Q \rangle \mid \mathsf{post}[\![\mathsf{S}]\!]P \subseteq Q\})$ ⎰def. (6) of $\mathcal{T}_{\mathrm{HL}}[\![\mathsf{S}]\!]$⎱

$\Leftrightarrow \neg(\mathsf{post}[\![\mathsf{S}]\!]P \subseteq Q)$ ⎰def. $\in$⎱

$\Leftrightarrow \neg(\{\sigma' \mid \exists \sigma \in P\,.\, \langle \sigma, \sigma' \rangle \in [\![\mathsf{S}]\!]\} \subseteq Q)$ ⎰def. post⎱

$\Leftrightarrow \neg(\forall \sigma'\,.\, (\exists \sigma \in P\,.\, \langle \sigma, \sigma' \rangle \in [\![\mathsf{S}]\!]) \Rightarrow (\sigma' \in Q))$ ⎰def. $\subseteq$⎱

$\Leftrightarrow \exists \sigma'\,.\, \exists \sigma \in P\,.\, \langle \sigma, \sigma' \rangle \in [\![\mathsf{S}]\!] \wedge \sigma' \notin Q$ ⎰def. negation $\neg$⎱

$\Leftrightarrow \exists \sigma \notin Q\,.\, \exists \sigma' \in P\,.\, \langle \sigma', \sigma \rangle \in [\![\mathsf{S}]\!]$ ⎰commutativity and renaming⎱

$$\Leftrightarrow \exists \sigma \in \Sigma \, . \, \exists \sigma' \in P \, . \, \langle \sigma', \sigma \rangle \in [\![\mathtt{S}]\!] \wedge \sigma \notin Q \qquad\qquad \wr\text{def. } \exists \wr$$

$$\Leftrightarrow \exists \sigma \in \Sigma \, . \, \forall \sigma'' \in \{\sigma\} \, . \, \exists \sigma' \in P \, . \, \langle \sigma', \sigma'' \rangle \in [\![\mathtt{S}]\!] \wedge \sigma \notin Q \qquad \wr\text{def. } \in \wr$$

$$\Leftrightarrow \exists \sigma \in \Sigma \, . \, \{\sigma\} \subseteq \{\sigma'' \mid \exists \sigma' \in P \, . \, \langle \sigma', \sigma'' \rangle \in [\![\mathtt{S}]\!]\} \wedge \sigma \notin Q \qquad \wr\text{def. } \subseteq \wr$$

$$\Leftrightarrow \exists \sigma \in \Sigma \, . \, \{\sigma\} \subseteq \mathsf{post}[\![\mathtt{S}]\!]P\} \wedge \sigma \notin Q \qquad\qquad \wr\text{def. } \mathsf{post}[\![\mathtt{S}]\!] \wr$$

$$\Leftrightarrow \exists \sigma \in \Sigma \, . \, \langle P, \{\sigma\} \rangle \in \{\langle P, Q \rangle \mid Q \subseteq \mathsf{post}[\![\mathtt{S}]\!]P\} \wedge \sigma \notin Q \qquad \wr\text{def. } \in \wr$$

$$\Leftrightarrow \exists \sigma \in \Sigma \, . \, \langle P, \{\sigma\} \rangle \in \mathcal{T}_{\mathrm{IL}}[\![\mathtt{S}]\!] \wedge \sigma \notin Q \qquad\qquad \wr\text{def. (7) of } \mathcal{T}_{\mathrm{IL}}[\![\mathtt{S}]\!] \wr$$

$$\Leftrightarrow \exists \sigma \in \Sigma \, . \, [P]\,\mathtt{S}\,[\{\sigma\}] \wedge \sigma \notin Q \qquad \wr\text{def. incorrectness logic triple, Q.E.D.} \wr$$

$$\Leftrightarrow \exists R \in \wp(\Sigma) \, . \, [P]\,\mathtt{S}\,[R] \wedge R \cap \neg Q \neq \emptyset$$

$\qquad \wr (\subseteq)$ take $R = \{\sigma\}$;

$\qquad (\supseteq)$ since $R \cap \neg Q \neq \emptyset$, we have $\exists \sigma \in R \, . \, \sigma \notin Q$ and $[P]\,\mathtt{S}\,[\{\sigma\}]$ since otherwise we would have $\neg(\forall \sigma'' \in \{\sigma\} \, . \, \exists \sigma' \in P \, . \, \langle \sigma'', \sigma' \rangle \in [\![\mathtt{S}]\!]) \Leftrightarrow \forall \sigma' \in P \, . \, \langle \sigma, \sigma' \rangle \notin [\![\mathtt{S}]\!])$, in contradiction with $[P]\,\mathtt{S}\,[R]$ and $\sigma \in R. \wr$ □

11   Calculational Design of Hoare Incorrectness Logic

Incorrectness logic being incomplete to prove Hoare incorrectness, we design a sound and semantically complete Hoare incorrectness logic $\overline{\mathrm{HL}}$.

Let us consider the negation of $X \in \wp(\mathcal{X})$, to be $\alpha^{\neg}(X) \triangleq \neg X$ (where $\neg X \triangleq \mathcal{X} \setminus X$) with Galois isomorphisms $\langle \wp(\mathcal{X}), \subseteq \rangle \xleftarrow{\;\;\alpha^{\neg}\;\;}_{\overrightarrow{\alpha^{\neg}}} \langle \wp(\mathcal{X}), \supseteq \rangle$ and $\langle \wp(\mathcal{X}), \supseteq \rangle \xleftarrow{\;\;\alpha^{\neg}\;\;}_{\overrightarrow{\alpha^{\neg}}} \langle \wp(\mathcal{X}), \subseteq \rangle$. The theory of Hoare incorrectness logic is

$$\mathcal{T}_{\overline{\mathrm{HL}}}[\![\mathtt{S}]\!] \triangleq \alpha^{\neg}(\mathcal{T}_{\mathrm{HL}}[\![\mathtt{S}]\!]) \qquad\qquad (13)$$

For iteration $\mathtt{W} = \mathtt{while}$ (B) S, the theory of Hoare incorrectness logic is

$$\mathcal{T}_{\overline{\mathrm{HL}}}[\![\mathtt{W}]\!] = \quad \{\langle P, Q \rangle \mid \exists n \geqslant 1 \, . \, \exists \langle \sigma_i \in I, i \in [1,n] \rangle \, . \, \sigma_1 \in P \wedge \forall i \in [1,n[.$$
$$\langle \mathcal{B}[\![\mathtt{B}]\!] \cap \{\sigma_i\}, \neg\{\sigma_{i+1}\} \rangle \in \mathcal{T}_{\overline{\mathrm{HL}}}[\![\mathtt{S}]\!] \wedge \sigma_n \notin \mathcal{B}[\![\mathtt{B}]\!] \wedge \sigma_n \notin Q\}$$
$$(14)$$

Proof (of (14)).

$\qquad \mathcal{T}_{\overline{\mathrm{HL}}}[\![\mathtt{W}]\!]$

$= \alpha^{\neg}(\mathcal{T}_{\mathrm{HL}}[\![\mathtt{W}]\!]) \qquad\qquad \wr\text{def. (13) of } \mathcal{T}_{\overline{\mathrm{HL}}}[\![\mathtt{W}]\!] \wr$

$= \alpha^{\neg}(\{\langle P, Q \rangle \mid \mathsf{post}[\![\mathtt{W}]\!]P \subseteq Q\}) \qquad\qquad \wr\text{def. (6) of } \mathcal{T}_{\mathrm{HL}}[\![\mathtt{W}]\!] \wr$

$= \{\langle P, Q \rangle \mid \neg(\mathsf{post}[\![\mathtt{W}]\!]P \subseteq Q)\} \qquad\qquad \wr\text{def. } \alpha^{\neg} \wr$

$= \{\langle P, Q \rangle \mid \mathsf{post}[\![\mathtt{W}]\!]P \cap \neg Q \neq \emptyset\} \qquad\qquad \wr\text{def. } \subseteq \text{ and } \neg \wr$

$= \{\langle P, Q \rangle \mid \mathsf{post}[\![\neg\mathtt{B}]\!](\mathsf{lfp}^{\subseteq} F'_P) \cap \neg Q \neq \emptyset\} \; \wr(5), F'_P(X) \triangleq P \cup \mathsf{post}([\![\mathtt{B}]\!] \, \mathring{,} \, [\![\mathtt{S}]\!])X \wr$

$= \{\langle P, Q \rangle \mid \mathsf{lfp}^{\subseteq} F'_P \cap \mathsf{pre}[\![\neg\mathtt{B}]\!](\neg Q) \neq \emptyset\}$

$\qquad\qquad\qquad\qquad\qquad \wr\mathsf{post}(R)P \cap Q \neq \emptyset \Leftrightarrow P \cap \mathsf{pre}(R)Q \neq \emptyset \wr$

$= \{\langle P, Q\rangle \mid \exists I \in \wp(\Sigma) . F'_P(I) \subseteq I \wedge \exists \langle W, \leqslant\rangle \in \mathfrak{Wf} . \exists \nu \in I \to W . \exists \langle \sigma_i \in I,$
$i \in [1\infty\rangle . \sigma_1 \in F'_P(\emptyset) \wedge \forall i \in [1, \infty] . \sigma_{i+1} \in F'_P(\{\sigma_i\}) \wedge \forall i \in [1, \infty] .$
$(\sigma_i \neq \sigma_{i+1}) \Rightarrow (\nu(\sigma_i) > \nu(\sigma_{i+1}) \wedge \forall i \in [1, \infty] . (\nu(\sigma_i) \not> \nu(\sigma_{i+1}) \Rightarrow \{\sigma_i\} \cap$
$\mathsf{pre}\llbracket \neg\mathsf{B}\rrbracket(\neg Q) \neq 0\}$ ⎧induction principle Th. 4⎭

$= \{\langle P, Q\rangle \mid \exists I \in \wp(\Sigma) . P \subseteq I \wedge \mathsf{post}(\llbracket\mathsf{B}\rrbracket \mathbin; \llbracket\mathsf{S}\rrbracket)I \subseteq I \wedge \exists \langle W, \leqslant\rangle \in \mathfrak{Wf} . \exists \nu \in$
$I \to W . \exists \langle \sigma_i \in I, i \in [1, \infty]\rangle . \sigma_1 \in P \wedge \forall i \in [1, \infty] . (\sigma_{i+1} \in P \vee \{\sigma_{i+1}\} \subseteq$
$\mathsf{post}(\llbracket\mathsf{B}\rrbracket \mathbin; \llbracket\mathsf{S}\rrbracket)\{\sigma_i\}) \wedge \forall i \in [1, \infty] . (\sigma_i \neq \sigma_{i+1}) \Rightarrow (\nu(\sigma_i) > \nu(\sigma_{i+1}) \wedge \forall i \in$
$[1, \infty] . (\nu(\sigma_i) \not> \nu(\sigma_{i+1}) \Rightarrow \sigma_i \in \mathsf{pre}\llbracket \neg\mathsf{B}\rrbracket(\neg Q)\}$
⎧def. $F'_P(X) \triangleq P \cup \mathsf{post}(\llbracket\mathsf{B}\rrbracket \mathbin; \llbracket\mathsf{S}\rrbracket)X$, $\subseteq$, and post, which is $\emptyset$-strict⎭

$= \{\langle P, Q\rangle \mid \exists I \in \wp(\Sigma) . P \subseteq I \wedge \mathsf{post}(\llbracket\mathsf{B}\rrbracket \mathbin; \llbracket\mathsf{S}\rrbracket)I \subseteq I \wedge \exists \langle W, \leqslant\rangle \in \mathfrak{Wf} .$
$\exists \nu \in I \to W . \exists \langle \sigma_i \in I, i \in [1, \infty]\rangle . \sigma_1 \in P \wedge \forall i \in [1, \infty] . \{\sigma_{i+1}\} \subseteq$
$\mathsf{post}(\llbracket\mathsf{B}\rrbracket \mathbin; \llbracket\mathsf{S}\rrbracket)\{\sigma_i\} \wedge \forall i \in [1, \infty] . (\sigma_i \neq \sigma_{i+1}) \Rightarrow (\nu(\sigma_i) > \nu(\sigma_{i+1}) \wedge \forall i \in$
$[1, \infty] . (\nu(\sigma_i) \not> \nu(\sigma_{i+1}) \Rightarrow \sigma_i \in \mathsf{pre}\llbracket \neg\mathsf{B}\rrbracket(\neg Q)\}$
⎧since if $\sigma_{i+1} \in P$, we can equivalently consider the sequence $\langle \sigma_j \in I,$
$j \in [i+1, \infty]\rangle\rangle$⎭

$= \{\langle P, Q\rangle \mid \exists I \in \wp(\Sigma) . P \subseteq I \wedge \mathsf{post}(\llbracket\mathsf{B}\rrbracket \mathbin; \llbracket\mathsf{S}\rrbracket)I \subseteq I \wedge \exists n \geqslant 1 . \exists \langle \sigma_i \in I, i \in$
$[1, n]\rangle . \sigma_1 \in P \wedge \forall i \in [1, n[. \{\sigma_{i+1}\} \subseteq \mathsf{post}(\llbracket\mathsf{B}\rrbracket \mathbin; \llbracket\mathsf{S}\rrbracket)\{\sigma_i\} \wedge \sigma_n \in \mathsf{pre}\llbracket \neg\mathsf{B}\rrbracket(\neg Q)\}$
⎧($\subseteq$) By $\langle W, \leqslant\rangle \in \mathfrak{Wf}$, $\nu \in I \to W$, $\forall i \in [1, \infty] . (\sigma_i \neq \sigma_{i+1}) \Rightarrow$
$(\nu(\sigma_i) > \nu(\sigma_{i+1}))$, the sequence is ultimately stationary at some rank n.
For then on, $\sigma_{i+1} = \sigma_i$, $i \geqslant n$ and so $\nu(\sigma_i) = \nu(\sigma_{i+1})$. Therefore $\forall i \in$
$[1, \infty] . (\nu(\sigma_i) \not> \nu(\sigma_{i+1}) \Rightarrow \sigma_i \notin Q$ implies that $\sigma_n \in \mathsf{pre}\llbracket \neg\mathsf{B}\rrbracket(\neg Q)$;

($\supseteq$) Conversely, from $\langle \sigma_i \in I, i \in [1, n]\rangle$ we can define $W = \{\sigma_i \mid i \in$
$[1, n]\} \cup \{-\infty\}$ with $-\infty < \sigma_i < \sigma_{i+1}$ and $\nu(x) = (\!| x \in \{\sigma_i \mid i \in [1, n] \,?$
$x : -\infty |\!)$ and the sequence $\langle \sigma_j \in I, j \in [1, \infty]\rangle$ repeats σ_n ad infimum
for $j \geqslant n$.⎭

$= \{\langle P, Q\rangle \mid \exists I \in \wp(\Sigma) . P \subseteq I \wedge \mathsf{post}(\llbracket\mathsf{B}\rrbracket \mathbin; \llbracket\mathsf{S}\rrbracket)I \subseteq I \wedge \exists n \geqslant 1 . \exists \langle \sigma_i \in I, i \in$
$[1, n]\rangle . \sigma_1 \in P \wedge \forall i \in [1, n[. \{\sigma_{i+1}\} \subseteq \mathsf{post}(\llbracket\mathsf{B}\rrbracket \mathbin; \llbracket\mathsf{S}\rrbracket)\{\sigma_i\} \wedge \sigma_n \notin \mathcal{B}\llbracket\mathsf{B}\rrbracket \wedge \sigma_n \notin Q\}$
⎧def. pre⎭

$= \{\langle P, Q\rangle \mid \exists n \geqslant 1 . \exists \langle \sigma_i \in I, i \in [1, n]\rangle . \sigma_1 \in P \wedge \forall i \in [1, n[. \{\sigma_{i+1}\} \subseteq$
$\mathsf{post}(\llbracket\mathsf{B}\rrbracket \mathbin; \llbracket\mathsf{S}\rrbracket)\{\sigma_i\} \wedge \sigma_n \notin \mathcal{B}\llbracket\mathsf{B}\rrbracket \wedge \sigma_n \notin Q\}$
⎧I is not used and can always be chosen to be Σ⎭

$= \{\langle P, Q\rangle \mid \exists n \geqslant 1 . \exists \langle \sigma_i \in I, i \in [1, n]\rangle . \sigma_1 \in P \wedge \forall i \in [1, n[. \mathsf{post}(\llbracket\mathsf{B}\rrbracket \mathbin;$
$\llbracket\mathsf{S}\rrbracket)\{\sigma_i\} \cap \{\sigma_{i+1}\} \neq \emptyset \wedge \sigma_n \notin \mathcal{B}\llbracket\mathsf{B}\rrbracket \wedge \sigma_n \notin Q\}$ ⎧since $x \in X \Leftrightarrow X \cap \{x\} \neq \emptyset$⎭

$= \{\langle P, Q\rangle \mid \exists n \geqslant 1 . \exists \langle \sigma_i \in I, i \in [1, n]\rangle . \sigma_1 \in P \wedge \forall i \in [1, n[. \mathsf{post}(\llbracket\mathsf{B}\rrbracket \mathbin;$
$\llbracket\mathsf{S}\rrbracket)\{\sigma_i\} \cap \neg(\neg\{\sigma_{i+1}\}) \neq \emptyset \wedge \sigma_n \notin \mathcal{B}\llbracket\mathsf{B}\rrbracket \wedge \sigma_n \notin Q\}$ ⎧def. $\neg X = \Sigma \setminus X$⎭

$= \{\langle P, Q\rangle \mid \exists n \geqslant 1 . \exists \langle \sigma_i \in I, i \in [1, n]\rangle . \sigma_1 \in P \wedge \forall i \in [1, n[. \neg(\mathsf{post}(\llbracket\mathsf{B}\rrbracket \mathbin;$
$\llbracket\mathsf{S}\rrbracket)\{\sigma_i\} \subseteq (\neg\{\sigma_{i+1}\})) \wedge \sigma_n \notin \mathcal{B}\llbracket\mathsf{B}\rrbracket \wedge \sigma_n \notin Q\}$ ⎧$\neg(X \subseteq Y) \Leftrightarrow (X \cap \neg Y \neq \emptyset)$⎭

$= \{\langle P, Q\rangle \mid \exists n \geqslant 1 . \exists \langle \sigma_i \in I, i \in [1, n]\rangle . \sigma_1 \in P \wedge \forall i \in [1, n[.$
$\neg(\mathsf{post}(\llbracket\mathsf{S}\rrbracket)(\mathcal{B}\llbracket\mathsf{B}\rrbracket \cap \{\sigma_i\}) \subseteq (\neg\{\sigma_{i+1}\})) \wedge \sigma_n \notin \mathcal{B}\llbracket\mathsf{B}\rrbracket \wedge \sigma_n \notin Q\}$
⎧def. post, $\llbracket\mathsf{B}\rrbracket$, and $\mathbin;$⎭

$= \{\langle P, Q\rangle \mid \exists n \geqslant 1 . \exists \langle \sigma_i \in I, i \in [1, n]\rangle . \sigma_1 \in P \wedge \forall i \in [1, n[. \langle \mathcal{B}\llbracket\mathsf{B}\rrbracket \cap \{\sigma_i\},$
$\neg\{\sigma_{i+1}\}\rangle \in \{\langle P, Q\rangle \mid \neg(\mathsf{post}(\llbracket\mathsf{S}\rrbracket)P \subseteq Q)\} \wedge \sigma_n \notin \mathcal{B}\llbracket\mathsf{B}\rrbracket \wedge \sigma_n \notin Q\}$ ⎧def. $\in$⎭

$$= \{\langle P,\, Q \rangle \mid \exists n \geqslant 1 \,.\, \exists \langle \sigma_i \in I,\, i \in [1, n] \rangle \,.\, \sigma_1 \in P \wedge \forall i \in [1, n[\,.\, \langle \mathcal{B}[\![B]\!] \cap \{\sigma_i\},$$
$$\neg\{\sigma_{i+1}\} \rangle \in \mathcal{T}_{\overline{HL}}[\![S]\!] \wedge \sigma_n \notin \mathcal{B}[\![B]\!] \wedge \sigma_n \in Q\} \qquad \langle \text{def. } \mathcal{T}_{\overline{HL}}[\![S]\!] \rangle \qquad \square$$

Defining $(\!| P |\!)\, \mathsf{S}\, (\!| Q |\!) \triangleq \langle P,\, Q \rangle \in \mathcal{T}_{\overline{HL}}[\![S]\!]$, the calculational design of incorrectness logic rules is as follows,

$$\frac{\begin{array}{c} \exists \langle \sigma_i \in I,\, i \in [1, n] \rangle \,.\, \sigma_1 \in P \wedge \\ \forall i \in [1, n[\,.\, (\!| \mathcal{B}[\![B]\!] \cap \{\sigma_i\} |\!)\, \mathsf{S}\, (\!| \neg\{\sigma_{i+1}\} |\!) \wedge \\ \sigma_n \notin \mathcal{B}[\![B]\!] \wedge \sigma_n \notin Q \end{array}}{(\!| P |\!)\, \mathtt{while\ (B)\ S}\, (\!| Q |\!)} \tag{15}$$

Proof (of (15)).

By structural induction (S being a strict component of $\mathtt{while\ (B)\ S}$), the rule for $(\!| P |\!)\, \mathsf{S}\, (\!| Q |\!)$ have already been defined. By Aczel method, the (constant) fixpoint $\mathsf{lfp}^{\subseteq} \lambda X \cdot S$ is defined by $\{\frac{\emptyset}{c} \mid c \in S\}$. So for $\mathtt{while\ (B)\ S}$ we have an axiom $\dfrac{\emptyset}{(\!| P |\!)\, \mathtt{while\ (B)\ S}\, (\!| Q |\!)}$ with side condition $\exists \langle \sigma_i \in I,\, i \in [1, n] \rangle \,.$ $\sigma_1 \in P \wedge \forall i \in [1, n[\,.\, (\!| \mathcal{B}[\![B]\!] \cap \{\sigma_i\} |\!)\, \mathsf{S}\, (\!| \neg\{\sigma_{i+1}\} |\!) \wedge \sigma_n \notin \mathcal{B}[\![B]\!] \wedge \sigma_n \notin Q$ where $(\!| \mathcal{B}[\![B]\!] \cap \{\sigma_i\} |\!)\, \mathsf{S}\, (\!| \neg\{\sigma_{i+1}\} |\!)$ is well-defined by structural induction. Traditionally, the side condition is written as a premiss, to get (15). $\qquad \square$

Rule (15) states that $\langle \sigma_i \in I, i \in [1, n] \rangle$ is a finite iteration in the loop starting with P true and finishing with Q false, which is obviously a counter example to Hoare triple $\{P\}\, \mathtt{while\ (B)\ S}\, \{Q\}$. Notice that, by structural induction, $(\!| \mathcal{B}[\![B]\!] \cap \{\sigma_i\} |\!)\, \mathsf{S}\, (\!| \neg\{\sigma_{i+1}\} |\!)$ enforces the execution of the loop body S to start in state σ_i and terminate in state σ_{i+1}.

It follows that Hoare incorrectness logic is nothing but debugging formalized as a logic. So Hoare incorrectness logic could also be called the debugging logic, to elevate debugging as the computer aided formal method of choice to prove the presence of bugs [10, page 7].

12   Conclusion

A Hoare style (or transformational) logic is an abstract interpretation of a relational semantics, and together with fixpoint induction and Aczel correspondence between set-theoretic fixpoint and deductive system, this leads to the calculational design of the logic proof system, which is semantically sound and complete, by construction.

In this paper, we have considered the abstractions of Fig. 1. [6] exploits this model theory-based point of view in greater details for many more logics.

We think that, in computer science, the Tarskian/model theoretic approach, which is semantic in nature, is superior to Gentzen/Prawitz proof-theoretic approaches, which are syntactic in nature. Whereas proof calculi are used in mathematics to define truth from which models are derived, we have, in computer science, the advantage that the models of interest are known a priori. They

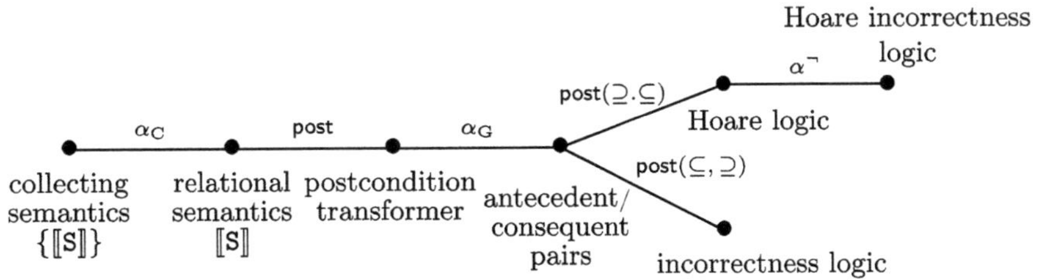

Fig. 1. Hoare style logic abstractions

are the semantics of programming languages and systems. Our approach simply exploits this advantage.

Although for most mathematicians and computer scientists, writing a fully formal proof is too pedantic and long-winded to be in common use, the study of program logics is useful to provide the intuition for informal reasonings on program behaviors. Showing that program logic are nothing but an abstract expression of the program semantics strongly supports that intuition. The only difference between logics and semantics is that logic offers ways of making deduction and inference, as made clear by our calculational design which shows that logic = semantics + abstraction + deduction + inference. We have shown

$$\text{Hoare logic} = \text{section } 2 + (4) + (6) + \text{theorem } 2$$
$$\text{Incorrectness logic} = \text{section } 2 + (4) + (7) + \text{theorem } 3$$
$$\text{Hoare incorrectness logic} = \text{section } 2 + (4) + (8) + \text{theorem } 4$$

which provides a simple way to explain and compare logics. All the rest is isomorphisms, as shown by the calculational designs only based on equality. This means that the automation of the calculational design might not need the full power of theorem provers since it is essentially rewriting [11].

Acknowledgements. I thank Thomas Wies for careful proofreading.

Disclosure of Interests. This paper is a written version of the talks I gave in London, UK, at Peter O'Hearn Fest on January 14th, 2024 and at POPL'24 on January 19th 2024, with a few simplifications and improved results.

References

1. Aczel, P.: An introduction to inductive definitions. In: Barwise, J. (ed.) Handbook of Mathematical Logic, chap. 7, pp. 739–782. North–Holland, Amsterdam (1977)
2. Cook, S.A.: Soundness and completeness of an axiom system for program verification. SIAM J. Comput. **7**(1), 70–90 (1978). https://doi.org/10.1137/0207005
3. Cook, S.A.: Corrigendum: soundness and completeness of an axiom system for program verification. SIAM J. Comput. **10**(3), 612 (1981). https://doi.org/10.1137/0210045

4. Cousot, P.: On fixpoint/iteration/variant induction principles for proving total correctness of programs with denotational semantics. In: Gabbrielli, M. (ed.) LOPSTR 2019. LNCS, vol. 12042, pp. 3–18. Springer, Cham (2020). https://doi.org/10.1007/978-3-030-45260-5_1

5. Cousot, P.: Principles of Abstract Interpretation. MIT Press, 1 edn. (2021)

6. Cousot, P.: Calculational design of [in]correctness transformational program logics by abstract interpretation. Proc. ACM Program. Lang. 8(POPL), 175–208 (2024)

7. Cousot, P.: Full version of "calculational design of [in]correctness transformational program logics by abstract interpretation", proc. ACM program. lang. 8, POPL (2024), 7:1–10:33. https://doi.org/10.1145/3632849 Zenodo p. 66 pages (Dec 2024)https://doi.org/10.5281/zenodo.10439108

8. Cousot, P., Cousot, R.: Constructive versions of Tarski's fixed point theorems. Pacific J. of Math. **82**(1), 43–57 (1979). https://doi.org/10.2140/pjm.1979.82.43

9. Cousot, P., Cousot, R.: Systematic design of program analysis frameworks. In: POPL, pp. 269–282. ACM Press (1979). https://doi.org/10.1145/567752.567778

10. Dijkstra, E.W.: Notes on structured programming. Tech. Rep. T.H.-Report 70-WSK-03, Department of Mathematics, Technological University Eindhoven, The Netherlands (Apr 1970). https://www.cs.utexas.edu/users/EWD/ewd02xx/EWD249.PDF

11. Durán, F., et al.: Programming and symbolic computation in Maude. J. Log. Algebraic Methods Program. **110** (2020)

12. Floyd, R.W.: Assigning meaning to programs. In: Schwartz, J. (ed.) Proceedings of the Symposium in Applied Math., vol. 19, pp. 19–32. American Mathematical Society (1967). https://doi.org/10.1007/978-94-011-1793-7_4

13. Hoare, C.A.R.: An axiomatic basis for computer programming. Commun. ACM **12**(10), 576–580 (1969). https://doi.org/10.1145/363235.363259

14. Kahn, G.: Natural semantics. In: Brandenburg, F.J., Vidal-Naquet, G., Wirsing, M. (eds.) STACS 1987. LNCS, vol. 247, pp. 22–39. Springer, Heidelberg (1987). https://doi.org/10.1007/BFb0039592

15. Karp, C.R.: Languages with Expressions of Infinite Length. North-Holland, Amsterdam (1964)

16. Naur, P.: Proofs of algorithms by general snapshots. BIT **6**, 310–316 (1966).https://doi.org/10.1007/BF01966091

17. O'Hearn, P.W.: Incorrectness logic. Proc. ACM Program. Lang. **4**(POPL), 10:1–10:32 (2020). https://doi.org/10.1145/3371078

18. Park, D.M.R.: Fixpoint induction and proofs of program properties. In: Mitchie, D., Meltzer, B. (eds.) Machine Intelligence Volume 5, chap. 3, pp. 59–78. Edinburgh Univ. Press (1969)

19. Tarski, A.: A lattice theoretical fixpoint theorem and its applications. Pacific J. of Math. **5**, 285–310 (1955). https://doi.org/10.2140/pjm.1955.5.285

20. Turing, A.: Checking a large routine. In: Report of a Conference on High Speed Automatic Calculating Machines, pp. 67–69. University of Cambridge Mathematical Laboratory, Cambridge, England (1949 [1950]). https://turingarchive.kings.cam.ac.uk/publications-lectures-and-talks-amtb/amt-b-8

21. de Vries, E., Koutavas, V.: Reverse Hoare logic. In: SEFM. Lecture Notes in Computer Science, vol. 7041, pp. 155–171. Springer (2011). https://doi.org/10.1007/978-3-642-24690-6_12

Reasoning About Hilbert's Choice Operator in SMT

Byron Cook[1,2]($\boxtimes$) and Andres Noetzli[3]

[1] Amazon, Seattle, USA
`byron@amazon.com`
[2] University College London, London, UK
[3] Cubist, New York, USA

Abstract. We describe a method of implementing support for Hilbert's ε-terms within solvers for satisfiability modulo theories (SMT), giving users access to a new logical choice primitive.

1 Introduction

Hilbert's ε-operator [10] can be used to create indeterminate terms with desired properties. For example, $\varepsilon x.P(x)$ represents a value where P holds. If there is no x such that $P(x)$ is possible, then $\varepsilon x.P(x)$ represents an arbitrary value. The meaning of $\varepsilon x.P(x)$ is specified by axioms from the ε-calculus [14,25] that enforce necessary conditions. We can use ε-terms as we do any other term, *e.g.* $(\varepsilon x.x > 0) + 5$, $f(\varepsilon x.x \neq \text{`foo'}) = g(y)$, etc.

Applications of ε-terms can be found throughout computer science, logic, and philosophy. For example, Hilbert and Bernays [3] use an ε-based schema to derive the principle of induction. Bourbaki [5] uses the expressiveness to formalize set theory. Reasoning based on the ε-calculus has also been used within formal methods procedures, *e.g.* justifying the encoding of invertibility conditions for quantified bit-vector constraints [18], or encoding non-deterministic language features [13]. Interactive theorem provers such as ISABELLE [12] or HOL [11] support them. Further applications can be found in proof theory, model theory, and linguistics. See Leisenring [14] or Zach [25] for comprehensive accounts.

The goal of this paper is to give users of satisfiability modulo theory (SMT) solvers easy and native access to ε-terms, combined with the usual theories such as strings, integers, and uninterpreted functions. See Leino [13] as an example of the difficulty users face when trying to encode ε-calculus reasoning into their queries without native support from the SMT solver. We also believe that our approach provides a foundation for using SMT solvers to automatically discharge proof goals from interactive theorem provers with ε-terms, extending existing approaches like Sledgehammer [4] and SMTCoq [7]. Furthermore, given that the ε-calculus was originally proposed as a semantics for quantifiers, our approach potentially provides new avenues for research on solving quantifiers in SMT.

In this work, we focus on proving formulas with ε-terms unsatisfiable. At a high level, we implement a counterexample-guided abstraction refinement. In

D. Dietsch et al. (Eds.): Podelski Festschrift, LNCS 14765, pp. 107–120, 2026.
https://doi.org/10.1007/978-3-032-13711-1_7

our initial abstraction we replace ε-terms with fresh constants and then generate and add refinement axioms until the underlying solver can prove a contradiction between the abstraction and the refinements. For every ε-term there is an infinite number of axioms that could be instantiated. Consequently, one of the challenges of our approach is to identify which refinement axioms to generate. We propose multiple approaches to do so. We present a simple heuristic that can quickly find simple axiom instantiations. To find more complicated axiom instances, we use existing quantifier instantiation approaches combined with Syntax-Guided Synthesis (SyGuS) [1].

Related Work

The aspect of our work that distinguishes it from previous research related to the ε-calculus is the focus on an encoding in the setting of SMT. Our proposal is complementary, for example, to the goals of interactive theorem prover developers that use ε-terms. We focus on automation, whereas interactive provers are aimed at expressiveness and human usability. Our work also explores a different avenue than that of Giese and Ahrendt [9], who describe how ε-terms can be supported in the internals of resolution-based theorem provers, rather than the internals of SMT solvers. Note that we focus exclusively on proving formulae unsatisfiable. While we believe that our work can aid the search for models, this is left as future work.

Our proposed procedure borrows from existing SMT-based methods. For example, SMT solvers often use E-matching [6] or model-based quantifier instantiation (MBQI) [8] to reason about quantifiers, and conjoin on additional constraints when needed as a method of refinement. We use the same technique. In fact, our refinement procedure can use these quantifier instantiation techniques as subprocedures. We also use Syntax-Guided Synthesis (SyGuS) techniques as a subprocedure (*e.g.* see [1] or [19]). Our method of instantiating axioms for nested ε-terms bears some resemblance to the synthesis of Skolem functions [20]. We expect that future research is likely to find additional techniques from existing tools (*e.g.* AVATAR [21], CVC4 [2], E [24], VAMPIRE [22], Z3 [15]) that can be tailored to improve performance of our approach for users looking to use ε-terms.

2   Illustrative Example

Before formally defining our procedure, we first informally demonstrate it on an example. Consider the first-order formula $\forall y.(P(y) \land \exists x. \neg P(x))$, where P is an uninterpreted function of type $P : \texttt{Int} \to \texttt{Bool}$. Our goal is to prove this formula unsatisfiable.

Using the standard embedding into the ε-calculus (see Leisenring [14] or Zach [25]), we can remove the two quantifiers using the equivalences $\forall x.Q(x) \equiv Q(\varepsilon x.\neg Q(x))$ and $\exists x.Q(x) \equiv Q(\varepsilon x.Q(x))$, for any Q. In our example we first apply $\forall x.Q(x) \equiv Q(\varepsilon x.\neg Q(x))$, which produces the mixed first-order/ε-calculus formula $\forall y.(P(y) \land \neg P(\varepsilon x.\neg P(x)))$. The term $\varepsilon x.\neg P(x)$ is a logical constant in the ε-calculus. Essentially, we are stating that x is a value such that $P(x)$ is false when possible. As we will see below, the ε-calculus axiom schema will use the syntactic form of this logical constant, *i.e.* $\neg P(x)$, to define axioms which can be used, if needed, to provide a precise semantic meaning. The phrase *"if needed"* is key to the practicality of our approach: even without the axioms used, the default interpretation in a theorem prover is still a sound (but imprecise) abstraction. That is, if the formula with the logical constants uninterpreted is unsatisfiable, then the formula with the constants interpreted by the ε-calculus is unsatisfiable. The level of abstraction we gain in our approach is controlled by how many axioms from the ε-calculus axiom schema are used.

To make our example easier to understand we will abbreviate the logical constant with $l_1 \equiv \varepsilon x.\neg P(x)$, thus our embedding can be expressed as $\forall y.(P(y) \land \neg P(l_1))$. To remove the universal quantifier, we map $\forall z.Q(z)$ to $Q(\varepsilon z.\neg Q(z))$. Again Q can be any formula, but in our setting $Q(y) \equiv P(y) \land \neg P(l_1)$. This introduction produces the quantifier-free ε-calculus formula $P(\varepsilon y.\neg(P(y) \land \neg P(l_1))) \land \neg P(l_1)$. We will abbreviate $l_2 \equiv \varepsilon y.\neg(P(y) \land \neg P(l_1))$, allowing us to write our embedding as:

$$P(l_2) \land \neg P(l_1)$$

We can then pass this quantifier- and ε-term-free formula to an SMT solver. If we do not provide specialized semantics for l_1 or l_2, then the SMT solver will treat them as it would any other logical constant. In this default abstraction our formula is satisfiable, with a model such as $l_1 = 0$, $l_2 = 1$, and $P(x) = \mathrm{ite}(x = 1, \mathtt{true}, \mathtt{false})$.

However, this model does not work for the ε-term that corresponds to l_2 because it interprets the body of the term, $\neg(P(l_2) \land \neg P(l_1))$, as $\mathtt{false}$. To rule out this case, we need to refine the abstraction of the ε-terms. Thus, the next step is to search for relevant axioms from the ε-calculus. In the ε-calculus, the set of possible axioms are defined as:

$$\{Q(t) \to Q(\varepsilon x.Q(x)) \mid Q \text{ is a well-formed formula, } t \text{ is a term, } x \text{ is a variable}\}$$

We can now see how the syntactic encoding of the ε-constants is important: the Q in the $\varepsilon x.Q(x)$ determines its semantics. For example, motivated by the $\neg P(x)$ from $l_1 \equiv \varepsilon x.\neg P(x)$, we can add axioms of the form $\neg P(t_1) \to \neg P(l_1)$. Here, t_1 can be any term, *e.g.* a simple value such as 5, or a more complex term such as $2 + l_2$. By contrapositive reasoning, we can rewrite $\neg P(t_1) \to \neg P(l_1)$ as $P(l_1) \to P(t_1)$. Looking at $l_2 \equiv \varepsilon y.\neg(P(y) \land \neg P(l_1))$, we might also try to add axioms of the form $\neg(P(t_2) \land \neg P(l_1)) \to \neg(P(l_2) \land \neg P(l_1))$. Here t_2 can also be any term. To make this easier to follow we again rewrite using contrapositive reasoning:

$$(P(l_2) \land \neg P(l_1)) \to (P(t_2) \land \neg P(l_1))$$

So imagine that we had previously conjoined the above two formulae (with t_1 and t_2 as fresh variables) onto our embedding $P(l_2) \land \neg P(l_1)$. Thus, instead of passing $P(l_2) \land \neg P(l_1)$ to the SMT solver, we passed the *equisatisfiable* formula:

$$\begin{aligned}
&[P(l_2) \land \neg P(l_1)] \\
&\land [(P(l_2) \land \neg P(l_1)) \to (P(t_2) \land \neg P(l_1))] \\
&\land [P(l_1) \to P(t_1)]
\end{aligned}$$

In the remainder of this paper, we will refer to these axioms that use free variables as *axiom templates*. Now, the SMT solver would return a model that interprets $P(l_2) = \texttt{true}$, $P(l_1) = \texttt{false}$, and $P(t_2) = \texttt{true}$. Notice that if $l_1 = t_2$, this model would be shown to be inconsistent. Why? Because the SMT solver will use the congruence axiom of uninterpreted functions (*i.e.* $\forall x, y, f.\ x = y \rightarrow f(x) = f(y)$) to infer that $l_1 = t_2 \rightarrow P(l_1) = P(t_2)$. But because $P(l_1) = \texttt{false}$ and $P(t_2) = \texttt{true}$, then $P(l_1) \neq P(t_2)$, which is a contradiction. Thus, to block the previous model $P(l_2) = \texttt{true}$, $P(l_1) = \texttt{false}$, $P(t_2) = \texttt{true}$ from our abstraction we can instantiate a new axiom to our formula $[(P(l_2) \wedge \neg P(l_1)) \rightarrow (P(\mathbf{V}) \wedge \neg P(l_1))]$, and insert the term l_1 for $\mathbf{V}$:

$$\begin{aligned}
&[P(l_2) \wedge \neg P(l_1)] \\
&\wedge \ [(P(l_2) \wedge \neg P(l_1)) \rightarrow (P(t_2) \wedge \neg P(l_1))] \\
&\wedge \ [P(l_1) \rightarrow P(t_1)] \\
&\wedge \ [(P(l_2) \wedge \neg P(l_1)) \rightarrow (P(l_1) \wedge \neg P(l_1))]
\end{aligned}$$

This formula is unsatisfiable. To simplify the presentation of the proof, we remove the t_1- and t_2-based axiom templates and show that the weaker formula is unsatisfiable:

$$\begin{aligned}
&[P(l_2) \wedge \neg P(l_1)] \\
&\wedge \ [(P(l_2) \wedge \neg P(l_1)) \rightarrow (P(l_1) \wedge \neg P(l_1))]
\end{aligned}$$

Because $(P(l_1) \wedge \neg P(l_1)) = \texttt{false}$, this reduces to

$$\begin{aligned}
&[P(l_2) \wedge \neg P(l_1)] \\
&\wedge \ [(P(l_2) \wedge \neg P(l_1)) \rightarrow \texttt{false}]
\end{aligned}$$

which equals $[P(l_2) \wedge \neg P(l_1)] \wedge \neg[(P(l_2) \wedge \neg P(l_1))]$, *i.e.* $\texttt{false}$.

Finally, because $[(P(l_2) \wedge \neg P(l_1)) \rightarrow (P(l_1) \wedge \neg P(l_1))]$ is a well-formed ε-axiom, we know that $P(l_2) \wedge \neg P(l_1)$ is unsatisfiable in the ε-calculus. As a consequence, we also know that $\forall y.(P(y) \wedge \exists x. \neg P(x))$ is unsatisfiable in first-order logic, which was our original goal.

To prove the input formula unsatisfiable, we had to find the right ε-term to instantiate axioms for and then to find the right term to instantiate the axiom with. For example, if we had instantiated an axiom for the other ε-term, we would not have been able to make progress. Similarly, if we had instantiated the axiom template with a constant value, say $t_2 = 0$, instead of l_1, the axiom would not have contributed towards our goal. With more complicated examples, multiple instantiations of multiple ε-terms are necessary. In the remainder of the paper, we discuss our approach to address those challenges.

3   Procedure

Following Leisenring [14] and Zach [25], the ε-calculus is a consistent extension to quantifier-free first-order logic. The theory adds constants of the form $\varepsilon x.Q$ (where x is a variable and Q is any formula), and axioms of the form $Q(t) \rightarrow Q(\varepsilon x.Q)$ for any well-formed formula Q, term t, and variable x. Nelson

```
def solve(F:Formula) → {UNSAT, UNKNOWN}:
    (F_T,T,M) = initialize(F)
    smt.assert(F_T)
    instantiated = ∅
    while true:
        match smt.solve() with
        | UNSAT =>  return UNSAT
        | SAT(m) => terms = refine(smt,m):
                    if terms ⊆ instantiated:
                        return UNKNOWN
                    for (t,term) ∈ terms:
                        Q = M(t)
                        k = T(t)
                        smt.assert(Q(term) → Q(k))
                    instantiated = terms ∪ instantiated
```

Fig. 1. ε-calculus satisfiability solver, using SMT and counterexample-guided abstraction refinement. F_T is an abstract version of the input formula F, with ε-constants replaced by fresh variables. T is the mapping from a set of fresh template variables to the fresh variables that encode the ε-constants. M maps the template variables to a representation of the original ε-constants. Procedures **initialize** and **refine** are defined below in Figs. 2 and 3, respectively. Note that our **solve** procedure only returns UNSAT or UNKNOWN. It does not prove that a F is satisfiable or attempt to find models.

and Oppen's guidelines [17] for combining decision procedures are: 1) the input expected must be quantifier-free, 2) and the signature of the theory must be disjoint from those of the other procedures. In our case, the axiom schema is quantifier-free. To establish 2), the signature of the theory (*i.e.* the set of ε-constants) can be made disjoint with purification [16]. For completeness of the overall procedure, Nelson and Oppen also require that we prove *stable infiniteness*, as well as showing termination of the search through the ε-axioms. However, because first-order logic is not decidable and the ε-calculus is more general than first-order logic, we know that we will not be able to prove completeness.

Figure 1 outlines our top-level procedure. Our strategy is to lazily use the models found by the SMT solver to help select needed axioms. Towards this goal the **initialize** procedure (Fig. 2, discussed in detail below) implements a template-instantiation step, where fresh free variables are introduced, *i.e.* t_1 and t_2 from the example in Sect. 2. The number of fresh variables is equal to the number of ε-constants in the input formula. F_T is a version of the input formula F, with ε-constants replaced by fresh variables. T is the mapping from a set of fresh template variables to the fresh variables that encode the ε-constants. M maps the template variables to the original ε-constants.

The procedure **refinement** (Fig. 3, discussed in detail below) is called by **solver** when the underlying SMT solver has found a satisfying model. The refinement uses the model to look for terms to instantiate new axioms. If we fail to refine, we return UNKNOWN to the user. If, on the other hand, we have found an unsatisfiable configuration then we return UNSAT to the caller. In the following, we elaborate on the different parts of the procedure and discuss its limitations.

```
def initialize(smt:Solver, F:Formula)
        -> (Formula, Set(Term * Term)
              , Set(Term   * (Var -> Formula))):
    M = ∅
    T = ∅
    X = F
    for k in subterms(F):
        match k with
        | εx.Q(x)
            (l,kind) = fresh_const(k)
            smt.add_const(l,kind)
            (t,kind) = fresh_const(k)
            smt.add_const(t,kind)
            R = Q[k:=l]
            X = X[k:=l] ∧ R(t) -> R(l)
            T = T ∪ {(t,l)}
            M = M ∪ {(t,λx.R(x))}
        | _ => skip
    return (X,T,M)
```

Fig. 2. Formula abstraction and axiom template instantiation. $f[s := t]$ represents substitution, where all instances of s are replaced by t in f. We assume that the $f[s := t]$ operation is defined for ε-terms with free variables in the same way that it is typically defined for $\forall$-terms and $\exists$-terms, $e.g.$ $(\varepsilon x.x + y)[y := 6] = \varepsilon x.x + 6$.

3.1   Initialization

Figure 2 shows the definition of `initialize`, which replaces ε-constants in the input formula by fresh theory constants and constructs the axiom templates. The constants in the axiom templates are left free and are used to synthesize terms that can be used to instantiate more axioms.

If we take the example from Sect. 2, `initialize` would return (X,T,M), where

$$
\begin{aligned}
\text{X} = \ &P(l_2) \wedge \neg P(l_1) \\
&\wedge \left[\neg (P(t_2) \wedge \neg P(l_1)) \to \neg (P(l_2) \wedge \neg P(l_1)) \right] \quad &&\text{(template formula for } l_2) \\
&\wedge \left[\neg P(t_1) \to \neg P(l_1) \right] \quad &&\text{(template formula for } l_1) \\
\text{T} = \ &\{(t_1, l_1), (t_2, l_2)\} \\
\text{M} = \ &\{(t_1, \lambda x.\neg P(x)), (t_2, \lambda y.\neg (P(y) \wedge \neg P(l_1)))\}
\end{aligned}
$$

When using the ε-calculus, we must be careful to appropriately α-rename when applying axioms in the context of bound variables. Renaming not only allows us to express all of the possible ε-terms we might need to construct during the search for the right axioms, renaming also avoids accidental name capture. In Sect. 2, there were no free variables in the ε-constants, so we avoided the issue. In our more general case, at initialization time functions are constructed that represent the possible ε-terms needed. The function `fresh_const` uses the structure of its parameter to define the sort of the fresh function constant. The result is a function of sort $\sigma_1 \times \ldots \times \sigma_n \to \sigma_r$, where the sorts of the arguments

$\sigma_1 \times \ldots \times \sigma_n$ correspond to the sorts of the free variables occurring in k (i.e. variables bound by ε-terms outside of k) and the co-domain sort σ_r matches the sort of k itself. This plays the same role as renaming. Furthermore, it also allows the SMT solver, during its proof search, to construct necessary abstractions of ε-terms. Because we are in the context of satisfiability, we only need to set up the constraint system such that all functions are possible, which is precisely the semantics of uninterpreted functions. That is: if the underlying SMT solver returns UNSAT, it has proved it unsatisfiable for all possible functions representing the ε-terms.

To illustrate why this is necessary, consider the case $\varepsilon x.(\neg \varepsilon y.y < x)$. Here y is bound. Our procedure will construct the encoding $l_1(l_2) < l_2$. During the proof search the SMT solver has to reason over all possible definitions for l_1, which acts as the dual to finding renaming in a validity-based proof. Note that this appears similar to Skolemization [23] but is serving a different purpose, and, unlike Skolemization, we apply this transformation regardless of the "polarity" of the term (with regards to its nesting within negations).

As alluded to in Sect. 2, the F_T that results from `initialize` is equisatisfiable to F, which is captured by the following lemma.

Lemma 1. *Assume that $(F_T, T, M) = $ `initialize`(F), $F_X \wedge X = F_T$, where X is the template, and template variables in T are disjoint from $vars(F_X)$. F is satisfiable iff $F_X \wedge X$ is satisfiable.*

Proof. X is the conjunction of formulae with shape

$$X = \bigwedge_{0 < i \leq n} Q(t_i) \to Q(k_i)$$

By induction on n. In the base case $X \equiv$ true, and thus F and $F_X \wedge X$ are equisatisfiable. By the inductive hypothesis we assume that F is equisatisfiable with $F_X \wedge X'$, where

$$X' = \bigwedge_{0 < i < n} Q(t_i) \to Q(k_i)$$

Let $F' \equiv F_X \wedge X'$. Assume (by assumption) that t_n is free in F_X, and thus by construction also free in F'. If F' is unsatisfiable, then clearly $F' \wedge [Q(t_n) \to Q(k_n)]$ is too. Thus our concern is the case where F' is satisfiable. Assume (by contradiction) that $F' \wedge [Q(t_n) \to Q(k_n)]$ is not satisfiable. Because F' alone is satisfiable then there is an (unsatisfying) interpretation m where $F' = $ true, but $Q(k_n) = $ false and $Q(t_n) = $ true. But because t_n is unconstrained, we can construct a satisfying model

$$m' = \{(a, b) \mid (a = t_n \to b = m(k_n)) \wedge (a \neq t_n \to b = m(a))\}$$

where $F' = $ true, $Q(k_n) = $ false, and $Q(t_n) = $ false. Thus $F' \wedge [Q(t_n) \to Q(k_n)]$ is satisfiable, which contradicts our premise. $\square$

Our `solve` procedure is sound as stated by the following lemma.

Lemma 2. *Assume that our SMT solver correctly implements first-order satisfiability, with consistent theory extensions T. Assume that F is a well-formed quantifier-free formula in the supported theory, with ε-constants. If* `solve(F)`*=UNSAT, then F is unsatisfiable in the ε-calculus combined with T.*

Proof. Let X be value of F_T at the beginning of execution, and X' be value of the instantiation at the end, constructed by the sequence of calls to `smt.assert`. Because `solve(F)`=UNSAT, we know that X' is unsatisfiable in the quantifier-free predicate logic with extensions T. Let W be a formula such that $W \wedge X = X'$. By Lemma 1 (on the equisatisfiablity of the template construction when all t variables are unconstrained), we know that $F \wedge W$ is also unsatisfiable, under appropriate renaming. Because W contains a well-formed ε-argument for F, F is unsatisfiable in the quantifier-free ε-calculus with extensions T. $\square$

Depending on the definition of the semantics of ε-terms, there is an additional *ε-extensionality axiom* to consider: $\forall x.(P(x) = Q(x)) \rightarrow \varepsilon x.P(x) = \varepsilon x.Q(x)$. Intuitively, this axiom ensures that if two ε-terms are equivalent, then they both choose the same value. For example, if both $\varepsilon x.x \geq 0$ and $\varepsilon x.x > -1$ where x is an integer, appeared in a formula, then they would always be equal. For the unsatisfiable case, our procedure is sound regardless of whether we consider the ε-extensionality axiom only restricts the possible values that a given ε-term can represent.

3.2   Refinement

We now discuss the core of our abstraction refinement loop, the `refine` procedure shown in Fig. 3, which is used to maintain a connection between the reasoning that the underlying SMT solver is performing, and our goal of finding necessary ε-axioms. The procedure returns the new terms for instantiating axioms as a mapping. We present two alternative approaches to implement such a procedure. The first approach lets the other cooperating decision procedures find terms—via the values in the found model—that we can use to instantiate more axioms. The second approach leverages existing quantifier instantiation and SyGuS approaches to instantiate axioms, assuming that the underlying SMT procedure supports it.

Recall the example from Sect. 2. In our procedure imagine that

$$\mathsf{F}_T = [P(l_2) \wedge \neg P(l_1)] \wedge [\neg(P(t_2) \wedge \neg P(l_1)) \rightarrow \neg(P(l_2) \wedge \neg P(l_1))] \wedge [\neg P(t_1) \rightarrow \neg P(l_1)]$$

When applied to F_T, our SMT solver might begin by finding a model that interprets P as follows

$$\mathtt{m} \equiv P(l_2) = \mathtt{true} \wedge P(l_1) = \mathtt{false} \wedge P(t_2) = \mathtt{true}$$

Because $\mathtt{m} \wedge l_1 = t_2$ is unsatisfiable, the refinement procedure would return the mapping $\{(t_2, l_1)\}$, which results in the axiom that we need to show the original formula unsatisfiable. When searching for suitable axioms, it is sufficient

```
def refine(smt: Solver, m: Model) → Set(Var * Term)
  terms = ∅
  for t, λx.R(x) in M:
    l = T(t)
    if !m(R(l)):
      for x ∈ vars(m) ∪ consts(m)
            ∪ const_heuristic(m,type(t)):
        smt.push()
        smt.assert(m ∧ x = t)
        if smt.check() == UNSAT:
          terms = terms ∪ {(t,x)}
        smt.pop()
  return terms
```

Fig. 3. Refinement procedure. `const_heuristic(m,t)` randomly generates a constant of type `t` that is not in `m`

to search for axioms for ε-terms that the model interprets as `false`, which is what the $!m(R(l))$ condition tests. If the model interprets the condition of an ε-term as `true`, then the model correctly interprets the ε-term, so finding axioms for other ε-terms is of higher priority. The `refine` procedure additionally explores constants that appear in the model `m` and other constants of a given type picked using a heuristic `const_heuristic`. In the following example, we show what a concrete implementation of such a heuristic may look like and why it is needed.

Example 1. Consider a first-order case like $\forall x, y.\ x = y$, where x and y have type `String`. In our translation to the ε-calculus we would have $F_T \equiv l_1 = l_2 \wedge (t_1 \neq t_2 \rightarrow l_1 \neq l_2)$. For this example the SMT solver may find a model where each of the variables equals the empty string. Our `consts_heuristic` can be designed to generate a randomly selected constant. Imagine that the refinement suggested is $\{((t_1, t_2), (\text{"foo"}, \text{"goo"}))\}$. Any strings not equal to the empty string suffice. We therefore add the axiom: $(\text{"foo"} \neq \text{"goo"} \rightarrow l_1 \neq l_2)$, which results in `UNSAT`. Where this approach fails is in a case like $\forall x.\texttt{str}.\texttt{substr}(x, 0, 3) \neq \text{"foo"}$. In these cases we rely on the quantifier instantiation procedure in `qrefine` to suggest the new axiom as discussed below.   □

Note that, if our underlying tools support them, we can make use of quantifier instantiation and function synthesis techniques to generate the refinement axioms. Figure 4 shows an alternative refinement procedure, `qrefine`, that leverages those techniques.

First, the procedure computes a partial model. The partial model is similar to the full model but with some details removed. The procedure `partial_model` acts as a heuristic that decides which parts of the model to keep. Examples of heuristics that we have found to work well include a `partial_model` procedure that only keeps the model at the propositional level (i.e. it removes all the theory-specific values) and a procedure that additionally keeps the model for uninterpreted functions. The choice of the heuristic has to balance how easy it

```
def qrefine(smt: Solver, m: Model) → Set(Var * Term)
  terms = ∅
  pm = partial_model(m)
  smt.push()
  smt.assert(pm)
  for t, λx.R(x) in M:
    l = T(t)
    if ¬m(R(l)):
      if !is_function(t):
        smt.push()
        smt.assert(∀t.R(t)→R(l))
        match smt.solve() with:
          | UNSAT(insts) =>
              terms = terms ∪ { (t,l) | t ∈ insts }
          | SAT => pass
        smt.pop()
      else:
        fvs = free_vars(R(x))
        c = consts(f)
        synth = sygus_solver()
        synth.synthesize(∃f.∀c.¬F_T[l:=f]∧pm)
        terms = terms ∪ { (tf(fvs),l) }
  smt.pop()
  return terms
```

Fig. 4. Alternative refinement procedure using available quantifier instantiation heuristics.

is for the rest of qrefine to find a refinement and how general the refinement will be. If we use the full model, then the refinement axiom will likely instantiate the axioms with concrete values. While those are valid refinements of ε-terms, they are not very general and may not be general enough to prove a formula unsatisfiable because they only refine the term for single values. If, on the other hand, we use no model at all, then the rest of the refinement has to find an instantiation of the axiom that directly proves the original formula unsatisfiable, which may not be possible.

Next, the procedure attempts to compute refinements for each ε-term. If the refinement that we are trying to find is a nullary constant, we use a quantifier instantiation procedure to find a refinement. Otherwise, we are looking for a *function*, which we have to synthesize.

In the former case, we assert $\forall t.R(t) \to R(l)$, where l is the fresh constant for $\varepsilon x.Q(x)$ introduced by initialize, and check whether the result is unsatisfiable. Intuitively, this corresponds to asserting all the possible ε-axioms at once. If the result is unsatisfiable, then we know that a conjunction of the formula and the partial model are in conflict with some axiom instantiations. The procedure asks the SMT solver to return all the instantiations that it made during its search. Naively, we can return all of those instantiations as axioms. If the underlying SMT solver supports proofs, then we could extract the relevant instantiations from the proof to get fewer axioms. The nature of these checks lends itself well to *incremental* solving because these refinement checks can be expressed in terms of additional assertions (for the partial model and quantified axiom template) on top of the current state of the solver.

In the latter case, we cannot quantify over t because t is a function, so we are trying to solve a higher-order problem where the goal is to synthesize a function with certain properties. Fortunately, this problem can be expressed in Syntax-Guided Synthesis (SyGuS) [1] form. SyGuS solves problems of the form $\exists f.\forall x_1, \ldots, x_n.\phi(f, x_1, \ldots, x_n)$ where f is the function to synthesize and $x_1, \ldots, x_n$ is a list of universal variables. In other words, the goal of a SyGuS solver is to find a function f such that ϕ is true for all possible values of $x_1, \ldots, x_n$. SyGuS optionally allows to restrict the grammar of the functions it synthesizes but in practice, we can rely on default grammars. A practical limitation of SyGuS is that the variables $x_1, \ldots, x_n$ cannot be of function types. To avoid this problem, our procedure uses the partial model to substitute occurrences of uninterpreted functions by their respective models.

To conclude this section, we illustrate two additional aspects of our refinement using examples. First, we revisit the handling of nested ε-terms.

Example 2. To see how our method handles nested ε-terms, consider the case of $\exists x.\forall y.x = y + 5$. Here y's abstraction would be a function $l_1 : \mathtt{Int} \to \mathtt{Int}$, where $(t_1, \lambda y.\neg(l_2 = (y(l_2)) + 5)) \in \mathsf{M}$ and $(t_1, l_1) \in \mathsf{T}$. Note that in the context of the ε-term the variable l_2 is free. The existential variable x meanwhile is represented with l_2, where $(t_2, \lambda x.x = (l_1(x)) + 5)) \in \mathsf{M}$ and $(t_2, l_2) \in \mathsf{T}$. In this instance, $\mathsf{F}_T \equiv l_2 = l_1(l_2) + 5$.

When examining F_T, the SMT solver would return **SAT** perhaps with a model that includes $l_2 = 0$ and $l_1(v) = \mathrm{ite}(v = 0, -5, 0)$. However, this interpretation is not a model for the original formula: If we consider the case where $x = 1$, then the interpretation would yield $1 = l_1(1) = 0$, which is false. To refine our abstraction, we can now use SyGuS to synthesize a function for t_1, that allows us to prove the original problem unsatisfiable. The SyGuS solver may return $\lambda v.v - 4$ for t_1. As a result, our procedure would add a new axiom:

$$\neg(l_2 = ((\lambda v.v - 4)(l_2)) + 5)) \to \neg(l_2 = l_1(l_2) + 5))$$

which can be simplified:

$$\begin{aligned}
&\neg(l_2 = ((l_2 - 4) + 5)) \to \neg(l_2 = l_1(l_2) + 5)) \\
\Leftrightarrow\ &\neg(l_2 = l_2 + 1) \to \neg(l_2 = l_1(l_2) + 5)) \\
\Leftrightarrow\ &\neg\mathtt{false} \to \neg(l_2 = l_1(l_2) + 5)) \\
\Leftrightarrow\ &\neg(l_2 = l_1(l_2) + 5))
\end{aligned}$$

Because $\mathsf{F}_T \wedge \neg(l_2 = l_1(l_2) + 5)$ is unsatisfiable, we know that $\exists x.\forall y.x = y + 5$ is unsatisfiable. □

So far, we have assumed that all quantifiers only have a single bound variable but that is not the case in general. In the following example, we show how we handle quantifiers with multiple bound variables.

Example 3. Consider the following constraints:

$$\forall x.\ g(s(x), x)$$
$$\wedge\ \forall x, y, z.\ g(x, y) \wedge g(y, z) \to g(x, z)$$
$$\wedge\ \neg(g(s(s(a)), a))$$

where $\mathtt{U}$ is an uninterpreted sort, $a : \mathtt{U}$, $s : \mathtt{U} \to \mathtt{U}$, and $g : \mathtt{U} \times \mathtt{U} \to \mathtt{Bool}$. When converting from first-order logic to the ε-calculus it is of practical importance to treat $\forall x, y, z.P(x, y, z)$ as $\forall(x, y, z).P(x, y, z)$ rather than $\forall x.\forall y.\forall z.P(x, y, z)$. We use the well-known trick of considering tuples of bound variables, thus avoiding fresh constants of function type, and subsequently avoiding using SyGuS in our refinement procedure. In practice, our implementation uses tuples in its representation and combines directly nested quantifiers of the same kind. For example, we begin with $((t_1, t_2, t_3), (l_1, l_2, l_3)) \in \mathtt{T}$, rather than $(t_1, l_1) \in \mathtt{T}$. Furthermore, we have $((t_1, t_2, t_3), \lambda(x, y, z).\neg((g(x, y) \wedge g(y, z)) \to g(x, z))) \in \mathtt{M}$. We also have $(t_4, l_4) \in \mathtt{T}$, and $(t_4, \lambda x.\neg g(s(x), x)) \in \mathtt{M}$. Our refinement procedure finds three axioms to prove the constraints unsatisfiable:

$$\neg(g(s(a), a) \to \neg(g(s(l_4), l_4)))$$
$$\wedge\ \neg(g(s(s(a)), s(a)) \to \neg(g(s(l_4), l_4)))$$
$$\wedge\ \neg(g(s(s(a)), s(a)) \wedge g(s(a), a) \to g(s(s(a)), a)) \to \neg(g(l_1, l_2) \wedge g(l_2, l_3) \to g(l_1, l_3))$$

□

3.3   Limitations

As mentioned previously, our current abstraction refinement only targets unsatisfiable cases. In the following example, we consider an example that has been slightly modified from the example in Sect. 2 and is satisfiable to illustrate the limitations of our approach. Our procedure will return $\mathtt{UNKNOWN}$ on this example, even though we will see that is satisfiable.

Example 4. Consider the constraint $\forall y.(P(y) \wedge \exists x.P(x))$. We can embed this into the ε-calculus as $P(l_2) \wedge P(l_1)$, where $l_1 \equiv \varepsilon x.P(x)$, and $l_2 \equiv \varepsilon y.\neg(P(y) \wedge P(l_1))$. We can then pass $P(l_2) \wedge P(l_1)$ to an SMT solver, which would return $P(l_2) = \mathtt{true}$ and $P(l_1) = \mathtt{true}$.

As we did before, we can conjoin the template axiom formulae (with t_1 and t_2 as fresh variables):

$$[P(l_2) \wedge P(l_1)]$$
$$\wedge\ [(P(l_2) \wedge P(l_1)) \to (P(t_2) \wedge P(l_1))]$$
$$\wedge\ [P(t_1) \to P(l_1)]$$

In this case we have $[P(t_2) \wedge P(l_1)]$ instead of $[P(t_2) \wedge \neg P(l_1)]$, as we had in the example from Sect. 2. Thus, the trick of connecting l_1 to t_2 will not suffice as a refinement. Previously, instantiating an axiom with l_1 had resulted in the falsifiable $P(l_1) \wedge \neg P(l_1)$, but in this instance it results in the satisfiable $P(l_1) \wedge P(l_1)$. In fact, if we define P as $P(v) \equiv \mathtt{true}$ (for any v), then the entire formula reduces to $\mathtt{true}$ and is therefore satisfiable for all possible values of t_1 and t_2. Thus, even if A is the set of all possible ε-axioms, we know that $A \wedge P(l_2) \wedge P(l_1)$ is still satisfiable, with a model where $P(v) \equiv \mathtt{true}$. As a consequence, we know that $\forall y.(P(y) \wedge \exists x.P(x))$ has a model, which was our original goal.

□

4 Discussion

Hilbert originally introduced the ε-operator with the goal of proving the consistency of first-order logic. But over time the expressive power of ε-terms has proved useful for both theoretical and practical purposes. This paper has outlined a method of adding native support for the ε-calculus into SMT solvers.

We believe that the relationship exploited here between the internals of SMT solvers and the ε-calculus's axiom schema potentially opens the door to new algorithms and proof strategies. For example, the axiomatic structure of the ε-calculus seems also to lend itself towards distributing SMT solving in a datacenter. Synthesis tools for inductive hypothesis may be able to exploit the axioms.

One of the practical challenges in our work is the problem of proving formulas satisfiable. In our example in Sect. 3.3, we demonstrate how it *can* be done, but we have not provided a procedure. An intriguing aspect of the problem is the possibility of proving the existence of a model, while not finding one. If we can prove that the conjunction of all possible (often uncountable) axioms still do not make the formula unsatisfiable, then we know that a model exists.

References

1. Alur, R., et al.: Syntax-guided synthesis. In: Dependable Software Systems Engineering, NATO Science for Peace and Security Series, D: Information and Communication Security, vol. 40 (2015)
2. Barrett, C.W., et al.: CVC4. In: CAV (2011)
3. Bernays, P., Hilbert, D.: Grundlagen der Mathematik. Springer (1934)
4. Blanchette, J.C., Böhme, S., Paulson, L.C.: Extending sledgehammer with SMT solvers. J. Autom. Reason. **51**(1), 109–128 (2013)
5. Bourbaki, N.: Théorie des Ensembles. Hermann (1954)
6. Detlefs, D., Nelson, G., Saxe, J.B.: Simplify: a theorem prover for program checking. JACM **52**(3), 365–473 (2005)
7. Ekici, B., et al.: SMTCoq: a plug-in for integrating SMT solvers into Coq. In: CAV (2017)
8. Ge, Y., de Moura, L.: Complete instantiation for quantified formulas in satisfiability modulo theories. In: CAV (2009)
9. Giese, M., Ahrendt, W.: Hilbert's ϵ-terms in automated theorem proving. In: TABLEAUX (1999)
10. Hilbert, D.: Neubegründung der mathematik: erste mitteilung. Abhandlungen aus dem Seminar der Hamburgischen Universität **1**, 157–177 (1922)
11. HOL88 theorem prover. https://github.com/theoremprover-museum/HOL88
12. Isabelle theorem prover. https://isabelle.in.tum.de/
13. Leino, K.R.M.: Compiling Hilbert's ε operator. In: LPAR (2018)
14. Leisenring, A.C.: Mathematical logic and Hilbert's ε-symbol. Macdonald & Co Publishers (1969)
15. de Moura, L.M., Bjørner, N.: Z3: an efficient SMT solver. In: TACAS (2008)
16. Nelson, G.: Techniques for program verification. Ph. D. dissertation, Harvard (1980)

17. Nelson, G., Oppen, D.C.: Simpliciation by cooperating decision procedures. TOPLAS **1**(42), 245–257 (1979)
18. Niemetz, A., Preiner, M., Reynolds, A., Barrett, C.W., Tinelli, C.: Solving quantified bit-vectors using invertibility conditions. In: CAV (2018)
19. Polgreen, E., Seshia, S.A.: SynRG: syntax guided synthesis of expressions with alternating quantifiers satisfiability modulo theories. arXiv:2007.10519 (2020)
20. Preiner, M., Niemetz, A., Biere, A.: Counterexample-guided model synthesis. In: TACAS (2017)
21. Reger, G., Bjorner, N., Suda, M., Voronkov, A.: AVATAR modulo theories. In: GCAI (2016)
22. Riazanov, A., Voronkov, A.: Vampire. In: CADE (1999)
23. Robinson, J.A., Voronkov, A. (eds.): Handbook of Automated Reasoning (in 2 volumes). Elsevier and MIT Press (2001)
24. Schulz, S., Cruanes, S., Vukmirovic, P.: Faster, higher, stronger: E 2.3. In: CADE (2019)
25. Zach, R.: Semantics and proof theory of the epsilon calculus. In: ICLA (2017)

PVS as a Proof Obligation Generator

Natarajan Shankar[(✉)]

SRI Computer Science Laboratory, Menlo Park, USA
shankar@csl.sri.com

Abstract. The PVS specification language extends simply typed higher-order logic with a number of useful features including predicate subtypes. The PVS typechecker verifies simple type correctness and generates proof obligations for subtype membership, type equivalence, and termination. These proof obligations can be discharged interactively or automatically using pre-defined proof strategies. By carefully crafting the type constraints, PVS can be used as a general-purpose proof obligation generator. This has already been illustrated in an elegant structural embedding of the B method in PVS by Muñoz and Rushby. We demonstrate a similar structural embedding of a variant of Floyd's method by defining a Floyd graph with a set of well-formedness conditions. When the graph is instantiated by an actual program annotated with assertions, the appropriate proof obligations are generated. The validity of these proof obligations implies the correctness of the program. The technique of defining templates for deriving proof obligations can be adapted to a number of other settings without the need for a specialized proof obligation generator or bespoke automation.

1 Introduction

Building verification tools is a daunting challenge. In order to build a static analyzer or a verifying compiler for a programming language, one must capture the syntax, define a range of syntactic and semantic operations on the syntax, and connect to various verification tools. Alternately, one could use a theorem prover to embed the target language and its semantics, thus leveraging the already built-in functionality. The PVS theorem prover has already been used to embed other logics and languages. These embeddings can leverage the expressibility of the type system, particularly the use of predicate subtyping, to connect the semantics of the embedded language with the automated theorem proving support in PVS. One early example of this kind of embedding is the PBR system which embeds the refinement technique of the B method into the PVS logic. We demonstrate the technique of embedding a formalism to automatically generate proof obligations by defining a version of Floyd's method [6] within PVS [18]. Andreas Podelski's contributions at the confluence of program logics, static analysis, termination analysis, and model checking has had a broad and deep impact on the theory and practice of automated verification. The work presented here also bears his clear influence.

Supported by NSF:CCRI Award #2016597.

1.1   The PVS Specification Language

We briefly introduce the PVS specification language which is used for the formalization. The language is based on higher-order logic. A PVS specification is a collection of files, where each file contains a sequence of theories. Each theory is a sequence of declarations of types, constants, or formulas (axioms, theorems, or generated proof obligations). Theories can have parameters, and include assumptions on the parameters. The basic types are Booleans **bool** and Reals **real**. New types can be constructed from existing ones as tuples $(T_1, \ldots, T_n)$, records $[\#l_1 : T_1, \ldots l_n : T_n\#]$, or functions $[T_1 \rightarrow T_2]$. Function, tuple, and record types can be dependent. Arrays are modeled as functions. Types can also be built as algebraic datatypes with a finite set of constructors, each with accessors/fields and a recognizer predicate. For any type T, a predicate p is an element of the type $[T \rightarrow$ **bool**$]$, and a predicate subtype $\{x : T \mid p(x)\}$ contains all the elements a of T where $p(a)$ holds. PVS expressions are built from constants and variables using equality, *if-then-else*, *case*-expressions, and tupling and projection, record construction and record field access, λ-abstraction and function application. In addition, there is an update construct that allows records, fields, and functions to be updated. PVS also admits structural subtyping, which we omit here, except to note that the update construct pairs up nicely with structural subtyping.

In a language like PVS with a form of subtyping where any predicate can serve as the constraint for defining a subtype, all kinds of questions become undecidable: typechecking, type containment and equality, emptiness. The main trick in handling undecidability is to generate proof obligations corresponding to the subtype constraints so that if we are checking that an expression e has type $\{x : T \mid p(x)\}$ in some context C, this yields a proof obligation $C \vdash p(a)$ in addition to $C \vdash a : T$. Subtyping is one source of proof obligations in PVS. Others include termination proof obligations for recursive functions, assumption proof obligations for assumptions on the parameters of a theory when it is imported, and theory interpretation proof obligations when a theory with axioms is interpreted. Proof obligations are liberating since one can add undecidable features to the typechecker as long as they are designed to decompose nicely into a decidable algorithmic check, e.g., basic type correctness, and proof obligation formulas. The heavy reliance on proof obligations is effective in PVS mainly because it is complemented with appropriate proof automation.

The PVS language is quite expressive in terms of capturing concepts with precision. Mathematical expressions are coherent: nonsense expressions like division by zero, real square-root of a negative real number, derivative of a non-differentiable function, are ruled out, as are bad programs with out-of-bounds array accesses, inappropriately applied accessors, and numeric overflow and underflow. Writing specifications is a creative process since there are many ways to leverage the generation of proof obligations, and some work more effectively with the typechecking and proof automation in PVS than others.

1.2   Structural Embeddings

Theorem provers such as ACL2 [12], Coq [3], HOL [8], and Isabelle/HOL [16] have been traditionally used as hosts for embedding other (guest) formalisms. These are either deep embeddings where the syntax and semantics of the entire formalism is captured in the host logic, or shallow embeddings where the semantics of the guest formalism is defined in the host logic in order to formalize individual specifications [7]. Formally, if we are embedding a guest logic G in a host logic H, then for some property A in the guest logic,

$$\vdash_G A \iff \overline{G} \vdash_H \overline{A},$$

where $\overline{G}$ and $\overline{A}$ are the embeddings of G and A, respectively. For a deep embedding, the equivalence is shown for all G and A, whereas for a shallow embedding it is established for each pair of G and A.

Here, we examine the use of PVS as a proof obligation generator for embedding other formalisms that rely on proof obligations. PVS has been used in this manner for a number of embeddings: temporal logics, duration calculus [20], Alloy [14] , the Z specification language [9], the B method [15,24], I/O Automata [1], the Ocsid [13], Hoare logic [19], Differential Dynamic Logic [21,23], and Java [5,11,22], among others. These are mostly semi-deep encodings that capture a surface syntax of the embedded formalism while retaining the PVS expression language for the mathematical content. Muñoz and Rushby [15] call these *structural embeddings*. The idea is to split the guest language G into a structural component G_S and a mathematical component G_M where G_M is just H. This makes sense since the mathematical component is usually shared across multiple formalisms. One then encodes G_S and $\overline{G_S}$ to show $\vdash_G A \iff \overline{G_S}, G_M \vdash_H \overline{A}$.

Munoz and Rushby demonstrate structural embeddings with succinct definition of the B method that allows the invariant and refinement proof obligations to be verified through the corresponding PVS proof obligations. This way, the theorem prover can be exploited for the mathematical reasoning in these embedded formalism obviating the need for custom automation. It is, of course, possible to recover these benefits with a shallow encoding, where we directly formalizes the semantics of the embedded language, or using a deep encoding which formalizes both the syntax and the semantics. What makes the PVS embeddings unusual is the way in which the proof obligation mechanism can be exploited to model the proof obligations one would expect to get in a bespoke implementation. There are of course overheads associated with embeddings and an abstraction engineer has to make prudent engineering choices on whether to build bespoke automation for a specific formalism or structurally embed the formalism in a suitable host system.

2   Floyd's Method

Floyd's seminal paper *Assigning Meaning to Programs* [6] introduces the idea of annotating flowcharts with assertions to generate proof obligations (verification conditions) that entail the correctness of the program, i.e., that any execution starting with a *start* state satisfying the precondition of the program terminates in a *halt* state satisfying the post-condition. Floyd presented a flowchart as a graph where the vertices are commands and the edges are control flows between commands. The flowchart has a distinguished *start* vertex with no incoming edges, and a distinguished *halt* vertex with no outgoing edges. Floyd's method decorates each edge with an assertion. The proof obligation is to show that if the assertion of an incoming edge holds of the prestate of a command and the command is executed to yield a post-state, then the assertion for the corresponding outgoing edge holds for this post-state. A flowchart is constructed from vertices that are assignments, branches, and merges, in addition to the *start* and *halt* vertices. Floyd axiomatizes the notion of a verification condition $VC_c(P; Q)$ as a formula that if verified ensures that when command c is applied to a pre-state satisfying P where the computation continues along the outgoing edge labeled by assertion Q, then the post-state satisfies Q.

We take a *dual* view of Floyd graphs where the vertices represent control points annotated with assertions and the edges represent commands. There are some technical reasons for formalizing dual Floyd graphs: each edge has a unique source and target vertex representing the precondition and post-condition, respectively. With Floyd graphs, each statement has multiple fan-in and fan-out edges complicating the generation of proof obligations. The dual Floyd graphs defined below are similar to the Floyd–Hoare automata introduced by Heizmann, Hoenicke, and Podelski [10] as the framework for a verification method based on language inclusion.

2.1   Capturing Basic Floyd Graphs in PVS

The PVS theory `floyd`, a portion of which is shown below, captures a simple formalization of dual Floyd graphs in PVS. This formalization is restricted to partial correctness. We later extend it to total correctness, define a semantics, prove soundness, and illustrate how the theory can be instantiated to generate the proof obligations needed to prove total correctness. The theory `floyd` introduces a (nonempty) type `Vertex` with constants `start` and `halt`. The type `Edge` has two operations `source` and `target` representing the source and target of an edge, respectively. The type `Vertex` has to be nonempty (indicated by `TYPE+` since we are declaring constants that inhabit it, whereas the type `Edge` may be nonempty. We next associate a computation with a graph. An assertion is a predicate on `State` which is just a function from `State` to `bool`. A transition is a two-place relation on `State`, relating the predstate to the post-state. We map vertices to assertions with the `assertions` operation, and edges to transitions with the `transitions` operation.

```
floyd  : THEORY

  BEGIN
   Vertex: TYPE+
   start: Vertex
   halt: Vertex
   Edge: TYPE
   source, target: [Edge->Vertex]
   State: TYPE
   assertions: [Vertex -> PRED[State]]
   transitions: [Edge -> PRED[[State, State]]]
   ...

  END floyd
```

There are three axioms associated with the graph. The first axiom asserts that
start has no incoming edges. The second asserts that halt has no outgoing
edges. The third axiom asserts that for any edge e, if the source assertion holds
and the transition relation for the e holds between the prestate and post-state,
then the assertions for the post-state holds.

```
   startVertex: AXIOM
      FORALL (e: Edge): target(e) /= start

   haltVertex: AXIOM
     FORALL (e: Edge): source(e) /= halt

   well_formed: AXIOM
     FORALL (e: Edge), (s1, s2: State):
     assertions(source(e))(s1) ∧ transitions(e)(s1, s2)
     ⇒ assertions(target(e))(s2)
```

To show that a concrete graph is correct, we merely perform a theory interpretation of the theory floyd with the concrete bindings for the uninterpreted
types Vertex, Edge, and State, and the uninterpreted constants start,
halt, source, target, assertions, and transitions. The instantiated
axioms are then generated as proof obligations. We first extend the floyd theory to cover total correctness before illustrating the theory interpretation.[1]

2.2   Total Correctness Floyd Graphs in PVS

The axioms in floyd only guarantee partial correctness. We therefore augment
the axioms to cover total correctness in the theory tfloyd. As in the theory
floyd, the theory tfloyd declares the same uninterpreted types and constants
and retains the three axioms startVertex, haltVertex, and well_formed.

---

[1] There are other mechanisms in PVS, e.g., *assumings*, for generating the same proof
obligations. We are using theory interpretations to highlight the use of this feature
for proof obligation generation.

```
tfloyd: THEORY
 BEGIN

   Vertex: TYPE+
   start: Vertex
   halt: Vertex
   Edge: TYPE
   source, target: [Edge->Vertex]
   State: TYPE
   assertions: [Vertex -> PRED[State]]
   transitions: [Edge -> PRED[[State, State]]]
   ...

END tfloyd
```

The type **Vstate** is declared as a tuple (pair) of **State** and **Vertex**. (Line comments are preceded by %.) The type **rankspace** serves as the range type for a ranking function **rank** which employs **Vstate** as the domain type. We also postulate the existence of a well-founded ordering **<=** on **rankspace**. These declarations might appear simple and straightforward, but there are many ways to formalize total correctness and this one happens to achieve a reasonable balance between flexibility and automation.

```
Vstate: TYPE = [State, Vertex]% state = v'1 , vertex = v'2
rankspace: TYPE+
rank: [Vstate -> rankspace]
<= : pred[[rankspace, rankspace]]
```

The additional axioms in **tfloyd** are shown below. The first axiom constrains the ordering relation on **rankspace** to be well-founded, i.e., there are no infinite decreasing chains. The **totality** axiom requires every state to have a successor along some edge. The graph may be nondeterministic so that there are multiple successors for a given state. The **termination** axiom asserts that the rank of a successor state must be smaller than its predecessor according to the well-founded ordering relation.

```
well_founded: AXIOM
  well_founded?(<=)

totality: AXIOM
  FORALL (v1 : Vertex), (s1 : State):
    v1 /= halt ∧ assertions(v1)(s1) =>
      (EXISTS (e : Edge), (s2 : State):
        source(e) = v1 ∧ transitions(e)(s1, s2))

termination: AXIOM
  FORALL (e: Edge), (s1, s2: State):
    assertions(source(e))(s1) ∧ transitions(e)(s1, s2) =>
      rank(s2, target(e)) <= rank(s1, source(e))
```

So, we have six axioms characterizing a (dual) Floyd graph. The key axioms for the Floyd graph are

1. The edges establish a Hoare triple between the precondition and post-condition assertions
2. For each non-halt vertex, there must be a feasible outgoing edge for any state satisfying vertex condition
3. The transition predicate must be well-founded

We next present a computational semantics for Floyd graphs to demonstrate soundness. The theory **tfloyd_semantics** describes the semantics. It first defines the type **path** through the graph as a finite sequence of edges such that the target of each edge matches the source of the subsequent one. (Finite sequences are dependent records with a **length** field and a **seq** field containing an array of size **length**.) The type **trace(p)** defines the sequences of elements of **Vstate** such that the vertices in trace match those in the path, and each pair of adjacent states satisfies the **transitions** relation. The **endpath?** predicate checks that a given path terminates in the **halt** vertex.

```
tfloyd_semantics: THEORY
BEGIN
 IMPORTING tfloyd

 path: TYPE =
 {p : finseq[Edge]  |
     p'length > 0 ∧
     FORALL (i : below(p'length - 1)): source(p'seq(i+1)) = target(p'seq(i))}

 trace(p: path): TYPE =
 {ss: finseq[Vstate] |
       ss'length = p'length + 1 ∧ ss'seq(0)'2 = source(p'seq(0)) ∧
       FORALL (i :below(p'length)):
          ss'seq(i+1)'2 = target(p'seq(i)) ∧
          transitions(p'seq(i))(ss'seq(i)'1, ss'seq(i+1)'1)}

 endpath?(p: path): bool = target(p'seq(p'length - 1)) = halt
```

We next prove soundness. The lemma **soundness** asserts that for any trace **ss** following a computation path **p** through the graph, if the (precondition) assertion for the initial vertex of the path **p** holds for the initial state (**ss'seq(0)'1** of the trace, then the (post-condition) assertion holds for each vertex along the path. The theorem **main_soundness** shows that if the precondition assertion holds for an endpath **p**, then the post-condition for **halt** holds of the last state. The lemma **totality_step** states that any vertex/state pair satisfying its assertion has an outgoing endpath, i.e., a path to the **halt** vertex, and an associated trace.

```
soundness: LEMMA
  FORALL (p: path), (ss: trace(p)), (i: below(ss'length)):
    assertions(ss'seq(0)'2)(ss'seq(0)'1)
      => assertions(ss'seq(i)'2)(ss'seq(i)'1)

main_soundness: THEOREM
FORALL (p: (endpath?)), (ss: trace(p)):
  assertions(ss'seq(0)'2)(ss'seq(0)'1)
      => assertions(halt)(ss'seq(ss'length - 1)'1)

totality_step: LEMMA
 FORALL (v : Vertex), (s: State):
   v /= halt ∧
   assertions(v)(s)
   => (EXISTS (p : (endpath?)), (ss : trace(p)):
        source(p'seq(0)) = v ∧ ss'seq(0)'1 = s)

END tfloyd_semantics
```

The proofs of these theorems are relatively straightforward and only take a
few step each. Multiple iterations are needed for discovering and refining the
proofs since early proof attempts point out a number of errors and gaps. In the
next section, we show how programs can be verified by constructing concrete
Floyd graphs.

3   Verifying Programs with Floyd Graphs

Theories in PVS can be imported or interpreted. Importing makes the declarations in the imported theory visible. Interpreting a theory creates a local clone
of the theory while generating proof obligations corresponding to the interpreted
axioms. We demonstrate this with a simple program that computes the maximal
element in an array of natural numbers. The theory **max** first defines the types
vertices and **edges** as intended interpretations of the abstract types **Vertex**
and **Edge**. The type **vertices** is a enumerated or scalar type (a trivial kind of
algebraic datatype) with elements **start**, **halt**, and **loop**. The type **edges** is
also a scalar type with elements **toloop**, **tohalt**, **branch1**, and **branch2**.

```
max: THEORY
  BEGIN
  vertices: TYPE = {start, halt, loop}
  edges: TYPE = {toloop, tohalt, branch1, branch2}
   .
   .
   .
END max
```

The graph for the **max** program can now be defined by spelling out the
source and target vertices of each edge. The function **source** indicates that the
toloop edge has **start** as its source, and all the remaining edges have **loop** as
their source. Similarly, the function **target** identifies **loop** as the target **halt**
as the target of the **tohalt** edge, and **loop** as the target of the remaining
edges.

```
source(e: edges): vertices
  = CASES e OF
        toloop: start
        ELSE loop
    ENDCASES


target(e: edges): vertices
  = CASES e OF
        tohalt: halt
        ELSE loop
    ENDCASES
```

The intended interpretation of the abstract **State** type is given by the type **state** which is defined as a record consisting of the following fields: an array **A** of size **N**, a cursor **i**, and a field **max** carrying the running maximum.[2] Some variable names are declared to range over states and edges, and there are two parameters (uninterpreted constants) to the algorithm: the array size **N** and the input array **X**.

```
N: nat

state: TYPE = [# A: ARRAY[below(N) -> nat],
                  i: nat,
                  max: nat #]

s, s1, s2: VAR state
e, e1, e2: VAR edges
X :   ARRAY[below(N) -> nat]
```

Next, we associate assertions with the vertices. The state predicate **startAssert** that goes with the vertex **start** constrains the field **A** to be equal to the uninterpreted constant **X**. The state predicate **loopAssert** the field **A** to be equal to **X**, the field **i** to be at most **N**, and the field **max** to be no smaller than any of the elements from 0 to $i - 1$. (The specification here does not check that **max** is an array element.) The state predicate **haltAssert** captures the post-condition, namely that **max** is the no smaller than the maximum of the elements in **A**, and that **A** remains equal to **X**.

```
startAssert(s): bool = (s'A = X ∧ s'i = 0 ∧ s'max = 0)
loopAssert(s): bool = (s'i <= N ∧ s'A = X ∧
                        FORALL (j : below(s'i)): s'A(j) <= s'max)
haltAssert(s): bool = (FORALL (j : below(N)): s'A(j) <= s'max) ∧ s'A = X
```

The mapping of vertices to assertions is given by the **assertions** operation defined below.

---

[2] The state representation here is simple but it is possible to introduce more sophisticated notions of program state that capture heap structure, class structure, allocation, and deallocation.

```
assertions(v: vertices)(s): bool =
  CASES v OF
    start: startAssert(s),
    loop: loopAssert(s),
    halt: haltAssert(s)
  ENDCASES
```

Next, we present the transitions. The four transitions are:

1. `toloopTransition` from `start` to `loop` which initializes `max` and `i` both to `0`.
2. `tohaltTransition` from `loop` to `halt` which checks that the `i` field is no smaller than `N` and preserves the state.
3. `branch1Transition` from `loop` to `loop` for the case where the current value `s1'A(s1'i)` is greater than the current maximum `max` and the new state `s2` updates `max` to `s1'A(s1'i)` and increments `i`.
4. `branch2Transition` from `loop` to `loop` for the alternative case where `max` is preserved and `i` is incremented.

```
toloopTransition(s1, s2): bool =
   (s2'max = 0 ∧ s2'i = 0 ∧ s2'A = s1'A)

tohaltTransition(s1, s2): bool =
   (¬ s1'i < N ∧ s2 = s1)

branch1Transition(s1, s2): bool =
(s1'i < N ∧ s1'A(s1'i) > s1'max ∧
 s2 = s1 WITH ['max := s1'A(s1'i), 'i := s1'i + 1])

branch2Transition(s1, s2): bool =
   (s1'i < N ∧ ¬ s1'A(s1'i) > s1'max ∧ s2 = s1 WITH ['i := s1'i + 1])
```

The transition map from edges to transitions is given by the function `transitions` below.

```
transitions(e)(s1, s2): bool =
   CASES e OF
      toloop: toloopTransition(s1, s2),
      tohalt: tohaltTransition(s1, s2),
      branch1: branch1Transition(s1, s2),
      branch2: branch2Transition(s1, s2)
   ENDCASES
```

The remaining part of the mapping deals with the bindings for the type `rankspace` and the ranking function `rank`. For the `max` program, we define the ranking space `frankspace` as the type of the primitive recursive sub-ϵ_0 ordinals `ordinals`. The function `vertexrank` defines one component of the ranking measure namely the ordering on graph vertices.

```
frankspace: TYPE = ordinal

vertexrank(v : vertices): below(3)
 = (CASES v OF
     halt: 0,
     loop: 1,
     start: 2
     ENDCASES)
```

The other component of the ranking measure is given by the function **stat-erank** defined below. to be the maximum of **0** and **N - s'i**. The full ranking function is given by **frank** as the two-lexicographic combination of **staterank** and **vertexrank**.

```
staterank(s: State): nat = max(0, N - s'i)

frank(s : state, v : vertices): ordinal = lex2(staterank(s), vertexrank(v))
```

The last step is to actually define the theory bindings which is done through a **THEORY** declaration.

```
maxtfloyd: THEORY = tfloydVertex := vertices, start := start, halt := halt,
                       Edge := edges, source := source, target := target,
   State := state, assertions := assertions,
   transitions := transitions,
   rankspace := frankspace,
   rank := frank,
   <= := ordinals.<
```

· This declaration generates six proof obligations for each of the six axioms. Since the **max** program is quite easy, these proofs are mostly one-liners. Half of them are discharged by the default strategy. Three of them require induction. The only nontrivial proof is that of **totality** since it involves the construction of a suitable successor state for each pre-state. This proof takes fourteen interactions.

Finally, we apply the above interpretation of **tfloyd** to construct an interpretation of the **tfloyd_semantics** theory to import the interpreted instances of the **main_soundness** and **totality_step** lemmas for the **max** program.

The formalization of structural embeddings can be improved and extended in a number of ways. Right now, there is a single proof obligation generated for each axiom, whereas it is desirable to generate a well-formedness and well-foundedness proof obligation for transition, and a totality proof obligation for each non-halt vertex. This can be achieved with a small amount of refactoring. There is really no significant scalability barrier to handling more complex programs with more complex states, assertions, and transitions. For example, one can add most structure to the atomic statements by introducing conditionals, assignments, and guarded assignments. The representation of state can also be extended to capture heaps and pointers, classes and subclasses, threads, and the program stack. The assertion logic can also be enriched with separation logic connectives. The Floyd graph can be enriched with assertions derived from static analysis, e.g., intervals, aliasing assertions, and ranking functions.

4   Conclusion

We have shown how the proof obligation mechanism for PVS can be used to define dual Floyd graphs in a form that makes it easy to generate proof obligations for concrete program graphs to establish soundness, totality, and termination. The mechanism can be easily adapted to richer notions of state and transitions to capture more realistic programming models. For example, one can formalize variations of the Boogie paradigm [2] in a similar manner. The advantage of this embedding is that type soundness and class invariants can be wired into the representation of state. It would also be interest to embed proof formalisms like the Proof Outline Logic of Owicki and Gries [17] and the UNITY formalism of Chandy and Misra [4].

The structural embedding approach can be emulated even in logics that do not support proof obligation generation by defining, for example, the concept of a Floyd graph along with a proof strategy for showing that specific program graphs satisfy the conditions of a Floyd graph. This approach does incur a fair amount of overhead compared to structural embeddings that directly produce the desired proof obligations needed to establish correctness.

There are pros and cons to the approach. The main pros are that there is very little overhead to defining such structural embeddings and there is a significant advantage to having the full power of the theorem prover for doing proofs. The disadvantage is that some of the expressiveness is limited by the expressiveness of the programming language. In the max example, the logic variable X had to be introduced as a constant parameter rather than as a logic variable. But overall, the pros easily outweigh the cons, and there is a great deal of power and flexibility to creating customized notation and automation for these embeddings while retaining the ability to bring in large volumes of background knowledge and powerful special-purpose and general-purpose theorem proving strategies. Metatheorems can be proved for the structural embedding so that proof techniques such as abstraction and refinement can be employed as part of the verification arsenal.

References

1. Archer, M., Heitmeyer, C.: TAME: a specialized specification and verification system for timed automata. In: Bestavros, A. (ed.) Work In Progress (WIP) Proceedings of the 17th IEEE Real-Time Systems Symposium (RTSS'96), pp. 3–6, Washington, DC (1996). The WIP Proceedings http://www.cs.bu.edu/pub/ieee-rts/rtss96/wip/proceedings
2. Barnett, M., Chang, B.-Y.E., DeLine, R., Jacobs, B., Leino, K.R.M.: Boogie: a modular reusable verifier for object-oriented programs. In: de Boer, F.S., Bonsangue, M.M., Graf, S., de Roever, W.-P. (eds.) FMCO 2005. LNCS, vol. 4111, pp. 364–387. Springer, Heidelberg (2006). https://doi.org/10.1007/11804192_17

3. Bertot, Y., Castéran, P.: Interactive Theorem Proving and Program Development. Springer, Heidelberg (2004). https://doi.org/10.1007/978-3-662-07964-5. Coq home page: http://coq.inria.fr/

4. Chandy, K.M., Misra, J.: Parallel Program Design: A Foundation. Addison Wesley (1988)

5. Dean, D.: Static typing with dynamic linking. In: Fourth ACM Conference on Computer and Communications Security, pp. 18–27, Zurich, Switzerland (1997)

6. Floyd, R.W.: Assigning meanings to programs. In: Mathematical Aspects of Computer Science, Proceedings of Symposia in Applied Mathematics, volume XIX, pp. 19–32. American Mathematical Society, Providence, Rhode Island (1967)

7. Gordon, M.J.C.: Mechanizing programming logics in higher order logic. Technical Report CCSRC-006, Cambridge Computer Science Research Center, SRI International, Cambridge, England (1988)

8. Gordon, M.J.C., Melham, T.F. (eds.): Introduction to HOL: A Theorem Proving Environment for Higher-Order Logic. Cambridge University Press, Cambridge (1993). HOL http://www.cl.cam.ac.uk/Research/HVG/HOL/

9. Gravell, A.M., Pratten, C.H.: Embedding a formal notation: experiences of automating the embedding of Z in the higher order logics of PVS and HOL, pp. 73–84. http://www.staff.ecs.soton.ac.uk/~amg/javalil/efn.ps.gz

10. Heizmann, M., Hoenicke, J., Podelski, A.: Software model checking for people who love automata. In: Sharygina, N., Veith, H. (eds.) CAV 2013. LNCS, vol. 8044, pp. 36–52. Springer, Heidelberg (2013). https://doi.org/10.1007/978-3-642-39799-8_2

11. Hensel, U., Huisman, M., Jacobs, B., Tews, H.: Reasoning about classes in object-oriented languages: logical models and tools. Technical Report CSI-R9718, Computing Sciences Institute, Katholieke Universiteit Nijmegen, Nijmegen, The Netherlands (1997)

12. Kaufmann, M., Manolios, P., Moore, J.S.: Computer-Aided Reasoning: An Approach, volume 3 of Advances in Formal Methods. Kluwer (2000)

13. Kellomäki, P.: A structural embedding of Ocsid in PVS. In: Boulton, R.J., Jackson, P.B. (eds.) TPHOLs 2001. LNCS, vol. 2152, pp. 281–296. Springer, Heidelberg (2001). https://doi.org/10.1007/3-540-44755-5_20

14. Moscato, M.M., Pombo, C.L., Frias, M.F.: Dynamite: a tool for the verification of Alloy models based on PVS. ACM Trans. Softw. Eng. Methodol. **23**(2), 20:1–20:37 (2014)

15. Muñoz, C., Rushby, J.: Structural embeddings: mechanization with method. In: Wing, J.M., Woodcock, J., Davies, J. (eds.) FM 1999. LNCS, vol. 1708, pp. 452–471. Springer, Heidelberg (1999). https://doi.org/10.1007/3-540-48119-2_26

16. Nipkow, T., Paulson, L.C., Wenzel, M.: Isabelle/HOL: A Proof Assistant for Higher-Order Logic. Springer, Heidelberg (2002). https://doi.org/10.1007/3-540-45949-9.Isabelle http://isabelle.in.tum.de/

17. Owicki, S., Gries, D.: An axiomatic proof technique for parallel programs. Acta Informatica **6**, 319–340 (1976)

18. Owre, S., Rushby, J., Shankar, N., von Henke, F.: Formal verification for fault-tolerant architectures: prolegomena to the design of PVS. **21**(2), 107–125 (1995). PVS http://pvs.csl.sri.com

19. Shankar, N.: Formalizing Hoare logic in PVS. In: Bowen, J.P., Liu, Z., Zhang, Z. (eds.) SETSS 2017. LNCS, vol. 11174, pp. 89–114. Springer, Cham (2018). https://doi.org/10.1007/978-3-030-02928-9_3

20. Skakkebæk, U.J., Shankar, N.: Towards a duration calculus proof assistant in PVS. In: Langmaack, H., de Roever, W.-P., Vytopil, J. (eds.) Formal Techniques in Real-Time and Fault-Tolerant Systems, vol. 863, pp. 660–679. Lübeck, Germany (1994)

21. Slagel, J.T., Moscato, M., White, L., Muñoz, C., Balachandran, S., Dutle, A.: Embedding differential dynamic logic in PVS. In: 18th Logical and Semantic Frameworks with Applications (2023)
22. van den Berg, J., Jacobs, B.: The loop compiler for Java and JML. In: Margaria, T., Yi, W. (eds.) Tools and Algorithms for the Construction and Analysis of Systems: 7th International Conference. TACAS 2001, volume 2031, pp. 299–312. Genova, Italy (2001)
23. White, L., Titolo, L., Slagel, J.T., Muñoz, C.: A temporal differential dynamic logic formal embedding. In: Proceedings of the 13th ACM SIGPLAN International Conference on Certified Programs and Proofs, pp. 162–176 (2024)
24. Zhou, J.M., Guo, J., Song, F.: Integrating the B-method into PVS. In: 2009 International Conference on Information Engineering and Computer Science, pp. 1–4. IEEE (2009)

Concurrent ∀∃-Hyperproperties

Bernd Finkbeiner[1](✉) and Ernst-Rüdiger Olderog[2](✉)

[1] CISPA Helmholtz Center for Information Security, Saarbrücken, Germany
`finkbeiner@cispa.de`
[2] Carl von Ossietzky University of Oldenburg, Oldenburg, Germany
`olderog@informatik.uni-oldenburg.de`

Abstract. Hyperproperties are system properties that relate multiple traces (executions) of a system. Typical applications of hyperproperties are found in information flow security. In a previous paper, we introduced *concurrent* hyperproperties, by generalizing traces to *concurrent* traces, defined as partially ordered multisets. We take Petri nets as the basic semantic model. To check concurrent hyperproperties, we extended the testing of processes due to De Nicola and Hennessy to the setting of concurrent traces, using the parallel composition of Petri nets. In this paper, we present new results on decidability and undecidability of may and must testing of universal and existential concurrent hyperproperties, and analyze the case of concurrent hyperproperties with quantifier alternation.

Keywords: Hyperproperties · concurrent traces · Petri nets · may and must testing · model checking · (un)decidability

1 Introduction

Clarkson and Schneider defined *hyperproperties* as system properties that relate multiple traces of a system [8]. Hyperproperties play a key role in information flow security, where policies like noninference [29], noninterference [21], and observational determinism [39] are formalized as hyperproperties; hyperproperties like robustness and symmetry are increasingly also studied in other areas (cf. [16]). For systems with true concurrency, such as those described by Petri nets, we recently introduced the notion of *concurrent hyperproperties* [17]. We showed that concurrent hyperproperties can be specified using a variation of De Nicola and Hennessy's *testing processes* [10,25].

As an example, consider the Petri net $\mathcal{N}_0$ shown on the left in Fig. 1. The concurrent hyperproperty we are interested in is *noninference* [29]. We partition the three actions of the net into the low-security actions l_1 and l_2, which are assumed to be publicly observable, and the high-security action h, whose occurrence should be kept a secret. Noninference requires that the low-security behavior must not change when all high-security actions are removed. We formalize noninference as the concurrent hyperproperty

D. Dietsch et al. (Eds.): Podelski Festschrift, LNCS 14765, pp. 135–153, 2026.
https://doi.org/10.1007/978-3-032-13711-1_9

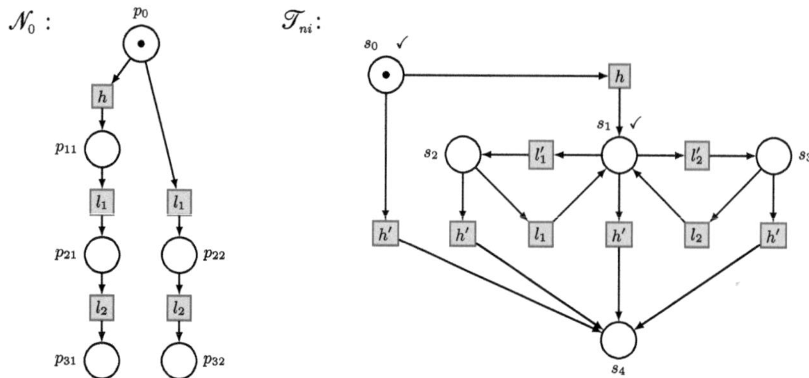

Fig. 1. Example system $\mathcal{N}_0$ and test $\mathcal{T}_{ni}$ for noninference.

$$\forall\,\rho.\ \exists\rho'.\ \mathcal{N}\,\|\,\mathcal{N}'\ \text{ must pass } \mathcal{T}_{ni},$$

where $\mathcal{T}_{ni}$ is the testing process shown on the right in Fig. 1. The definition of the concurrent hyperproperty refers to two runs ρ and ρ' of $\mathcal{N}_0$, where ρ is chosen universally and ρ' is chosen existentially: for every ρ there must exist a ρ', such that the two runs pass the test described in the following. The test analyzes the net $\mathcal{N}$ of ρ and the net $\mathcal{N}'$ of ρ', where, in $\mathcal{N}'$, the actions l_1, l_2, h have been renamed to l_1', l_2', h', respectively. The testing process $\mathcal{T}_{ni}$ then synchronizes with $\mathcal{N}$ and $\mathcal{N}'$ on the full set of actions $h', h, l_1', l_1, l_2', l_2$. The test is successful if the combination of $\mathcal{N}$, $\mathcal{N}'$ and $\mathcal{T}_{ni}$ either runs forever or terminates in a marking where all places of $\mathcal{T}_{ni}$ are marked with a checkmark $\checkmark$. Our testing process $\mathcal{T}_{ni}$ ensures that this occurs exactly if either $\mathcal{N}$ does not begin with h or the low-security events of $\mathcal{N}$ and $\mathcal{N}'$ exactly match up, and, additionally, $\mathcal{N}'$ does not contain an occurrence of h'.

Checking our system $\mathcal{N}_0$ against this concurrent hyperproperty, we note that the nondeterministic choice in place p_0 results in two possible runs. For each such run ρ, we must choose a run ρ' so that the test is successful. If we choose the run on the left (with action h renamed into h') for ρ', the test $\mathcal{T}_{ni}$ will unsuccessfully deadlock in place s_4. However, if we choose the run to the right (without h) as ρ', there is no action h' in ρ'. If then ρ has an action h, the actions l_1' and l_2' in ρ occur in the same order as l_1 and l_2 in ρ'. Hence, $\mathcal{T}_{ni}$ successfully terminates in place s_1. If ρ has no action h, the test $\mathcal{T}_{ni}$ stays in the success place s_0.

The model checking problem of (safe) Petri nets against concurrent hyper-properties is, in general, undecidable. Specifically, we previously showed that the model checking problems is undecidable for "$\forall$ may" hyperproperties and decidable for "$\forall$ must" hyperproperties [17]. The distinction between "may" and "must" clarifies the result of the test if the testing process has multiple runs. A "may" test is successful if there is a successful run of the testing process; a "must" test is successful if all runs are successful. The class of "$\forall$ must" hyperproperties refers to "must" hyperproperties where all quantifiers are universal, and "∀ may" refers to "may" hyperproperties where all quantifiers are universal.

Table 1. Decidability results on model checking concurrent hyperproperties. Bold entries are new.

Property class	Model checking problem
∀ must	decidable ([17])
∃ may	**decidable** (Theorem 1)
∀ may	undecidable ([17])
∃ must	**undecidable** (Theorem 2)
∀∃/∃∀ must/may	**undecidable** (Corollary 1)

In this paper, we complete this analysis of the decidability of the model checking problem, resulting in the classification shown in Table 1. We show that the model checking problem is decidable for "∃ may" and undecidable for "∃ must" concurrent hyperproperties. As a corollary, we obtain that concurrent hyperproperties that contain both existential and universal quantifiers are always undecidable: all four "∀∃ must/may" property classes (resulting from the choice between ∀∃ and ∃∀ quantifier alternation and the choice between "must" and "may") either contain the undecidable "∀ may" class or the undecidable "∃ must" class as a special case. This is unfortunate, because many hyperproperties of interest involve a quantifier alternation. For example, the noninference property of our example, and, similarly, the notion of generalized noninterference [28], both need a ∀∃ quantifier alternation.

We address this situation by identifying a special case of ∀∃ hyperproperties where the model checking problem remains decidable. Concurrent hyperproperties of the form "∀∃ may" can be simplified to "∀ may" by combining the testing process with a copy of the original Petri net. If the resulting tester is *deterministic*, then "must" and "may" coincide, and "∀ may" can therefore be further reduced to the decidable "∀ must" case. Likewise, "∀∃ must" is, for deterministic testers, equivalent to "∀∃ may," and can therefore also be reduced to "∀ must" if the intermediate tester is again deterministic. Hence, under the (admittedly strong) assumption that deterministic testers suffice, both "∀∃ may" and "∀∃ must" are decidable.

Our paper is organized as follows. In Sect. 2, we recall from [17] the notion of concurrent hyperproperties and consider examples. In Sect. 3, we define basic concepts from Petri nets as needed in our approach. In Sect. 4, we adapt the concept of testing processes developed by De Nicola and Hennessy to Petri nets. In Sect. 5, we discuss how the concurrent hyperproperties of Sect. 2 can be tested. In Sect. 6, we establish the new results on the decidability and undecidability of the model checking problem. In Sect. 7, we discuss related work, and in Sect. 8, we conclude the paper.

Dedication. We dedicate this paper to Andreas Podelski. The choice of topic was motivated by a series of inspiring discussions between Andreas Podelski and the first author on the role of hyperproperties in the verification of multi-threaded programs. Andreas has a strong interest in concurrency, in particular the verification of concurrent programs [15], also by using Petri nets as representations [11]. Both authors have fond memories of the close collaboration with Andreas as part of the Collaborative Research Center AVACS (Automatic Verification and Analysis of Complex Systems) between the universities of Oldenburg, Freiburg, and Saarbrücken, which provided for many years a rich source of very pleasant interaction and exchange.

2   Concurrent Hyperproperties

Clarkson and Schneider defined *hyperproperties* as a generalization of trace properties, which are sets of traces, to sets of sets of traces [8]. To give an analogous definition of *concurrent* hyperproperties, we generalized traces to *concurrent* traces, defined as partially ordered multisets (pomsets) [17].

Let Σ be a set of labels. A Σ-labeled partially ordered set is a triple $(X, <, \ell)$ where $<$ is an irreflexive partial order on a set X and $\ell : X \to \Sigma$ is a labeling function. Two such sets $(X, <, \ell)$ and $(X', <', \ell')$ are *isomorphic* if there exists a bijective mapping $f : X \to X'$ such that $f(x) < f(y) \Leftrightarrow x < y$ and $\ell'(f(x)) = \ell(x)$. A *partially ordered multiset (pomset)* over Σ is an isomorphy class of Σ-labeled partial ordered sets, denoted as $[(X, <, \ell)]$. A *totally ordered multiset (tomset)* is a pomset where $<$ is a total order [35].

We then refer to tomsets over Σ as *traces* and pomsets over Σ as *concurrent traces*. A *trace property* is a set of traces; a *hyperproperty* is a set of sets of traces. Analogously, a *concurrent trace property* is a set of concurrent traces, and a set of sets of concurrent traces is a *concurrent hyperproperty*. We denote with $\mathbb{T}(\Sigma)$ the set of all concurrent traces over Σ.

Example 1. Consider the hyperproperty that every pair of concurrent traces agrees on the occurrence of the low-security events, independent on any other event. Let Σ_{low} be the set of low-security events. The requirement can then be formalized as the following concurrent hyperproperty H_1 employing two universal quantifiers [17]:

$$H_1 = \{ \, T \subseteq \mathbb{T}(\Sigma) \ \mid \forall [(X, <, \ell)] \in T. \ \forall [(X', <', \ell')] \in T.$$
$$\exists \text{ bijection } f : X_{low} \to X'_{low}. \forall x \in X_{low}. \ell'(f(x)) = \ell(x) \, \},$$

where $X_{low} = \{x \in X \mid \ell(x) \in \Sigma_{low}\}$ and $X'_{low} = \{x \in X' \mid \ell'(x) \in \Sigma_{low}\}$.

Example 2. The hyperproperty of *noninference* [29] requires that the behavior observable by a low-security observer must not change when all high-security inputs are removed. We identify the events as low-security and high-security:

$\Sigma = \Sigma_{low} \cup \Sigma_{high}$. The requirement can then be formalized as the following concurrent hyperproperty H_2 using a quantifier alternation:

$$H_2 = \{\ T \subseteq \mathbb{T}(\Sigma)\ \mid \forall\,[(X, <, \ell)] \in T.\ \exists[(X', <', \ell')] \in T.$$
$$\exists\ \text{bijection}\ f : X_{low} \to X'_{low}.$$
$$(\ \forall x \in X_{low}.\,\ell'(f(x)) = \ell(x)$$
$$\wedge\,\forall x, y \in X_{low}.\,f(x) <' f(y) \Leftrightarrow x < y\,)$$
$$\wedge\,\forall x \in X'.\,\ell'(x) \notin \Sigma_{high}\ \},$$

where X_{low} and X'_{low} are as above.

3   Petri Nets

As a model for concurrent systems we take Petri nets because they distinguish the fundamental concepts of causal dependency, nondeterministic choice, and concurrency explicitly. We consider here safe Petri nets [4,36], with the transitions labeled by actions which serve as synchronization points in a parallel composition of such nets. We use the notation from [31], which is inspired by [22]. A *Petri net* or simply *net* is a structure $\mathcal{N} = (A,\ Pl,\ \longrightarrow,\ M_0)$, where

1. A is a finite communication alphabet, denoted by $\alpha(\mathcal{N})$, with $\tau \notin A$,
2. Pl is a possibly infinite set of *places*,
3. $\longrightarrow\ \subseteq \mathscr{P}_{nf}(Pl) \times (A \cup \{\,\tau\,\}) \times \mathscr{P}_{nf}(Pl)$ is the *transition relation*,
4. $M_0 \in \mathscr{P}_{nf}(Pl)$ is the *initial marking*.

Let p, q, r range over Pl. The notation $\mathscr{P}_{nf}(Pl)$ stands for the set of all nonempty, finite subsets of Pl. An element $(I,\ u,\ O) \in\ \longrightarrow$ with $I, O \in \mathscr{P}_{nf}(Pl)$ and $u \in A \cup \{\tau\}$ is called a *transition* (*labeled with the action* iuyt) and written as

$$I \xrightarrow{\ u\ } O.$$

For a transition $t = I \xrightarrow{\ u\ } O$ its *preset* or *input* is given by $pre(t) = I$, its *postset* or *output* by $post(t) = O$, and its action by $act(t) = u$. The letter τ is intended to model an *internal* action.

In the graphical representation of a net $\mathcal{N} = (A,\ Pl,\ \longrightarrow,\ M_0)$ we mention the alphabet A separately and display the components $Pl, \longrightarrow$ and M_0 as usual. Places $p \in Pl$ are represented as circles $\bigcirc$, usually with the name p outside, and transitions

$$t = \{p_1, \ldots, p_m\} \xrightarrow{\ u\ } \{q_1, \ldots, q_n\}$$

as boxes $\boxed{u}$ carrying the label u inside, connected via directed arcs from the places in $pre(t){=}\{p_1, \ldots, p_m\}$ and to the places in $post(t){=}\{q_1, \ldots, q_n\}$. Since $pre(t)$ and $post(t)$ need not be disjoint, some of the outgoing arcs of $\boxed{u}$ may actually point back to places in $pre(t)$ and thus introduce *cycles*. Graphically, we employ then double-headed arrows between $\boxed{u}$ and the places in $pre(t) \cap post(t)$. The initial marking M_0 is represented by putting a token $\bullet$ into the circle of each

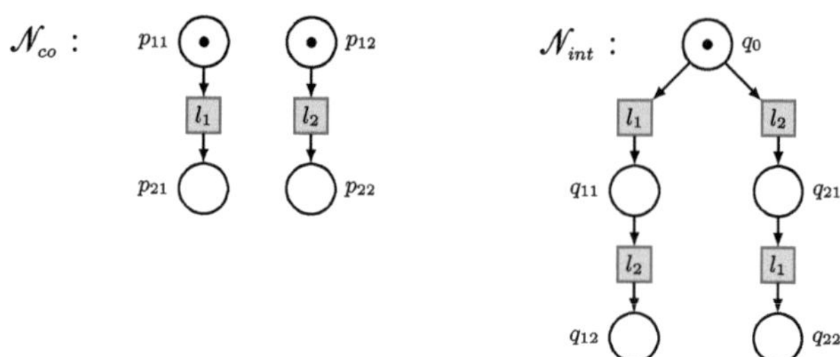

Fig. 2. The net $\mathcal{N}_{int}$ shows an interleaving of l_1 and l_2, consisting of a nondeterministic choice at place q_0 between two sequential behaviors of first l_1 and then l_2 (here the occurrence of l_2 causally depends on l_1) or of first l_2 and then l_1 (here the occurrence of l_1 causally depends on l_2).

$p \in M_0$. Figure 2 shows how concurrency, nondeterministic choice and sequential behavior (causal dependency) appears graphically.

Starting from the initial marking, the firing of transitions creates new markings $M \in \mathscr{P}_{nf}(Pl)$, which represent the global states of a Petri net. Formally, a transition t is *enabled* at a marking M if $pre(t) \subseteq M$. *Firing* such a transition t at M yields the successor marking $M' = (M - pre(t)) \cup post(t)$. We write then $M[t\rangle M'$. We assume here that $\cup$ is a disjoint union, which is satisfied if the net is *contact-free*, i.e., if for all $t \in \mathscr{T}$ and all reachable markings M

$$pre(t) \subseteq M \Rightarrow post(t) \subseteq (Pl - M) \cup pre(t).$$

The set of *reachable markings* of a net $\mathcal{N}$ is defined by

$$reach(\mathcal{N}) = \{M \mid \exists n \in \mathbb{N}.\, \exists\, t_1,\ldots,t_n \in \mathscr{T}.\ M_0[t_1\rangle M_1[t_2\rangle \ldots [t_n\rangle M_n = M\}.$$

For $n = 0$ inside this set, it is understood that $M_0 = M$ holds, so $M_0 \in reach(\mathcal{N})$. In the present setting, all reachable markings are non-empty, finite sets of places. Such Petri nets are called *safe* or *1-bounded* because every reachable marking contains at most one token per place. In general place/transition nets, the reachable markings can be multisets representing multiple tokens per place.

3.1   Causal Nets and Runs

Concurrent computations of a net can be described by *causal nets* [33,36]. Informally, a causal net is an acyclic net where all choices have been resolved. It can be seen as a net-theoretic way of defining a partial order among the occurrences of transitions in a net to represent their causal dependency.

We need more notation for a net $\mathcal{N} = (A, Pl, \longrightarrow, M_0)$. For a place $p \in Pl$ its *preset* is defined by $pre(p) = \{t \in \longrightarrow \mid p \in post(t)\,\}$ and its *postset* by $post(p) = \{t \in \longrightarrow \mid p \in pre(t)\,\}$. A net is *deterministic* if $\forall p \in Pl\,.\, |post(p)| \leq 1$, i.e., there are no choices among transitions leaving the same place. Otherwise, the net is *nondeterministic*.

The *flow relation* $\mathscr{F}_{\mathcal{N}} \subseteq Pl \times Pl$ on the places of $\mathcal{N}$ is given by

$$p \; \mathscr{F}_{\mathcal{N}} \; q \quad \text{if} \quad \exists\, t \in \longrightarrow . \; p \in pre(t) \text{ and } q \in post(t).$$

$\mathscr{F}_{\mathcal{N}}$ is *well-founded* if there are no infinite backward chains $\cdots p_3 \; \mathscr{F}_{\mathcal{N}} \; p_2 \; \mathscr{F}_{\mathcal{N}} \; p_1$.
A net $\mathcal{N} = (\,A,\,Pl,\,\longrightarrow,\,M_0)$ is called a *causal net* if the following holds:

(1) all places are unbranched, i.e., $\forall p \in Pl . \; |pre(p)| \leq 1$ and $|post(p)| \leq 1$,
(2) the flow relation $\mathscr{F}_{\mathcal{N}}$ is well-founded, and
(3) the initial marking consists of all places without an ingoing arc, i.e.,

$$M_0 \; = \; \{p \in Pl \mid pre(p) \; = \; \emptyset\}.$$

By condition (1), $\mathcal{N}$ is in particular deterministic. Condition (2) implies that
the transitive closure of $\mathscr{F}_{\mathcal{N}}$ is irreflexive. Thus a causal net $\mathcal{N}$ is acyclic, so
each transition occurs only once. Conditions (1)–(3) ensure that there are no
superfluous places and transitions in causal nets: every transition can fire and
every place is contained in some reachable marking. Every causal net is safe.

Following Petri's intuition, causal nets should describe the concurrent computations of a net. Thus we explain how causal nets relate to ordinary (safe)
nets. To this end, we use the following notion of embedding.

Let $\mathcal{N}_1 = (A_1,\, Pl_1,\, \longrightarrow_1,\, M_{01})$ be a causal net and $\mathcal{N}_2 = (A_2,\, Pl_2,\, \longrightarrow_2,$
$M_{02})$ be a safe net, where M_{01} and M_{02} denote the initial markings of $\mathcal{N}_1$ and
$\mathcal{N}_2$, respectively. $\mathcal{N}_1$ is a *causal net of* $\mathcal{N}_2$ if $A_1 = A_2$ and there exists a mapping
$f : Pl_1 \longrightarrow Pl_2$, which is extended elementwise to subsets $X \subseteq Pl_1$ by putting
$f(X) = \{f(p) \in Pl_2 \mid p \in X\}$, such that the following holds:

1. $f(M_{01}) = M_{02}$,
2. $\forall M \in reach(\mathcal{N}_1) . \; f \downarrow M$, the restriction of f to $M \subseteq Pl_1$, is injective,
3. $\forall\, t \in \longrightarrow_1 . \; (f(pre(t)), act(t), f(post(t))) \in \longrightarrow_2 ,$

The mapping f is called an *embedding of* $\mathcal{N}_1$ *into* $\mathcal{N}_2$. Note that f distributes
over the flow relation:

$$\forall\, p, q \in Pl_1 . \; (p \; \mathscr{F}_{\mathcal{N}_1} \; q \Rightarrow f(p) \; \mathscr{F}_{\mathcal{N}_2} \; f(q)).$$

In net theory, the pair $(\mathcal{N}_1, f)$ is called a *process* of $\mathcal{N}_2$ [3,33]. We call it a
(*concurrent*) *run* of $\mathcal{N}_2$ and use the (possibly decorated) letter ρ for runs. A run
$\rho = (\mathcal{N}_1, f)$ of $\mathcal{N}_2$ is called *maximal* if

$$\forall\, p \in Pl_1 . \; (\exists\, q \in Pl_2 . \; f(p) \; \mathscr{F}_{\mathcal{N}_2} \; q \Rightarrow \exists\, p' \in Pl_1 . \; p \; \mathscr{F}_{\mathcal{N}_1} \; p'),$$

so the run ρ cannot stop at a place p if there is an extension possible at the
corresponding place $f(p)$ in $\mathcal{N}_2$. Every net has at least one maximal run.

3.2   Causal Nets Corresponding to Concurrent Traces

A causal net $\mathcal{N}$ *corresponds to* the concurrent trace (pomset) $[(X, <, \ell)]$, where

- $X = \longrightarrow$, the set of transitions of $\mathcal{N}$,
- $<$ is the transitive closure of the *immediate causal successor* relation $<_m$ between transitions: $t_1 <_m t_2$ holds for $t_1, t_2 \in \longrightarrow$ if $post(t_1) \cap pre(t_2) \neq \emptyset$,
- $\ell(t) = act(t)$ for every $t \in \longrightarrow$.

The irreflexive partial order $t_1 < t_2$ expresses that transition t_2 can occur only after transition t_1 has happened, so t_2 *causally depends* on t_1. If for transitions $t_1 \neq t_2$ neither $t_1 < t_2$ nor $t_2 < t_1$ holds, t_1 and t_2 are *causally independent* and can occur *concurrently*. Graphically, we represent these pomsets by showing each transition t labeled with $\ell(t) = u$ as a box $\boxed{u}$ and connecting these boxes with arcs representing the immediate causal successor relation $<_m$.

Also, vice versa, if a concurrent trace $[(X, <, \ell)]$ is given, it is easy to construct a causal net $\mathcal{N}$ corresponding to the trace in the above sense. One just has to add the missing places to turn the trace into a causal net.

3.3   Parallel Composition

Petri nets with disjoint sets of places, but possibly overlapping communication alphabets can be composed in parallel. Thereby transitions with different actions are performed asynchronously, whereas transitions with the *same* action synchronize. For $\mathcal{N}_i = (A_i, Pl_i, \longrightarrow_i, M_{0i})$, $i = 1,2$, with $Pl_1 \cap Pl_2 = \emptyset$ their *parallel composition* is defined as follows:

$$\mathcal{N}_1 \parallel \mathcal{N}_2 = (A_1 \cup A_2, Pl_1 \cup Pl_2, \longrightarrow, M_{01} \cup M_{02}),$$

where

$$\longrightarrow = \quad \{\ (I, u, O) \in \longrightarrow_1 \cup \longrightarrow_2 \mid u \notin A_1 \cap A_2\ \} \quad \text{(asynchrony)}$$
$$\cup \{\ (I_1 \cup I_2, a, O_1 \cup O_2) \mid a \in A_1 \cap A_2 \text{ and} \quad \text{(synchrony)}$$
$$(I_1, a, O_1) \in \longrightarrow_1 \text{ and } (I_2, a, O_2) \in \longrightarrow_2\ \}.$$

The synchronization of actions depends on the choice of the alphabets A_1 and A_2. Actions labeled with the internal action τ never synchronize because τ does not appear in any alphabet A_i. Up to bijective renaming of places, the parallel composition of nets is commutative and associative.

4   Testing

The idea of *testing* processes is due to De Nicola and Hennessy [10,25]. There the interaction of a (nondeterministic) process and a user is explicitly formalized using a synchronous parallel composition. The user is formalized by a *test*, which is a process with some states marked as a *success*. The authors distinguish between two options: a process may or must pass a test. A process P *may*

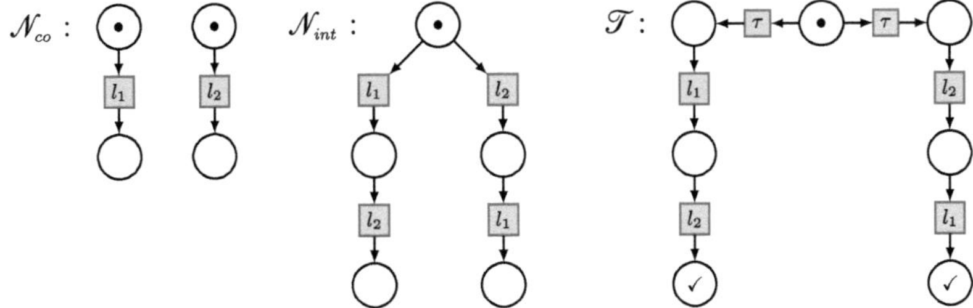

Fig. 3. We consider again the nets $\mathcal{N}_{co}$ and $\mathcal{N}_{int}$ of Fig. 2, showing two actions l_1 and l_2 in concurrent and interleaved fashion, respectively. The test $\mathcal{T}$ can initially choose between two orders of the actions l_1 and l_2 and has final places marked with $\checkmark$.

pass a test T if in *some* maximal parallel computation with P, synchronizing on transitions with the same label, the test T reaches a *success* state. A process P *must* pass a test T if in *all* such computations the test T reaches a *success* state.

We transfer this notion of testing to Petri nets. A *test* is a Petri net, extended by a distinguished set $\checkmark \subseteq Pl$ of *successful* places: $\mathcal{T} = (\, A,\, Pl,\, \checkmark,\, \longrightarrow,\, M_0)$. In the graphical notation, we mark each place of this subset by the symbol $\checkmark$.

To perform a test $\mathcal{T}$ on a given Petri net $\mathcal{N}$, we consider the parallel composition $\mathcal{N} \parallel \mathcal{T}$. A run $\rho = (\mathcal{N}_R,\, f)$ of $\mathcal{N} \parallel \mathcal{T}$ is *deadlock free* if it is infinite, and it *terminates successfully* if it is finite and all places of $\mathcal{T}$ inside the parallel composition without causal successor are marked with $\checkmark$. A net $\mathcal{N}$ *may pass* a test $\mathcal{T}$ if there exists a maximal run of $\mathcal{N} \parallel \mathcal{T}$ which is deadlock free or terminates successfully. A net $\mathcal{N}$ *must pass* a test $\mathcal{T}$ if all maximal runs of $\mathcal{N} \parallel \mathcal{T}$ are deadlock free or terminate successfully.

Figure 3 shows that tests can distinguish runs of concurrent and interleaved systems. The test $\mathcal{T}$ offers two alternatives, one performing first l_1 and then l_2, the other performing first l_2 and then l_1. In parallel composition with the single run of the concurrent net $\mathcal{N}_{co}$, both alternatives are successful, but in parallel composition with the two runs of the net $\mathcal{N}_{int}$, the run that first performs l_1 and then l_2 will lead to a deadlock when put in parallel with the alternative of the test $\mathcal{T}$ that first chooses l_2 and then l_1. Thus the run of $\mathcal{N}_{co}$ must pass $\mathcal{T}$, but it is not the case that all runs of $\mathcal{N}_{int}$ must pass $\mathcal{T}$. However, they may pass $\mathcal{T}$.

Another notion of testing that can distinguish concurrency and interleaving is *causal testing* due to Goltz and Wehrheim [23]. The authors use it to define an equivalence relation on event structures that respects action refinement. Here, we do not aim at a notion of equivalence, but at a concept for checking concurrent hyperproperties.

To *check a hyperproperty* relating k concurrent traces on a system represented by a net $\mathcal{N}_0$, we investigate maximal runs $\rho_i = (\mathcal{N}_i, f_i)$ with $i = 1, \cdots, k$ of $\mathcal{N}_0$, where the causal nets $\mathcal{N}_i$ correspond to the concurrent traces of the hyperproperty, except that in $\mathcal{N}_i$ we relabel every action u of $\mathcal{N}_0$ into u_i. So the alphabet $\alpha(\mathcal{N}_i)$ is $\alpha(\mathcal{N}_0)$, but with every action u renamed into u_i. We will test the parallel composition $\mathcal{N}_1 \parallel \cdots \parallel \mathcal{N}_k$. The purpose of this relabeling is to have nets

$\mathcal{N}_1, \ldots, \mathcal{N}_k$ that do not synchronize in this composition. To represent the hyperproperty, we suitably quantify existentially or universally over these k runs of $\mathcal{N}_0$ and thus arrive at the following possibilities of testing:

$$Q_1 \rho_1, \cdots, Q_k \rho_k. \; \mathcal{N}_1 \parallel \cdots \parallel \mathcal{N}_k \; m \; \text{pass} \; \mathcal{T},$$

where $Q_i \in \{\exists, \forall\}$ and $m \in \{\text{may}, \text{must}\}$. $\mathcal{T}$ uses the subscripted labels of the form $u_1, \ldots, u_k$ to synchronize with the actions in $\mathcal{N}_1, \ldots, \mathcal{N}_k$.

We also use primed copies like u' and u'' instead of subscripts. For example, for $k = 2$, we use one causal net $\mathcal{N}$ having the original actions of $\mathcal{N}_0$ and one causal $\mathcal{N}'$ with every action u of $\mathcal{N}_0$ relabeled into a primed copy u'. Then the above pattern specializes to

$$Q \rho. \, Q' \rho'. \; \mathcal{N} \parallel \mathcal{N}' \; m \; \text{pass} \; \mathcal{T},$$

where $Q, Q' \in \{\exists, \forall\}$ and $m \in \{\text{may}, \text{must}\}$. Whereas $\mathcal{N}$ and $\mathcal{N}'$ have no common actions to synchronize on, the test $\mathcal{T}$ will synchronize with $\mathcal{N}$ and $\mathcal{N}'$ via common (unprimed and primed) actions, thereby checking the hyperproperty. Note that the explicit quantifiers refer to runs of the system $\mathcal{N}_0$ under test. Once these runs are fixed, may and must corresponds to existential and universal quantification over runs originating from the test.

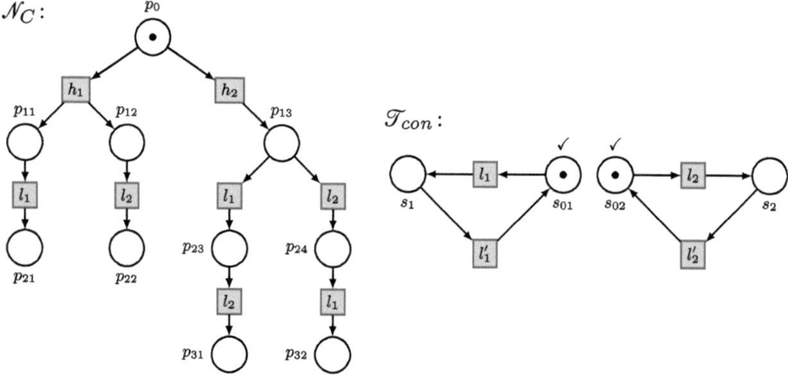

Fig. 4. System $\mathcal{N}_C$ showing concurrent and sequential behavior and a concurrent test $\mathcal{T}_{con}$ [17]. $\mathcal{N}_C$ has three runs: the concurrent run ρ_1 is obtained by choosing at p_0 the left branch starting with h_1 (after which l_1 and l_2 can occur concurrently), the sequential run ρ_2 is obtained by choosing at p_0 the right branch starting with h_2 and then at p_{13} the left branch starting with l_1, and the sequential run ρ_3 is obtained by choosing at p_0 the right branch starting with h_2 and then at p_{13} the right branch starting with l_2.

5   Examples

5.1   Testing H_1

In Fig. 4, we show a system $\mathcal{N}_C$ with high-level actions h_1 and h_2 and low-level actions l_1 and l_2, and a concurrent test $\mathcal{T}_{con}$ for the concurrent hyperproperty H_1 of Example 1 whether every pair of concurrent traces π and π' agrees on the occurrence of the low-security events l_1 and l_2. The test checks whether each l_1 is matched by l'_1, but l_2 may occur in between, and vice versa for l_2 and l'_2 and a possibly intervening l_1. Figure 5 shows the outcomes of testing the runs ρ_1 and ρ'_3 (which is ρ_3 with all actions renamed into primed copies) with their nets $\mathcal{N}_1$ and $\mathcal{N}'_3$. We see that the test is successful. More generally, we have

$$\forall \rho. \, \forall \rho'. \, \mathcal{N} \, \| \, \mathcal{N}' \ \text{ must pass } \mathcal{T}_{con}.$$

This shows that $\mathcal{N}_{\mathscr{C}}$ satisfies the concurrent hyperproperty H_1.

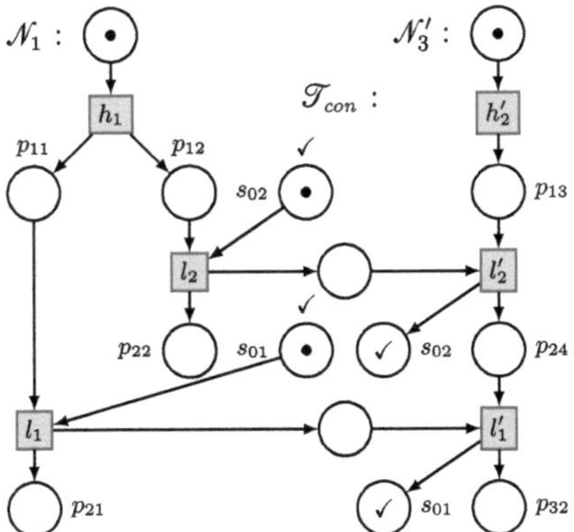

Fig. 5. Testing the concurrent hyperproperty H_1 with $\mathcal{T}_{con}$ [17]. We consider the unique maximal run of the parallel composition $\mathcal{N}_1 \, \| \, \mathcal{T}_{con} \, \| \, \mathcal{N}'_3$, where $\mathcal{N}_1$ and $\mathcal{N}'_3$ are the nets of the runs ρ_1 and ρ'_3. The maximal run terminates successfully because both concurrent components of the test end in a place marked with ✓.

5.2   Testing H_2

In Fig. 1, we showed a system $\mathcal{N}_0$ with a high-level action h and low-level actions l_1 and l_2, and a test $\mathcal{T}_{ni}$ for *noninference* (see Example 2). This is a $\forall\exists$-hyperproperty that can be checked by requiring

$$\forall \rho. \, \exists \rho'. \, \mathcal{N} \, \| \, \mathcal{N}' \ \text{ must pass } \mathcal{T}_{ni}.$$

The test $\mathcal{T}_{ni}$ synchronizes with the net $\mathcal{N}$ of the universally quantified run ρ of $\mathcal{N}_0$ and the net $\mathcal{N}'$ of the existentially quantified run ρ' of the copy $\mathcal{N}'_0$

of $\mathcal{N}_0$ on all actions $h', h, l'_1, l_1, l'_2, l_2$. The system $\mathcal{N}_0$ has two runs corresponding to choosing one of the nondeterministic branches starting in the place p_0. As explained in the introduction, if the net $\mathcal{N}'$ has an action h', the test $\mathcal{T}_{ni}$ will deadlock in the place s_4. However, for $\mathcal{N}_0$ the run to the right can be chosen as ρ'. Then the test $\mathcal{T}_{ni}$ will terminate for any of the two runs of $\mathcal{N}_0$ chosen as ρ in one of the places s_0 or s_1 signalling success.

6   Decidability

We now turn to Table 1 and prove the new entries on (un)decidability of testing concurrent hyperproperties on finite nets.

Theorem 1 ($\exists$ may). *Existential may testing is decidable.*

Proof. Existential may testing of a finite net $\mathcal{N}_0$ is of the form

$$(*) \qquad \exists \rho_1. \ldots \exists \rho_k. \ \mathcal{N}_1 \parallel \cdots \parallel \mathcal{N}_k \ \text{may pass } \mathcal{T},$$

where $\mathcal{N}_1, \ldots, \mathcal{N}_k$ are the nets belonging to the runs $\rho_1, \ldots, \rho_k$ of $\mathcal{N}_0$. Instead of referring to k runs of $\mathcal{N}_0$ we can equivalently refer to k copies $\mathcal{N}_{0,1}, \ldots, \mathcal{N}_{0,k}$ of $\mathcal{N}_0$, with suitably renamed action labels, and check the net

$$\mathcal{N} = \mathcal{N}_{0,1} \parallel \cdots \parallel \mathcal{N}_{0,k} \parallel \mathcal{T},$$

with $\longrightarrow$ denoting its transition relation and $Pl_{\mathcal{T}}$ the set of places inside $\mathcal{T}$, for the following properties:

(1) the unfolding of $\mathcal{N}$ is infinite
or (2) $\exists M \in reach(\mathcal{N}). \ \forall p \in Pl_{\mathcal{T}} \cap M. \ p \in \checkmark \wedge \neg \exists t \in \longrightarrow. \ pre(t) \subseteq M.$

The unfolding of a net is a maximal branching process, which is like a maximal run but additionally recording nondeterministic branches [12,13]. Since $\mathcal{N}$ is a finite, safe net, property (1) is decidable by checking whether there is a loop in the reachability graph of $\mathcal{N}$. Property (2) is a reachability problem for Petri nets, which is decidable [27]. Since we consider safe Petri nets, this reachability is PSPACE-complete [14]. Thus, it is decidable whether $(*)$ holds. $\square$

Theorem 2 ($\exists$ must). *Existential must testing is undecidable.*

We reduce the *infinite* Post Correspondence Problem (ω-PCP) to existential must testing. The ω-PCP is defined as follows [19]:

- The input consists of two finite lists $(u_1, \ldots, u_n)$ and $(v_1, \ldots, v_n)$ of the same length n of finite, non-empty words over some alphabet Γ.
- The question is whether there exists an *infinite correspondence*, i.e., an infinite sequence of indices $i_1, i_2, \ldots, i_k, \ldots$ such that the infinite words $u_{i_1} u_{i_2} \ldots u_{i_k} \ldots$ and $v_{i_1} v_{i_2} \ldots v_{i_k} \ldots$ over Γ are identical.

It has been shown that for alphabets Γ with at least two elements, the ω-PCP is undecidable [19,20,37].

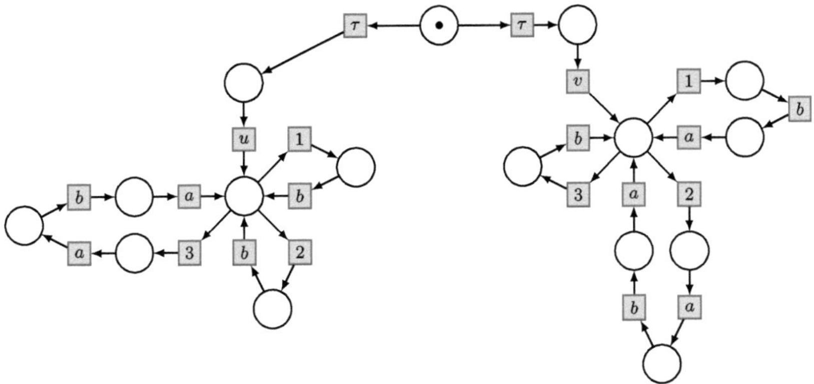

Fig. 6. Petri net $\mathcal{N}_I$ simulating the input I of the ω-PCP

Proof. We present the proof idea for the ω-PCP over the alphabet $\{a,b\}$. As input I, we consider the lists (u_1, u_2, u_3) and (v_1, v_2, v_3), where

$$u_1 = b, \; u_2 = b, \; u_3 = aba \;\; \text{and} \;\; v_1 = ba, \; v_2 = aba, \; v_3 = b.$$

The ω-PCP with this input is solvable by the infinite (ω-regular) correspondence $1 \cdot (3 \cdot 2)^\omega$ because

$$u_1\, u_3\, u_2\, u_3\, u_2 \cdots = b \,|\, a\,b\,a \,|\, b \,|\, a\,b\,a \,|\, b \cdots$$
$$v_1\, v_3\, v_2\, v_3\, v_2 \cdots = b\,a \,|\, b \,|\, a\,b\,a \,|\, b \,|\, a\,b\,a \cdots$$

Note that the input I has no solution as a normal, finite PCP [34] because for attempted finite correspondences the lengths of the two sides never agree.

The ω-PCP input I is simulated by the Petri net $\mathcal{N}_I$ shown in Fig. 6. It consists of two branches that are selected by an initial choice between two internal actions. For distinguishing them in a test, the left branch starts with a transition labeled with u and the right branch with a transition labeled with v. Afterwards, their tokens reside in their center places from where they can nondeterministically choose which of the words u_i or v_i for $i \in \{1, 2, 3\}$ to perform next. For example, the left branch simulates $u_3 = aba$ by the sequence of actions 3, a, b, and a, after which the token is again on the center place so that the next choice can be performed.

In general, the ω-PCP with input I simulated by a net $\mathcal{N}_I$ of the form above has an infinite correspondence if and only if

$$\exists\, \rho.\, \exists\, \rho'.\, \mathcal{N} \,\|\, \mathcal{N}' \;\; \text{must pass} \;\; \mathcal{T}_\omega$$

for the test $\mathcal{T}_\omega$ shown in Fig. 7. Here $\mathcal{N}$ and $\mathcal{N}'$ are the nets of the runs ρ and ρ' of $\mathcal{N}_I$, respectively. Note that $\mathcal{T}_\omega$ has no place labelled with $\checkmark$. Thus it can be successful only if it interacts with $\mathcal{N}$ and $\mathcal{N}'$ infinitely long.

The left branch of $\mathcal{T}_\omega$ checks whether $\mathcal{N}$ and $\mathcal{N}'$ produce letter by letter the same word. Here the transitions labeled with unprimed symbols refer to $\mathcal{N}$

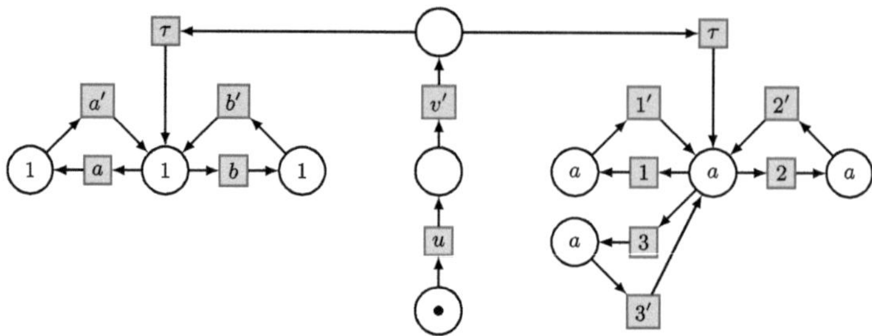

Fig. 7. Test $\mathscr{T}_\omega$ for checking whether two runs of $\mathscr{N}_I$ simulate a correspondence of the ω-PCP. The left branch checks that the runs produce letter by letter the same word, the right branch checks that the runs have chosen the same sequence of indices.

and transitions labeled with primed symbols refer to $\mathscr{N}'$. The initial transitions labeled with u and v' ensure that the unprimed symbols refer to the left-hand side of $\mathscr{N}_I$ simulating the u-part and that the primed symbols refer to (the primed version of) right-hand side of $\mathscr{N}_I$ simulating the v-part of the proposed correspondence.

The right branch of $\mathscr{T}_\omega$ checks whether $\mathscr{N}$ and $\mathscr{N}'$ have chosen the same sequence of indices $1, 2, 3$ in producing the common infinite word. Note that this branch checks the same runs $\mathscr{N}$ and $\mathscr{N}'$ than the left branch because $\mathscr{N}$ and $\mathscr{N}'$ are fixed initially.

There is one technical detail. Whereas the runs $\mathscr{N}$ and $\mathscr{N}'$ have no symbols in common because $\mathscr{N}$ uses only unprimed symbols and $\mathscr{N}'$ only primed versions of the symbols, the test $\mathscr{T}_\omega$ synchronizes in the parallel composition with $\mathscr{N} \parallel \mathscr{N}'$ on all its symbols except τ, i.e., on $a, b, a', b', u, v', 1, 2, 3, 1', 2', 3'$. To avoid unintended deadlocks we have to enable the left branch of $\mathscr{T}_\omega$ to be able to synchronize at every place marked with 1 with any transition labeled with $1, 2, 3, 1', 2'$ or $3'$, and vice versa, the right branch of $\mathscr{T}_\omega$ to be able to synchronize at every place marked with a with any transition labeled with a, b, a', b', u or v'. To enhance visibility, we dropped the loop transitions attached to these places allowing for these synchronizations. □

Corollary 1 (Quantifier alternation). *For a single quantifier alternation we can extend the above results:*

1. *$\forall\exists$ may testing and $\exists\forall$ may testing are undecidable.*
2. *$\forall\exists$ must testing and $\exists\forall$ must testing are undecidable.*

Proof. Re: (1). Suppose $\forall\exists$ may testing is decidable. Then also $\forall$ may testing would be decidable as a special case, where the $\exists$ quantifier is not employed in the test. Contradiction to the result in [17] (see Table 1). An analogous argument applies for $\exists\forall$ may testing.

Re: (2). Suppose $\forall\exists$ must testing is decidable. Then also $\exists$ must testing would be decidable as a special case, where the $\forall$ quantifier is not employed in the test. Contradiction to Theorem 2. An analogous argument applies for $\exists\forall$ must testing. □

By Corollary 1, $\forall\exists$ may testing is in general undecidable. However, for a special case we can show decidability.

Theorem 3 (Deterministic $\forall\exists$ may testing). *Consider $\forall\exists$ may testing of a finite net $\mathcal{N}_0$ of the form*

$$(*) \qquad \forall\,\rho.\,\exists\,\rho'.\,\mathcal{N}\,\|\,\mathcal{N}'\ \ may\ pass\ \mathcal{T},$$

where $\mathcal{N}$ and $\mathcal{N}'$ are the nets belonging to the runs ρ and ρ' of $\mathcal{N}_0$ and where $\alpha(\mathcal{T}) = \alpha(\mathcal{N}) \cup \alpha(\mathcal{N}')$. Suppose the parallel composition $\mathcal{N}'\,\|\,\mathcal{T}$ yields a deterministic net. Then it is decidable whether $(*)$ holds.

Proof. By the definition of testing, $(*)$ means that we check the maximal runs of $\mathcal{N}\,\|\,\mathcal{N}'\,\|\,\mathcal{T}$, where the parallel composition is associative. We consider the second composition $\mathcal{N}'\,\|\,\mathcal{T}$ as a new test $\mathcal{T}_{det}$ and examine instead the maximal runs of $\mathcal{N}\,\|\,\mathcal{T}_{det}$. Since by assumption $\mathcal{T}_{det}$ is deterministic, there is only one run to be examined. So may testing coincides with must testing. Thus, $(*)$ reduces to $\forall$ must testing. Therefore, it is decidable whether $(*)$ holds. $\square$

We give an example deterministic $\forall\exists$ may testing.

Example 3. From Fig. 1 we consider the system $\mathcal{N}_0$ and the test $\mathcal{T}_{ni}$ for noninference. Figure 8 shows the parallel composition of the net $\mathcal{N}'$ corresponding to the run to the right of $\mathcal{N}_0$ with $\mathcal{T}_{ni}$. The result is a deterministic system.

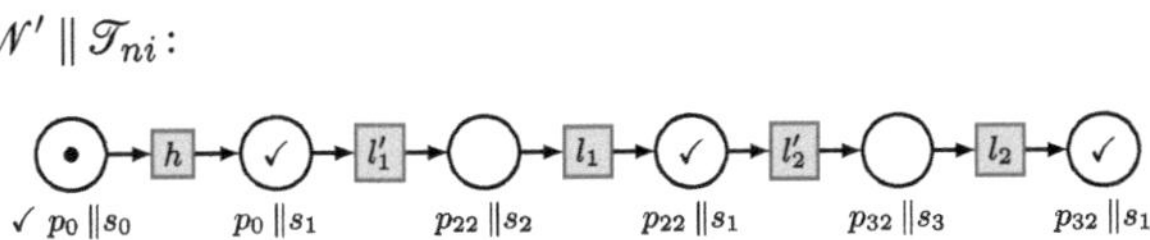

Fig. 8. Parallel composition of $\mathcal{N}'$ and test $\mathcal{T}_{ni}$, yielding a deterministic net.

7   Related Work

The notion of hyperproperties as sets of sets of execution traces was introduced by Clarkson and Schneider [8]. Before their seminal work, specific types of hyperproperties have long been studied in information flow security (cf. [21,26,38]). For the specification of hyperproperties, several extensions of temporal logic have been proposed. Notably, *HyperLTL* [7] adds universal and existential quantification over traces to standard propositional linear-time temporal logic (LTL). While HyperLTL has a strictly synchronous semantics, several extensions have been proposed that allow for the specification of asynchronous hyperproperties: *trajectory quantifiers* [2] allow for multiple schedulings between the traces; *Stuttering HyperLTL* [6] eliminates stuttering steps from the traces. The *temporal* *fixpoint calculus H_μ* [24] furthermore integrates the quantifiers from HyperLTL into the modal μ-calculus. Asynchronous hyperproperties can also be expressed in *second-order HyperLTL* [5].

While all these logics allow for the specification of $\forall\exists$ hyperproperties, the standard model checking approach for such hyperproperties, which eliminates the existential quantifier via an exponential complementation construction [18], is usually too expensive for practical applications. This problem has been addressed with an approximation technique that replaces the trace quantifiers with strategies in a two-person game between an $\exists$-player, who simulates existential trace quantifiers, and a $\forall$-player, who simulates universal trace quantifiers [9]. This technique is, however, in general incomplete.

Our specification technique for concurrent hyperproperties is based on testing processes. De Nicola and Hennessy [10,25] introduced the notion of testing to define an *equivalence* on nondeterministic, communicating processes. The processes are drawn from Milner's Calculus of Communication Systems (CCS) [30]. Two processes are equivalent if they pass the same tests, where a test is a process equipped with some states marked as a *success*. May testing leads to 'may equivalence' and must testing to 'must equivalence' of processes. De Nicola and Hennessy showed that for establishing may and must equivalence it suffices that the processes pass only a certain subset of all tests.

Our use of tests is different. For checking whether a system satisfies a particular hyperproperty, we consider a *single test* that formalizes this hyperproperty. When the system passes the test, it satisfies the hyperproperty. We do not use tests for defining an equivalence on systems. Employing a single test is often applied as a reduction technique in model checking, for example of real-time systems [32]. To check a complex system property that is not directly expressible in the logic of the model checker, a test process with a designated 'bad state' is designed to interact with the system. The system satisfies the property if and only if the test never reaches its bad state when interacting with the system. In contrast to our work here, these applications typically represent parallel composition by interleaving.

Whereas De Nicola and Hennessy considered systems expressed in CCS with its interleaving semantics, we consider here Petri nets as the system model, thereby distinguishing concurrency from interleaving. Notions of testing that define equivalences distinguishing concurrency and interleaving have also been studied in the setting of event structures [1,23]. Specifically, Goltz and Wehrheim propose the notion of *causal testing* to define an equivalence relation on event structures that respects action refinement [23]. In our approach we do not aim at a notion of equivalence, but at a concept for checking concurrent hyperproperties.

8   Conclusion

In this paper, we studied the model checking problem for concurrent hyperproperties. Our main result is that the model checking problem is undecidable for concurrent hyperproperties that combine existential and universal quantification. This result is in contrast to the situation for standard (non-concurrent) hyperproperties, as specified, for example as formulas of the temporal logic HyperLTL [7]. For HyperLTL, the model checking problem remains decidable for arbitrary quantifier alternations, albeit with nonelementary complexity [18]. In this paper, we identified deterministic testers as a special case where quantifier alternations can be allowed, because, in this case, *may* and *must* testing coincides. Generalizing this result to some class of nondeterministic testers is an important open problem for future work.

Acknowledgement. This work was supported by the European Research Council (ERC) Grant HYPER (No. 101055412).

References

1. Aceto, L., De Nicola, R., Fantechi, A.: Testing equivalences for event structures. In: Zilli, M.V. (ed.) Mathematical Models for the Semantics of Parallelism. LNCS, vol. 280, pp. 1–20. Springer, Heidelberg (1987). https://doi.org/10.1007/3-540-18419-8_9

2. Baumeister, J., Coenen, N., Bonakdarpour, B., Finkbeiner, B., Sánchez, C.: A temporal logic for asynchronous hyperproperties. In: Silva, A., Leino, K.R.M. (eds.) CAV 2021. LNCS, vol. 12759, pp. 694–717. Springer, Cham (2021). https://doi.org/10.1007/978-3-030-81685-8_33

3. Best, E., Fernández, C.: Nonsequential Processes. Springer (1988). https://doi.org/10.1007/978-3-642-73483-0

4. Best, E., Devillers, R.: Petri Net Primer – A Compendium of the Core Model, Analysis, and Synthesis. Computer Science Foundations and Applied Logic, Birkhäuser (2024). https://doi.org/10.1007/978-3-031-48278-6

5. Beutner, R., Finkbeiner, B., Frenkel, H., Metzger, N.: Second-order hyperproperties. In: Enea, C., Lal, A. (eds.) Computer Aided Verification - 35th International Conference, CAV 2023, Proc., Part II. LNCS, vol. 13965, pp. 309–332. Springer (2023). https://doi.org/10.1007/978-3-031-37703-7

6. Bozzelli, L., Peron, A., Sánchez, C.: Asynchronous extensions of HyperLTL. In: 36th Annual ACM/IEEE Symposium on Logic in Computer Science, LICS 2021, pp. 1–13. IEEE (2021).https://doi.org/10.1109/LICS52264.2021.9470583

7. Clarkson, M.R., Finkbeiner, B., Koleini, M., Micinski, K.K., Rabe, M.N., Sánchez, C.: Temporal logics for hyperproperties. In: Abadi, M., Kremer, S. (eds.) Principles of Security and Trust – Third International Conference, POST 2014, Held as Part of ETAPS 2014, Proceedings of the LNCS, vol. 8414, pp. 265–284. Springer (2014). https://doi.org/10.1007/978-3-642-54792-8

8. Clarkson, M.R., Schneider, F.B.: Hyperproperties. J. Comput. Secur. **18**(6), 1157–1210 (2010). https://doi.org/10.3233/JCS-2009-0393

9. Coenen, N., Finkbeiner, B., Sánchez, C., Tentrup, L.: Verifying hyperliveness. In: Dillig, I., Tasiran, S. (eds.) CAV 2019. LNCS, vol. 11561, pp. 121–139. Springer, Cham (2019). https://doi.org/10.1007/978-3-030-25540-4_7

10. De Nicola, R., Hennessy, M.: Testing equivalences for processes. TCS **34**, 83–134 (1984). https://doi.org/10.1016/0304-3975(84)90113-0

11. Dietsch, D., Heizmann, M., Klumpp, D., Naouar, M., Podelski, A., Schätzle, C.: Verification of concurrent programs using Petri net unfoldings. In: Henglein, F., Shoham, S., Vizel, Y. (eds.) VMCAI 2021. LNCS, vol. 12597, pp. 174–195. Springer, Cham (2021). https://doi.org/10.1007/978-3-030-67067-2_9

12. Engelfriet, J.: Branching processes of Petri nets. Acta Informatica **28**(6), 575–591 (1991). https://doi.org/10.1007/BF01463946
13. Esparza, J., Heljanko, K.: Unfoldings - A Partial-Order Approach to Model Checking. Springer (2008). https://doi.org/10.1007/978-3-540-77426-6
14. Esparza, J., Nielsen, M.: Decidability issues for Petri nets - a survey. Bull. EATCS **52**, 244–262 (1994)
15. Farzan, A., Klumpp, D., Podelski, A.: Sound sequentialization for concurrent program verification. In: Jhala, R., Dillig, I. (eds.) PLDI '22: 43rd ACM SIGPLAN Intern. Conf. on Programming Language Design and Implementation, 2022. pp. 506–521. ACM (2022). https://doi.org/10.1145/3519939.3523727
16. Finkbeiner, B.: Logics and algorithms for hyperproperties. ACM SIGLOG News **10**(2), 4–23 (2023). https://doi.org/10.1145/3610392.3610394
17. Finkbeiner, B., Olderog, E.R.: Concurrent hyperproperties. In: Bowen, J.P., Li, Q., Xu, Q. (eds.) Theories of Programming and Formal Methods - Essays Dedicated to Jifeng He on the Occasion of His 80th Birthday. LNCS, vol. 14080, pp. 211–231. Springer (2023). https://doi.org/10.1007/978-3-031-40436-8
18. Finkbeiner, B., Rabe, M.N., Sánchez, C.: Algorithms for model checking Hyper-LTL and HyperCTL*. In: Kroening, D., Păsăreanu, C.S. (eds.) CAV 2015. LNCS, vol. 9206, pp. 30–48. Springer, Cham (2015). https://doi.org/10.1007/978-3-319-21690-4_3
19. Finkel, O.: The exact complexity of the infinite post correspondence problem. Inf. Process. Lett. **115**(6–8), 609–611 (2015). https://doi.org/10.1016/J.IPL.2015.02.009
20. Gire, F.: Two decidability problems for infinite words. Inf. Process. Lett. **22**(3), 135–140 (1986). https://doi.org/10.1016/0020-0190(86)90058-X
21. Goguen, J.A., Meseguer, J.: Security policies and security models. In: Proc. IEEE Symposium on Security and Privacy, pp. 11–20. IEEE Computer Society (1982). https://doi.org/10.1109/SP.1982.10014
22. Goltz, U.: On representing CCS programs by finite Petri nets. In: Chytil, M., Janiga, L., Koubek, V. (eds.) Proc. Math. Found. of Comput. Sci. 1988,. LNCS, vol. 324, pp. 339–350. Springer (1988). https://doi.org/10.1007/BFb0017157
23. Goltz, U., Wehrheim, H.: Causal testing. In: Penczek, W., Szalas, A. (eds.) Mathematical Foundations of Computer Science 1996, 21st International Symposium, Proceedings LNCS, vol. 1113, pp. 394–406. Springer (1996). https://doi.org/10.1007/3-540-61550-4
24. Gutsfeld, J.O., Müller-Olm, M., Ohrem, C.: Automata and fixpoints for asynchronous hyperproperties. Proc. ACM Program. Lang. **5**(POPL) (2021). https://doi.org/10.1145/3434319
25. Hennessy, M.: Algebraic Theory of Processes. MIT Press (1988)
26. Mantel, H., Reinhard, A.: Controlling the what and where of declassification in language-based security. In: De Nicola, R. (ed.) ESOP 2007. LNCS, vol. 4421, pp. 141–156. Springer, Heidelberg (2007). https://doi.org/10.1007/978-3-540-71316-6_11
27. Mayr, E.W.: An algorithm for the general Petri net reachability problem. SIAM J. Comput. **13**(3), 441–460 (1984). https://doi.org/10.1137/0213029
28. McCullough, D.: Noninterference and the composability of security properties. In: Proceedings IEEE Symposium on Security and Privacy, pp. 177–186. IEEE Computer Society (1988). https://doi.org/10.1109/SECPRI.1988.8110
29. McLean, J.: A general theory of composition for trace sets closed under selective interleaving functions. In: 1994 IEEE Computer Society Symposium on Research

in Security and Privacy, pp. 79–93. IEEE Computer Society (1994). https://doi.org/10.1109/RISP.1994.296590
30. Milner, R.: A Calculus of Communicating Systems, LNCS, vol. 92. Springer (1980). https://doi.org/10.1007/3-540-10235-3
31. Olderog, E.R.: Nets, Terms and Formulas: Three Views of Concurrent Processes and Their Relationship. Cambridge University Press (1991). https://doi.org/10.1017/CBO9780511526589
32. Olderog, E.R., Dierks, H.: Real-Time Systems - Formal Specification and Automatic Verification. Cambridge University Press (2008). https://doi.org/10.1017/CBO9780511619953
33. Petri, C.: Non-sequential processes. Tech. Rep. Internal Report GMD-ISF-77-5, Gesellschaft Math. Datenverarb., St. Augustin (1977)
34. Post, E.L.: A variant of a recursively unsolvable problem. Bull. Am. Math. Soc. **54**(4), 264–268 (1946). https://doi.org/10.1007/978-3-642-19835-9
35. Pratt, V.: The pomset model of parallel processes: unifying the temporal and the spatial. In: Brookes, S.D., Roscoe, A.W., Winskel, G. (eds.) CONCURRENCY 1984. LNCS, vol. 197, pp. 180–196. Springer, Heidelberg (1985). https://doi.org/10.1007/3-540-15670-4_9
36. Reisig, W.: Petri Nets - An Introduction. Springer (1985). https://doi.org/10.1007/978-3-642-69968-9
37. Ruohonen, K.: Reversible machines and Post's correspondence problem for biprefix morphisms. J. Inf. Process. Cybern. **21**(12), 579–595 (1985)
38. Sabelfeld, A., Sands, D.: Declassification: dimensions and principles. J. Comput. Secur. **17**(5), 517–548 (2009). https://doi.org/10.3233/JCS-2009-0352
39. Zdancewic, S., Myers, A.C.: Observational determinism for concurrent program security. In: 16th IEEE Computer Security Foundations Workshop (CSFW-16 2003), pp. 29–43. IEEE Computer Society (2003). https://doi.org/10.1109/CSFW.2003.1212703

Author Index

If you have any concerns about our products,
you can contact us on
ProductSafety@springernature.com

In case Publisher is established outside the EU,
the EU authorized representative is:
Springer Nature Customer Service Center GmbH
Europaplatz 3, 69115 Heidelberg, Germany

Printed by Libri Plureos GmbH
in Hamburg, Germany